Still
Standing

NATALIE QUEIROZ

Still Standing

A pregnant woman.

A brutal attack.

An inspirational fight for survival.

JOHN BLAKE

Published by John Blake Publishing,
The Plaza,
535 Kings Road,
Chelsea Harbour,
London SW10 0SZ

www.johnblakebooks.com

www.facebook.com/johnblakebooks
twitter.com/jblakebooks

First published in paperback in 2019

ISBN: 978 1 78946 065 0

British Library Cataloguing-in-Publication Data:
A catalogue record for this book is available from the British Library.

Design by www.envydesign.co.uk

Printed and bound in Great Britain by Clays Ltd, Elcograf S.p.A.

1 3 5 7 9 10 8 6 4 2

John Blake Publishing is an imprint of Bonnier Books UK
www.bonnierbooks.co.uk

*To my three precious daughters who fill me with pride
and inspire me every single day*

Contents

Prologue

'TO NEW ADVENTURES!'

THE CORKS POPPED AND THE GLASSES FIZZED AS WE RAISED THEM TO TOAST OUR FRIENDS PREPARING TO LEAVE for South Korea. A new life awaited them and their three children. It was early August 2015 as we stood together in the garden of their parents' house in Birmingham. As my eyes panned our assembled group, I smiled at the easy familiarity we still enjoyed over twenty-five years on from our first meeting. Drawn together during school years, our group of teenage girls then befriended pupils at the neighbouring boys' grammar school. Memories of house parties still hung in the air: smuggled alcohol, surreptitious kisses, hormones flying. Bobby, my now true love, and I shared a kiss at one such party, until I somewhat unceremoniously almost choked on the Polo mint I was sucking – something we had joked about many times since. But our relationship developed no further back then as I was the recent ex of one of his close friends and the 'mate code' had kicked in. I chuckled to myself as I glanced at that very guy, ironically now happily married to my former 'bestie' from school, with a family unit of their own.

Quite a few of the girls ended up marrying the boys from back then. Bobby and I were a late addition to this coupling trend. After school we lost contact as we went our separate ways to different universities. I always heard about him through the other girls, though. Whilst he stayed single, playing the role of the doting and loyal eldest son to his strict Muslim parents, I married Ian at twenty-eight and we had two children, Emily and Isabel. Unfortunately, the marriage didn't go to plan and we split when the youngest, Isabel, was only three years old. Luckily, we maintained a very amicable relationship and despite not being together, still showed care and consideration to each other, happily attending events as a couple when necessary.

Bobby and I got together the year after my marriage failed. A genuine, loving, caring and fun guy, I was over the moon. Even today, he was still holding court with the group. Always the high-spirited centre of fun, he was full of energy. I'll never forget the time we all did a twenty-six mile walk around the city, an event organised by the local radio station. He bounced along to SL2 'On a Ragga Tip' and House of Pain 'Jump Around' whilst the rest of us tried not to focus on our sore, blistered feet. His energy was infectious, as was his smile.

I turned and caught his eye across the group. He shot me a dazzling smile and with a slight nod mouthed, 'You OK?' I reassured him with a smile and return nod. We were holding a special secret between us. Only two weeks previously, we had found out I was pregnant! We were embarking on our very own new adventure. Thirty-nine, divorced and with two relatively independent children, I never expected to have another baby, but Bobby's absolute life desire to have a child, and the fact I was madly in love with him, led to us taking the bold step of having a baby of our own. It felt so right. However, it was early days in the pregnancy and nausea flowed through me. I had driven to the party to explain why I wasn't drinking, a weak excuse bearing in mind Bob had always been the group's nominated driver as he didn't drink due to his cultural beliefs. Fortunately, no one seemed to notice.

The party was full of laughter, reminiscences and talk of future paths. As we stood on the lawn hugging our goodbyes, discussing when we would be able to meet up again as a group, little did any of us know this was to be one of our very last times together. In that happy moment, none of us knew what was to happen in just under seven months' time.

No one could have predicted what that day in March 2016 was to bring.

Chapter 1

And So It Began

06.30, Friday, 4 March 2016

I WOKE IN THE DARK, MY PEACE SHATTERED BY THE INCESSANT BEEPING OF MY PHONE'S ALARM. BLEARY-EYED, I PRODDED at the screen, almost knocking it off the bedside table in the process. Another night of disturbed sleep – my burgeoning bump had woken me numerous times throughout the night for toilet visits or because my unborn daughter decided to take a gym class in my belly. The joy of the third and final trimester. At thirty-six weeks and two days pregnant, I only had a short way left to go.

Nearing the end of a week's annual leave from my job as a project manager at a large pharmaceutical company, leading into maternity leave, I was looking forward to some rest and an opportunity to get everything together for the baby's imminent arrival. The week to this point had been far from restful and included a few days in hospital with threatened premature labour. But today was Friday. Clear of all those challenges, I ran through a mental checklist of what had to be done: eldest daughter's school assembly, going to the gym, doing food shopping at some point and perhaps meeting up with my partner, Bobby, to sort out money or have a late lunch in Sutton Coldfield, our hometown.

At that moment, he stirred and rolled towards me, lazily smiling a 'Good morning' and attempting to pull me to him, the lump of our daughter in my belly keeping a chaste distance between us. I knew that twinkle in his eye very well – it's what got me in this way in the first place!

'No way, mister! Not this morning, you've got to get to work,' I told him with as much sternness as I could muster.

A slight pout of defeat. 'OK,' he conceded, 'But tonight when the girls are in bed, you and I are having an early night.'

'Deal!' I laughed, rolling my heavily pregnant self out of bed. As I stood brushing my hair and pinning it up in a clip for the gym, Bobby came back into the bedroom ready for work. He said he was off to the bank at lunchtime and suggested we meet after for lunch. He had money from his business that he wanted to transfer to my account to help cover my maternity leave period, but the bank had stopped the initial payment to guard against money laundering. He asked for my identification, so he could prove I was his partner and that nothing untoward was happening, so I handed him a couple of utility bills in my name and my driving licence since I couldn't find my passport – knowing me, I'd shoved it away somewhere. He rolled up the documents, popped the licence in his wallet, gave me and my two girls a kiss goodbye, shouted, 'Love you, see you later,' and was gone – leaving our home for the last time ever.

I arrived at school in plenty of time for the assembly. Ian, my former husband, was already there, ready to go and grab us a seat in the front row. Emily, our eldest, was playing the mother part in a rewrite of the famous tale of the prodigal son (or daughter, here), so she had taken one of my smart jackets to wear. She looked so grown-up and I was so proud of her. Afterwards, I gave her the big hug she'd earned and she asked if she could keep the jacket until the end of the school day. I conceded on her absolute promise that she'd look after it. She ran off with a cheeky grin and our youngest, Isabel, waved shyly from amongst a knot of her friends as they filed back to class. Of course I didn't know that I wouldn't see their beautiful faces at the end of the school day, let alone be fighting for my life in just over five hours' time.

Ian and I strolled out of school together and then went our separate ways. I jumped in my car to head to the gym. He had a rare day off from work and we joked about how I wouldn't be following suit. Eight months pregnant and there was me, the unstoppable machine! As I got in my car, I checked my phone – a message from Bobby sat there, unread. 'Please apologise to Emily. I forgot to tell her to "break a leg"! xxx'.

Grinning, I dropped the phone onto the passenger seat and set off for the gym. The usual crowd were in and the personal trainers looked at me warily, asking if I really should be there with the bump as they knew I'd been in hospital. I reassured them that I was fine and would take it easy – after all, I certainly couldn't manage running on the treadmill without a sturdy pair of absorbent pants on!

Whilst I gave the cross-trainer a good workout, a friend of my ex-boyfriend Jason came over to me to chat and my heart sank: I was worried that Jason, who turned out to have a very nasty temper, would find out where I'd gone. I had moved away from my first gym to get away from him and I didn't want him to find out I had a new life and was pregnant to boot. As soon as I was done on the trainer, I texted Bobby to tell him about it. His reply came back, typically supportive, saying 'Fuck him, do your thing and ignore him. Are you OK? and telling me he loved me.

This was followed by another message, six minutes later, an angry message telling me his meeting had moved – and calling the people responsible bitches and c*nts.

The message surprised me – Bobby didn't usually swear that much in texts. We exchanged a couple more messages, with his last-ever text to me asking, 'Is Ian picking up the kids? xxx'

I finished my workout, showered and left the gym. Heavy clouds filled the sky, there was a slight chill in the air and rain threatened to come pouring down. With more time to spare than I initially planned, I decided to face the weekly food shop. As I wandered the aisles, aimlessly throwing stuff in the trolley, I called Bobby. We discussed the usual mundane couple stuff and his promise to the kids to help them make me breakfast in bed that weekend on Mother's Day before our talk turned to business. He said it would be good if I could attend the bank appointment, so I finished the call and rang to ask my mum about doing the school run. Knowing we had a money issue to deal with, she immediately agreed.

As I neared the end of the shop, my ever-expanding bump getting in the way as I navigated a full trolley, I ran into a woman from my previous gym. She was completely surprised by my pregnancy and I delighted in telling her how Bobby and I planned on marrying when I could see my hips again! As one of the last people to see me unharmed, it would be something she would report to the police in the coming days.

Back home, I tackled the dull job of unpacking. Bobby rang: his appointment had been shifted back even later to 3.30pm. When I told him I'd walk in, he wasn't keen at all, insisting he'd pick me up. I didn't want him putting pressure on himself by diverting home before the meeting so I made it clear I was fine walking in. He then asked a strange question: 'If you did walk, which way would you go?'

'Stalker!' I laughed down the phone.

'Hey, it's not like that with us! Just tell me which way you'd go,' he said in an annoyed tone.

'The normal way – past the hospital, then up over Trinity Hill and down into Sutton,' I told him.

'OK, but you aren't walking anyway, so it doesn't matter. I'll come and get you in the next half hour,' he said, his impatience vanished. I could hear the warmth return to his voice.

I hung up, a little confused. Dead time filled the room so I started making Emily's favourite chocolate cake, given she'd done so well in assembly. I got as far as getting out the ingredients before losing interest. It was 2.55pm. Spurred on, I got my stuff together to set off. Despite Bobby's insistence, he still hadn't arrived.

Sod it! I thought, *I'll walk.*

When I called Bobby to tell him I'd left, he answered quickly: 'I'm stuck in traffic on the other side of town, still not even on the Expressway yet. Where are you?'

'Not to worry, babe. I set off when I didn't hear from you. I thought you were probably stuck at work, so I'm walking down now.'

'Oh, OK. Sorry, I should have called.'

He sounded slightly distracted, but he was driving.

'It's honestly no problem. I'm just turning into Rectory Road now, just call me when you arrive.'

'OK, baby, I'll call you when I get there. Love you,' he replied smoothly.

'Love you, too,' I said and hung up.

He was talking without hands-free and had to be quick, I guessed. But I wasn't to know that Bobby wasn't really in his car, that he wasn't really on the other side of Birmingham.

The rain pelted down as I walked down Rectory Road and the air got quite cold, as if on the point of snowing. As I approached the end of the road, I chewed my bottom lip nervously. Ahead was Trinity Hill, the cut through behind the church to Sutton Coldfield town centre. I've always hated Trinity Hill. When I was home from university one Christmas, a girl was murdered there on New Year's Eve. It rocked Sutton Coldfield. A massive manhunt ensued and it was many years before her killer was eventually found, through a chance arrest for an unrelated event. A memorial based on a piece of artwork she'd created was placed at the top of Trinity Hill. Every time I passed it, I thought of her and grew cold at the thought of what she must have endured. This was a place that always made me feel slightly uneasy. But as I crossed the shortcut, I saw a woman walking up with her shopping bags. The rain was still coming down, I was getting drenched and it was the middle of a Friday afternoon. There was no need to worry. I reprimanded myself inside for being so ridiculous. I could have walked the long way around the front of the church, sticking to the main road, but I overrode my gut feeling and strode down behind the church garden wall passing under the overgrown, oppressive trees.

It was then that I heard the footsteps behind me. Heavy steps, moving at a faster pace than mine. As I turned to look over my shoulder, a shiver ran through me. A hooded man, wearing a dark top, rough jeans and scruffy trainers, had his head down as he powered down the lane behind me at a pace. Clamping down on the instinctive twinge of fear, I reminded myself that there was no reason to be nervous – in a moment he'd be past me and life would go on, there was nothing to worry about.

Chapter 2

So, How Did I Get Here?

AND *PAUSE*... WE WILL RETURN!

MANY PEOPLE HAVE ASKED ME, 'WHAT HAPPENED BEFORE THE ATTACK? YOU MUST SURELY HAVE SEEN IT COMING?'

The simple answer is no. If you asked anybody who knew Bobby, they would all say the same: he seemed happy, excited about the baby, and in love with me. A calm, non-violent, caring individual. So, the question is: what happened?

Let me take you through the journey to meeting Bob again, how our relationship developed, the day it fell terminally (almost literally) apart and the aftermath with my recovery and what I found out about the man I thought I knew so well.

I believe our lives and experiences change and shape us. Our experiences prepare us sometimes in ways we could never have imagined until we are faced with a circumstance that draws on all our resilience to get us through. Without further ado, let's go back in time...

March 2013: after three years of problems, arguments, issues and numerous attempts to get things back on track,

Ian's and my nearly nine-year marriage failed irreversibly and he moved out. It was an exceptionally tough decision to go our separate ways. As you step towards your beloved in your big white dress, you believe this will be for life – your 'Happy Ever After'. It was a very sad time.

Our daughters were just seven and three years old. I really struggled with how this could affect them. Little did I know they would have so much more to deal with in their very young lives, just three years on from this point.

The realisation soon hit me that I was the most responsible person in the house: the kids' rock, their stability. Left with no other choice, I began to find my feet as a single mother.

I sought solace in the gym to burn off the frustrations and stresses of the week. I've been a gym-goer for many years, training all the way through my pregnancies. Unfortunately, I managed to prolapse a spinal disc spectacularly after having Isabel and swimming became the main form of exercise for my rehabilitation. That's how I met Jason. As I powered up and down the pool, I didn't notice him watching me. When I came up for a break, he was there greeting me. It was a couple of months after Ian had left that I referred in conversation to being a single mum. Instantly, he came back with the line, 'Well, I have to take you out for a coffee and you have no excuse!'

I laughed, not taking the offer particularly seriously. Jason asked me out a number of times and eventually I threw caution to the wind and agreed to a drink. The first date, just a few drinks in Birmingham city centre, went well. Our second date was at the Tate Modern in London. But the rosy start of the relationship soon faded as I began to notice Jason's temper. The more time we spent together, it became clear that my independence, something he was so attracted to initially, actually caused him an issue. After just a few months I called time on the relationship.

For my first summer as a single mother, with my family, I took the girls to the South of France. On the morning of the holiday the kids sat together on a big leather beanbag in the front bay window watching TV whilst I pulled the last few bits and pieces together. I called them through to the kitchen and with the radio blaring, the girls munched their way through cereal and toast.

Then it happened: *Bang!*

It sounded like an explosion in the front room. I raced out of the kitchen into the now smoke-filled front room, trying desperately to work out what had happened. Then I saw it: the back of my car had come *through* the bay window. Bricks lay strewn across the beanbag the kids had been sat on, just ten minutes before. A neighbour from three doors down had somehow knocked his wife's automatic car into reverse, shot backwards off his drive, completed a full semi-circle backwards before hitting my car, parked on my drive, pushing it through the window!

The front bay had to be completely rebuilt. It was a horrible experience but I got through and it was another step forwards towards my independence and resilience. I remember catching my breath and thinking, *Wow, I can get through more than I thought.*

In the October of that year, I had major surgery to fuse my lower spine where the disc was repeatedly prolapsing. The surgeon, a brilliant man, wanted to make an incision through my lower abdomen and access my spine from the 'front'. Horrified at the thought of a scar down my stomach, I refused and so he went through my back. How ridiculous that seems now, with my scar-filled abdomen. The surgery

11

went well and, to my surprise, it was only a day later that they got me out of bed to try walking. I nearly passed out during the first few attempts, but determinedly pushed on – I had to, I couldn't give in.

But the challenges of the year weren't over. Friday the 13th (this time in December), generally a day feared by so many, Jason called to ask to see me and as the children were with Ian that day, he came to my house. The conversation soon deteriorated and it only took a few minutes before I realised I couldn't take his abuse, so I told him I was moving on with my life without him. That was met with a stream of obscenities and hurtful comments. He went to walk towards the door, his temper growing as he realised I meant it, then without warning he turned on me and pinned me against the wall. His right hand was clenched around my windpipe like a vice as he lifted me. I put my hands up to pull at his fingers and panic set in as I struggled to breathe. He dragged me across the hallway and pinned me against the opposite wall before throwing me down backwards.

I was dumbstruck. I'd never had a man lay a hand on me in anger before. Previously, every man I'd known or been partner to knew the cardinal rule that you don't lay a hand on a woman. Rubbing my neck and staring up at him in disbelief, I said nothing. Panicked, he crouched down, begging me to forgive him. But I just stared at him and after a few minutes quietly asked him to leave. I got to my feet, wobbling slightly, trying my hardest to disguise the sheer terror running through me. As calmly as I could, I repeated, 'Please leave. I've heard your apology and I just want you to leave now.'

As I held the door open, he bolted out, screaming apologies as he went. After jumping in his car parked outside, he screeched away. Completely bewildered, I shut the door. I didn't know quite what to do next but two of my friends, who I called after he left, begged me to report it. Later that evening, I rang the police non-emergency line and was questioned in some detail about the incident. I made it clear that I didn't want to press charges, just have it recorded. However, two officers turned up at my house. The next day, they arrested Jason and took him into Sutton Coldfield police station for questioning. He was issued with a Community Resolution Order, recording what he had done. The police updated me later that he had admitted to common assault. In the following days I was so nervous, wondering if there would be a backlash from reporting him to the police. I left my gym, where I had been a member for twelve years, to get away from Jason and looked for a new one – I needed to take charge of the situation.

The year 2013 had been vile: separation, both house and car smashed in and then assaulted by a new partner. As I happily waved the year off, my Facebook account pinged with a Friend request from Bobby (Babur Raja) Karamat. Bob from my old school days! I hadn't heard from him for years. Occasionally, I'd seen him around and had friends who still saw him regularly, taking holidays together even. I accepted the request, smiling to myself as it was good to hear from him. Messenger soon pinged through a message from him asking how I was, what I'd been up to and wanting to catch up. Quite a few messages later, we had caught up on what each of us were doing. He too was now back living in Sutton Coldfield and so we agreed to meet for a drink and catch up. But, as Christmas took over, we never got round to it.

Chapter 3

Internet Dating and Other Crazy Decisions

1 JANUARY 2014 – A TIME WHEN WE VOW TO MAKE THE YEAR AHEAD OUR BEST YET AND I WAS ADAMANT THIS YEAR WAS GOING TO BE BETTER THAN THE LAST.

I wanted the happiness that everyone else seemed to have in their relationships, although whether that perception is real or fabricated through social media is a matter for debate. I'd never considered online dating before, but I felt it was my only way forward so I paid the subscription fee for a mini-trial and set up my profile. I went out on dates with three different men. The first man lasted one date as I soon found out, through a very quick social media background check, that he was in fact engaged. The next man was lovely. We met a couple of times but the spark just wasn't there. Somewhat disastrously, I told him this after our third date, in a leisure club car park, as he went in for a goodbye kiss. I then forgot the barrier code to get out and had to call after him. His face lit up, only to drop again as I asked for the code (he was so nice, he even told me the right number combination!).

My final attempt was calamitous: a good-looking guy, into his weightlifting. Unfortunately, he talked for hours about how much protein he consumed each day and frequently referred to himself in the third person. Eventually, I blurted out, 'Natalie finds it very annoying when ******* refers to himself in the third person all the time.' Things finally came to a head after I'd been on a work conference abroad. He couldn't handle my job or independence and spent the week drinking himself into a stupor and calling all hours. That's when I knew it was over and finished the relationship, resigning myself to a life of singledom. My short trial had ended on the internet dating site and so I deactivated the account.

With my internet dating experience firmly behind me, I decided to focus on myself. This began with a long-anticipated operation: my boob job, or 'breast augmentation' as it's more technically known. I appreciate people have very mixed opinions about this procedure, but it was important to me for very personal reasons. After breastfeeding two children and losing weight when I got divorced, it would be fair to compare my chest to two wet teabags hanging off a spoon. I felt terrifically self-conscious, even embarrassed, and had to do something about it. Little did I know taking this first step to fill out my chest would be a key reason why I would survive the most horrific event of my life. The operation had mixed success, the one implant didn't 'sit' quite right. I was told to wait to see how they settled, which I reluctantly agreed to.

As I recovered from the operation Jason got back in contact, apologising profusely for what he had done nearly six months before. He blurted out how he had sought anger management counselling. Of course I was exceptionally wary, but listened carefully. If he had gone to a counsellor, I knew this would be a massive step for him. There were positive qualities which Jason possessed and so, warily, I gradually let him back into my life and decided to give him a second chance. Doesn't everyone deserve one?

Things seemed really good at first, but it didn't take long for the cracks to show through, most notably when my childhood friend Anita and I went on holiday with my girls to Spain and his jealousy grew. The holiday was incredible – the kids spent practically the entire week in the pool, almost diving in in their pyjamas some mornings! Our evenings were generally very quiet and once the kids were tucked up in bed, Anita and I spent our evenings out on the patio, by the open doors to hear the children. Most nights consisted of a drink, a chill, a chat and a perusal through social media.

Summer 2014 was the year of the Ice Bucket Challenge to raise money and awareness of Amyotrophic lateral sclerosis (ALS). Social media was full of videos of people chucking buckets of iced water over their heads, whilst we laughed at them and donated money via text. Bobby posted a video of himself doing the Ice Bucket Challenge outside his work. Anita and I watched with intrigue: we hadn't seen Bobby in the flesh for years and he had really changed! The video reminded me that I hadn't contacted him back for months. The events with Jason had made me lose track of time, so I messaged him that night to say hi and commented that Anita and I could barely believe the man in the video was actually him. Almost straight away, he messaged back and we caught up on the last eight months. He asked how Anita was and suggested the three of us should meet for a drink to catch up when we got back.

We agreed, but I was concerned about how Jason would be about it. I knew he would probably start an argument, but it was Anita and I meeting up with an old school mate, nothing more, so he'd have to understand.

Anita and I flew back with the children, sun-kissed and relaxed. Jason seemed happy to see us back and for a week he was calm. However, that soon diminished and his paranoia grew about any man whom I came into contact with. One Saturday evening in late September, it all came to a head during a meal out with the children. We ended up on a table by Isabel's young male swimming instructor and his exuberant friends, who chatted to us animatedly. Jason's face turned to thunder, and tension radiated from him. We left the restaurant before we had even ordered. Later that night, with the children tucked up in bed, I told Jason it was clear he hadn't changed and I finished the relationship before anything else happened. The next night, he came back to collect some of his stuff that was at my house whilst the kids were at Ian's. His mood was stormy and trouble was clearly brewing. Luckily, I got him out of the house quickly and closed the door. As I turned and headed into the lounge, I heard my phone beep: ironically, it was Bobby.

'So, shall we get a date and time sorted for this catch-up for the three of us, then?'

Chapter 4

The First Drink, First Date...

MY MOBILE LAY ON THE ARM OF THE SOFA, *IMESSAGE: BOBBY KARAMAT* EMBLAZONED ACROSS THE SCREEN. I OPENED THE MESSAGE AND SMILED AS I TEXTED ANITA TO SEE WHEN SHE was free. She texted back that she was busy with work the next few weeks but told me to get a couple of dates and she would see what she could do.

Bobby and I got a couple of dates I knew I could get a babysitter for and I asked Anita. She wasn't sure she could make the ones we had chosen but said to go ahead and she would try her best to join us. We arranged it for the following week and I popped it in my diary, confirming with my mum the babysitting duties and texting Anita the date we planned to meet.

In the week that followed, Bobby and I swapped some more messages. His sense of humour was still there and we laughed about things from many years back. Sunday soon came around and my phone beeped with a group text from Bobby. As I read it, my heart sank: his father had passed away that morning. Bobby had spent the last couple of years caring for his father, who had been very ill with kidney failure, amongst other health issues. Still the family-focused, kind and caring man I had always known, Bobby lived at home with his parents and his life revolved around his family. A long-awaited son (his father's first marriage produced four daughters), his mother adored him.

As I sat staring at my phone, I wondered how best to write a message to convey how sad I was for Bobby and his family without sounding patronising or crass. I told him to focus on his family and that I would be there for a coffee and chat when he needed to talk to someone else. His life would be crazy for the weeks that followed, I knew. The eldest son, his mother had relied on him heavily for support before his father's death, so I could only imagine the responsibility placed on him now. He had to focus on them all and so I stood back to let them have space to grieve. Bobby kept in contact though, just to talk about what was happening. As with Muslim tradition, the funeral happened very quickly and from what he told me, the house was flooded with visitors.

I assumed we would not meet for quite some time, which was fine. We hadn't caught up face to face in such a long time, a few more weeks wouldn't make a difference. However, after a week, Bobby was desperate for a distraction, some normality away from the intense grief and so he asked to meet me for a drink. He was due to fly out to Pakistan on Tuesday, 14 October for a family wedding, which would see him away for a couple of weeks. We arranged to meet the Wednesday before at a local bar. Anita couldn't make it as she was busy, but I knew Bobby would be feeling emotional and assumed we would have a quick, quiet chat before going our separate ways, so I didn't change it. I still remember what I wore: skinny jeans, vest top and brown fitted leather jacket – the jacket I wore on the day of my horrific attack, the same jacket worn for our first and last date.

On arrival, Bobby had already saved two large sofas by an open roaring fire. His dark hair had gone grey and it was strange meeting someone so familiar but now considerably older. Always the light-hearted joker, a mischievous look still glinted in his eye though. We both broke into a huge grin as we hugged 'hello'.

It didn't take long before we were chattering away about everything and anything – what the gang from school were up to and the parties we'd been to, including the one where we once kissed. We laughed for hours until we realised the bar was emptying and I remembered I should be getting back home to Mum and the kids. Bobby walked me back to my car. It was a cold, dark night and we huddled together to keep warm. As we reached my car, he pulled me towards him and kissed me full on the lips. I was a little taken aback, but it felt right and so we stood there like a pair of teenagers, snogging away. Soon, the cold set in and I pulled away as I knew I had to get back. After unlocking the car, I jumped in. Bobby leant in and asked to see me again before he flew out on the Tuesday to Islamabad. I said I would see what I could arrange – the weekend was packed with parties and family celebrations, but Monday night was a possibility.

One last kiss and I shut the door and pulled away.

I smiled, a little confused; it was certainly something I hadn't planned, but it seemed so natural. It was only a short drive back to my house and I bounded in, a look of slight bewilderment on my face. When I filled my mum in on the events of the evening, she just laughed – 'Oh well, at least it's someone you've known a long time, so see what happens.'

I woke the next morning to a text from Bobby, saying what a lovely evening he'd had and how he was looking forward to seeing me again. It was Mum's birthday, so I popped in after work to see her with my middle sister Mand. I'm the youngest and most headstrong of three girls. Mum is my role model and inspiration, strong, loving and never giving in. Bringing up three children alone, the bond between us all was strong.

When I headed home, my phone beeped: Jason still had tools at my house and I needed to give him money for some painting he'd done. Back home, I stacked the bag of tools and cash by the front door for when he came past to collect them on his way home from the gym.

It was 9pm and there was a knock at the door. My heart raced slightly. Mum and Mand had offered to come over, knowing Jason was due round and not trusting him, but I had reassured them that it would be alright.

I was wrong. His anger at me refusing to try again at our relationship caused him to advance at me once more and in a desperate attempt to keep him out of the house, I found myself trapped in the porch with him. Once more his hand was around my throat and he pushed me up high against the door. I pulled at his fingers and screamed for help. He pushed me down to the side, smacking my ribcage off the low internal brick wall in the porch and threw me to the ground. As I fell at his feet, he grabbed me by the wrist. Luckily, he stepped back and tripped, losing his balance and grip on me, so I took my chance to shove him out the way and ran to my neighbour's house, pounding on their door for help. He came quickly to the door and told Jason to leave.

Once I was back in my house, I collapsed into tears and, with shaking hands, called Anita. Red marks were all around my throat where his fingers had gripped me, my wrist was bruised and cut, my ribs hurt from bashing the wall as he pushed me to the floor. Anita came over and she sat me down, then ran her hands through her hair in frustration,

'Right, have you phoned the police yet?' was the first inevitable question.

'No, and I'm not going to,' I replied, an edge of fear in my voice.

I explained that Jason would be charged automatically, which would mean me having to go to court and I just couldn't face it. I was sure it was over now that he'd done this – how wrong I was.

The next morning, I was bruised and sore. Throughout the day my mobile filled with voicemails and text messages from Jason. A couple of texts from Bobby came too – our evening out just forty-eight hours earlier a world away. His messages made me smile for the first time that day. He asked about my day and whether we could confirm a meet-up before he left on the Tuesday. I didn't tell him what had happened.

On the Monday night, I saw Bobby before he left for Pakistan the next day. It was really good to see him again. We'd been texting the whole weekend and then when we met, we chatted non-stop. He asked what had been happening with me and so I decided to tell him, not knowing how he would react. He was brilliant – supportive, concerned and understanding about my feelings around the police and not reporting it yet. But he was appalled at what Jason had done – he couldn't believe a man would do that to a woman. The irony!

Bobby flew out the next day and I had regular updates and photos about what was happening. I joked he had to be careful not to be married off too whilst out there, to which he replied his mother had tried many times and it hadn't worked. He was adamant he would choose his own partner and although he was forty and still hadn't found that special person, he hoped that was now changing.

Early evening on Saturday, 18 October 2014, Bobby – via the wonders of FaceTime – asked me to be his girlfriend. The relationship would have its challenges, we both knew (namely, his mother), but he reassured me it would be fine. Despite having lived in England for the best part of forty years, Bobby's mother was – and still is – a very traditional Pakistani Muslim. His two younger sisters, however, were both married to white British men (who converted to Islam to help smooth the acceptance). However, Bobby was his mother's beloved eldest son and I wasn't going to have an easy time in terms of acceptance. But as happens in the early days of relationships, you don't think too much about the consequences. I knew that Bobby's mother had cut off his youngest brother because he had married a Sikh girl. She refused point blank to have anything to do with him and his little brother wasn't held in such esteem as Bobby. I should have seen the signs from the start. You only live once, I thought – it didn't cross my mind that this notion would go anywhere near what it did. Little did I know this was the beginning of the end of that life. I was to learn so much more about Bobby and the complicated family picture and life he led and weaved but, unfortunately, most of it too late. For now, I was happy and certain that cultural hurdles might be overcome with time, patience and a little persistence.

During the time Bobby was away in Pakistan, Jason refused to give up in his pursuit of me. Voicemails stacked up. In a couple of the messages he actually admitted to assaulting me. He continued to harass me, even leaving a note through my door and writing on my window sill in Biro. That was when I realised enough was enough. Knowing I had no other choice, on Sunday, 26 October 2014, with a heavy heart I walked into Sutton Coldfield police station, my heart pounding.

'I've come to report an assault and continuing threats from my ex-partner. He has already had a Community Resolution Order placed on him from assaulting me before, but I didn't want to press charges then,' I told the officer as I stood at the desk.

She looked at me and could see how distressed I was. She smiled and said she would get an officer to come and speak to me. I spent seven hours in the police station going through everything; my statement went on for about twelve pages. They told me they would send officers out to arrest him for assault and harassment, and bring him in.

Chapter 5

A Whole New World

AFTER THE MONUMENTAL MOVE AT THE WEEKEND OF ACTUALLY TURNING UP AT THE POLICE STATION AND PRESSING CHARGES, I EXPECTED THE MONDAY TO BRING NEWS of Jason's arrest and everything to change. But it took until the New Year before he was arrested. He was sent off to the magistrates court and pleaded not guilty to both counts. The trial date was set for Monday, 13 April 2014 – over six months after the assault. My heart sank.

Back to that Monday and a welcome distraction came later as PIA (Pakistan International Airline) flight PK791 touched down at Birmingham airport from Islamabad, carrying Bobby. *He was home!* A warm glow flowed through me, knowing he was back on UK soil. I hadn't told him about my day at Sutton Coldfield police station as I didn't want to weigh him down with that sort of news whilst he was away with his family. Instead, we arranged to meet up soon and I was so excited to see him.

Bobby and I developed into a very serious relationship quickly. Only two weeks after he had landed from Pakistan, he declared his love for me as we left a restaurant. It was a rare night that I had driven. Bob got in the passenger side of my car and asked me to wait before turning the engine on. He looked me straight in the eye and said, 'I know this is going to sound crazy, I know we have only been dating a few weeks, but I'm totally and utterly in love with you.'

Flabbergasted, I wasn't quite sure what to say. I knew Bobby was completely different to Jason – calm, loving, secure and protective of me. From the start I adored him, but I wasn't sure I was ready to say 'I love you' back. So, I was honest. I told him I thought a lot of him, but I didn't want to say it back until I was one hundred per cent sure. My lack of reciprocation didn't hinder our relationship, though.

Christmas was soon upon us, and despite Bobby never having really celebrated it before, we both went to town on gifts. He had once told me about a personal car registration number plate his dad used to have. The plate ended up getting sold, but I knew it meant a lot to him so I investigated various private number plate specialists until I found one very close to it. He was overwhelmed when he opened it, tears prickled his eyes, and he said no one had ever done something so thoughtful for him.

We were a truly loved-up couple. Mutual friends we had known since our school days were so pleased to see old friends together like this in a couple. *My fairytale end may just be happening*, I thought. Bobby even made work colleagues of mine envious as every training course or meeting I went away on, which involved staying at a hotel, he arranged for a bouquet to be delivered to my room in time for when I got there. I felt a glow that someone had put so much thought and effort into making me feel special.

Unfortunately, not everyone was so happy for us. Bobby

had never told his mother about any partner before me. As far as she was concerned, whether she truly believed it or not, her precious son had had no previous girlfriends. He was attached to the family, catering for all their needs in terms of support. The prize son, who had only gone against her wishes in relation to an arranged marriage, as he flatly refused any introductions she tried to engineer. He wanted to choose his own partner, and that choice fell to me. I believe his mother thought he would either stay faithful to his family for life, living at home with her, looking after her until her dying day, or give in eventually and take up an arranged marriage (as time passed and he had no child). I was certainly not what she was expecting, let alone wanting.

He told his mother at the end of the November. She was furious. He broke the news one evening when he went to his youngest sister's house, where his mother was staying, helping her with her then newborn twins. From what I was told, an almighty row broke out in which his mother told him in no uncertain terms that she was ashamed of him and he had betrayed her. He had, according to her, devastated her life with this news and she would not forgive him if he continued with the relationship. His sister, Shazan, despite being married to a white British man and with three children, condemned him too. She added that she could not believe he would upset and betray their mother, especially so soon after their father had passed away. Clearly having forgotten the ethnicity of her own husband who was in the house at the time, she questioned how he could have chosen a partner like myself. Both his mother and sister laid into him verbally. I believe he never thought his family would actually turn on him so badly. For the first time in his life he was condemned and told he was a point of shame for the family because he chose me, a white British Catholic, as his partner.

I remember the broken look on his face when he came back to me that evening. The hurt was palatable. He had never crossed his mother like this before, he had always done things to please her, yet that counted for nothing it seemed. All because I didn't fit what she wanted. I'm not perfect, but I'm honest, loving and supportive and I loved and adored Bobby; I would stand by his side for life. They couldn't ask for a more loyal partner, but they didn't give me a chance. I hugged him tight and told him that he had to do what was best for him – I couldn't cause a rift in his family as I knew they meant the world to him. I told him I loved him and would be there for him for life, if he wanted. Breaking free of my grasp, he looked me straight in the eye: 'I want you, I choose you. My family will have to accept you. They will accept you with time, they just need time to settle and adjust to it.'

Though not entirely convinced even then that his family would change, I wanted so badly to believe we could get over this hurdle. I was eager to show his mother that I wasn't the Devil incarnate. I knew I wouldn't convert to Islam, but I would always respect Bobby's religion and support him in the cultural practices he undertook. So I hugged and reassured him that we would get through this together – I truly meant it.

The day after he had broken the news, Bobby's phone filled with messages, mainly from his youngest sister. She repeated her disbelief in his choice of partner, admonished him for having chosen a white non-Muslim and told him, in no uncertain terms, that he must finish with me. Though I did my best not to react, inside I could feel my anger welling up. I could almost accept his mother's stance: a Pakistani-Muslim woman who wanted her eldest son to have the traditional marriage to a Pakistani-Muslim girl, preferably of her choice. I didn't agree with her, but I could almost see why she was like she was. But I could not abide his sister, who had chosen a white male for her partner. *She* had the partner of *her* choice, she hadn't had an arranged marriage, she hadn't even married an Asian or original Muslim. She knew her husband did not abide by traditional cultural practices, yet I was deemed unacceptable. I bit my tongue, held my opinion as best I could, and saved the ranting and venting for my closest friends and Mum.

One subject his sister did raise with him was children. From the start of our relationship, Bobby made it clear that he wanted at least one child. His time was running out for such things, but it was something he so badly wanted. Already he had asked me if I could have another child. It was a crucial question as if I hadn't wanted any more, he told me he would have to walk away to pursue his dream of becoming a dad. When I was married, I had wanted a third child, but with my divorce, I had come to accept that having another child was out of the question. My older two had started to grow up and become less dependent, with time with their dad one day and night every week (which gave me the chance to catch up with myself), so the need for a third child flitted away. I even had a coil fitted to prevent any 'accidents', but I knew I had to consider this. Committing to this relationship with Bob would mean committing to having another child. For a short while, I reflected and concluded I would have another child. Just one more. For him. For *us*. I told him, so when the text came through from his sister, asking if I would have a child

31

for him, his answer went back quickly: Yes. Definitely. I was fine with this commitment – I loved him and saw my life with him.

Despite family disproval, Bobby and I continued our intense relationship. He took me away to London for the New Year to his old university haunt of South Kensington. We went to bars, restaurants and nightclubs and stayed in a beautiful boutique hotel. He treated me in a way I had never been treated before. We went sightseeing, saw a show and were probably cringeworthy as we cuddled up against the cold in places such as Trafalgar Square. The photos and images of that trip are still etched on my brain, our smiles and laughter as we leapt on and off the Tube. Joint selfies at Tube stations, in museums and nightclubs. Faces pressed together as we grinned at the camera, so happy and so in love. Suddenly I wasn't having to be the strong one in the relationship, I had someone who could lead and I was happy to follow. I trusted him completely. This whole new world, despite its challenges, was turning out to be not that bad: we were invincible, we could overcome anything.

Things went from strength to strength. February saw my birthday and Bobby was keen to introduce me to some of his family that approved of us. He had a cousin out in Germany and they had been close since childhood. Bobby even confided they actually had a sexual relationship in their teens, which few knew about. At first I found it very strange to deal with – she was his first cousin, a complete no-no in my head. But it seemed more 'normal' in his view of the world. In fact, Bobby's relationship before me had been with another first cousin, who at the time was living in Pakistan. They were unofficially engaged, but the relationship fizzled out after a couple of years. She now lives in the UK with her husband and child. Back in Germany, his cousin there was now married with two children. We arrived in time for their 'Karnival' and before I knew it, we were lining the streets of the small German village. I was wearing furry tiger dungarees whilst he stuck to his own clothes firmly. It was completely not Bob's thing. A wry smile crossed his face as I bounced about in my borrowed attire.

On our final evening there, Bob arranged a meal for the two of us at a lovely restaurant. On our return to the hotel, he turned to me and said, 'I want to marry you, Natalie Queiroz. One day, I want you to be my wife with our child. You are everything I have ever wanted.' He looked me deep in the eyes and I felt so happy and secure. This man had turned my world around, shown me things I had never seen, given me a new lease of life. Germany only served to enforce on me that Bobby and I really were for life.

On Valentine's Day, he presented me with a handwritten poem he had penned and placed in a frame. It read:

I know that I am not perfect,
I get angry and I am stubborn,
I just hope that you (are) able to look past all my faults
   and forgive all my mistakes,
Because I also know that I have found the one person
   I want to spend the rest of my life with,
I love you.

All this made it clear in my mind that I wanted him to be forever a part of my life. It was time for him to meet the children, I decided, having waited until we knew we were in a stronger, more secure place. We set 1 March as the date to meet and to ease the pressure of the day, planned a day trip to Warwick Castle. It was a great day. The air was cold and the sky cloudy, but in true Brit fashion, we pushed on and had our picnic (although the rug was used to cover our laps as we sat on benches, rather than on the grass). Afterwards, we looked around the castle and the kids seemed to really take to Bobby. We rounded the day off with dinner out in a warm restaurant and happy and settled back home, Bobby left us to it.

Obviously, alongside all these positive moves forward, the case against Jason at the magistrates' court drew near. My happy bubble had to be temporarily halted as the harsh reality of my unfinished business had to be faced and dealt with. But with Bob's strong reassurance, I knew it was possible.

Anything was possible.

Chapter 6

Birmingham Magistrates' Court

BIRMINGHAM MAGISTRATES COURT IS A BEAUTIFUL AND INTRICATE BUILDING. A DEEP TERRACOTTA, IT HAS STATUES SET IN ITS FASCIA. QUEEN VICTORIA'S STATUE STANDS ABOVE THE main entrance, a tribute to Her Majesty, who ruled at the time of its build. The inside of the main building is equally breathtaking, with vast decorated ceilings and chandeliers resembling Victoria's Coronation crown.

Before the day of the trial I was taken around the court with Mum to familiarise myself with the place and its procedures. We stepped out of the court slightly bemused, crossed the road and headed for a coffee shop. As I sat there, cradling my tea, I stared out at the imposing building opposite, incredulous that my life had come to this. In a couple of weeks, I would be standing in a dock, giving evidence against a man who scared me. I shook my head, but knew it must be done.

Monday, 13 April 2015 soon came around. The trial was to start at 2pm. Nervously, I went through everything I had to do, then my phone rang. My work colleague, Mike, who had seen me bruised and battered the following day, was one of my witnesses. He couldn't get himself to the court as he had caught a flu-type illness. Sat opposite me, Bobby watched my concerned face then stepped in with the offer to drive up to Mike's house if he still wanted to attend court, to collect him and take him there himself. He still wanted to come so Bobby set off.

I drove Mum and Anita to the court, meeting my sister Mand there. We were led briskly to the Victim Support room. My neighbour, another of my witnesses, was there waiting; we were just missing Bobby with Mike. A short while later, the door opened and they walked in, Bobby looking concerned about how I was doing. The barrister briefed us all and as he left, I let out a tiny sigh. Bobby came over and hugged me tightly. He was smartly dressed, the stiffness of his blazer pressed against my face as I embraced him. 'I'm so, so proud of you for doing this. You are so brave and strong, you can do this. You have come so far, I am here for you every step of the way,' he whispered to me.

As I pulled away, I looked into his dark brown eyes and they gazed back into mine. My rock, my supporter and protector, I knew he meant every word. As I sat back down, he kept his eyes on me the whole time. Mand commented later about how Bobby watched me with complete love and adoration. I felt safe with him there, knowing he would stand by me come what may.

'He's here, by the way,' said Bobby, breaking the silence. 'He walked in behind us as we came through the entrance. He was on his own, with a pair of sunglasses on, and wearing a suit with a shirt far too large for him.'

Despite myself, I gently chuckled and shook my head, imagining Jason trying to 'style out' walking into the court as if he had done absolutely nothing wrong. We all read our statements in silence, our study broken by the code being punched in the lock of the door and the barrister's entrance.

'He has made an offer, a plea bargain. If you drop the assault charge, he will plead guilty to harassment. If not, he will keep his plea as not guilty to both.'

How dare he, I thought, incredulous.

'Not a chance,' I replied calmly. 'Absolutely no deal. He assaulted me and he knows it, the evidence is clear and I'm not dropping that charge. He can stick to pleading not guilty for both and be trialed for both.'

The barrister looked at me levelly and nodded before saying, 'The evidence is exceptionally strong, so I agree you are doing the right thing pushing on. I will tell him no deal and we will get proceedings started.' With that, he swept out once more.

'No way!' I defiantly said. 'No way have I come this far to be intimidated by him and dropping that charge. He assaulted me and he will stand trial for that.'

Bobby smiled. He called me his 'little warrior', not afraid to go into battle when needed. This was about doing the right thing.

It wasn't too long before a court usher came in and led Mum, Mand and Bobby to the public dock to listen to the trial. Each gave me one last tight hug and filed out behind her. My heart pounded in my chest.

She soon returned and nodded kindly at me with a smile of encouragement, 'Natalie, they are ready for you now if you would like to follow me.'

My legs were similar to those of a newborn giraffe as I stood up and made my way across the room. I followed her to a side door for the courtroom, which took me straight into the dock, shielded by the screens from Jason, but facing the judge. My heart was ready to burst out of my chest. I stepped up into the dock and was handed a copy of the Bible to swear the oath on. The prosecution barrister, 'my' lawyer, started with questions and outlining evidence. I went through the evening of the assault on 9 October in detail – it was all OK at this point.

The defence lawyer then took up the questioning. Despite being warned he would do his best to tear my case apart, I was not prepared for the ruthless and relentless line of questioning that was to follow. I was questioned in the dock for over an hour, with no break. Eventually, the judge stepped in and reprimanded the defence, stating that I had clearly answered his questions, repeatedly, and if he didn't have anything new to add, then please could he wrap up his questioning. I silently wept as I was thanked for my evidence and dismissed, the torture over. The court usher quietly helped me down and led me out. As we turned the corner into the main corridor, Mand stood there, her arms wide open. I collapsed into her and sobbed like a child. As she held me tight, she said, 'Well done, you held it together so well. That was so much harder than I expected.' I nodded in agreement.

Time was marching on and the court was finishing for the day, so Mum and Bobby soon returned. Both of them hugged me tight and Bobby whispered words of comfort and reassurance in my ear about how well I'd done and how well I'd come across. My barrister soon followed and updated us with where we were with the case and how it would need to continue now the next day. He too congratulated me on how well I'd done in the dock.

Everyone took their leave. Bobby took Mike home, giving

me one last extra-tight hug as he left, and promised to come straight back to mine. The day had been exhausting and we still had the next day to get through.

When Bobby returned, we had a proper chance to catch up. He repeated how proud of me he was, and said that for him the hardest part was hearing me cry as I spoke. He had wanted to just come and hold me, and it had killed him to hear me so upset behind a screen. They had all been sat behind Jason during the evidence. He had looked round to see them all. Bobby couldn't hide his disdain for him and what he had done. He said he couldn't believe a man could do such a thing to a woman, especially me, and how he would never lay a hand on me to hurt me.

I guess he forgot that less than a year later.

All too soon, the next day was upon us. My witnesses gave their evidence first before Jason was called to give evidence. From what I believe, he was his usual fairly arrogant self. He became unstuck when texts and transcripts of the voicemails were read out and he said in them, 'I'm sorry for assaulting you, grabbing you' – he had no explanation for these.

As the hearing progressed, Mand and I had to leave the court to go and get the children from school. At just gone 4pm, a one-word text arrived from Bobby: Guilty.

I broke down in tears. It was over, justice had been done and the pressure of the last two days came flooding out. I was confused by my reaction as I had expected to be jumping around, punching the air. Instead, I felt whacked out.

Sentencing was set for 9 June 2015. Bobby went in to listen whilst my friend Annabel and I sat in the coffee shop across the road. He was gone some time, with the odd text update sent across to us. Eventually, he came out of the building and ran across to the shop where we were sitting.

Jason's sentence hadn't been light. He was sentenced to 180 hours Community Service, issued with a twelve-month Community Order with supervision, instructed to complete a twenty-one-day Victim Awareness Programme and was issued with an indefinite restraining order, prohibiting him from ever contacting me directly or indirectly through any channel or third party. There was a total of £920 in costs to him. Justice had been done and he had been found guilty of the crime he had committed. Although hell to go through, it was truly worth it, I felt.

I let out a long sigh. It was over, truly over. With the support of my family, friends and Bobby, I'd got through it.

I have only ever bumped into Jason once since that day. It was in the local supermarket. I was nearly six months pregnant. As his eye caught mine, he did a double-take. I could see that familiar anger well up in him but I held his gaze, determined not to be intimidated. My only concern was my bump. I leant forwards on the trolley to allow my coat to hang down, scared that if he decided to risk lashing out at me, I must protect my baby. When I got home and told Bobby what had happened, he gave me a huge hug and asked why I hadn't called him, to which I replied I was independent. Although he shook his head in exasperation, he knew I liked to tough it out and there was nothing he could do to change that so he held me tight, stroked my hair and told me how I was home with him and I was safe now…

Chapter 7

Next Steps

COURT DONE, THAT CHAPTER BEHIND ME, AND LIFE CARRIED ON. AT THIS POINT MY BREAST IMPLANTS HAD BEEN IN PLACE FOR JUST UNDER A YEAR AND THEY WERE STILL DEFORMED on one side. I WAS so disappointed, it wasn't what I was wanting or expecting. My friend Annabel pushed me into doing something about it when I essentially flashed her as she wouldn't believe me that the one implant wasn't 'right'.

'Oh! Oh dear… Yep, I see what you mean, it is deformed. It's shaped like a camel with two humps' was essentially her thoughtful analysis of the sight she was greeted with.

The problem clearly needed sorting out. It took a few meetings with my surgeon, with Bobby present every step of the way, to get her agreement it hadn't turned out well. The surgeon covered the cost of the operation and new implants to be put in. I chose new implants – larger volume to fill the loose skin. Little did I know this very decision and procedure almost certainly contributed significantly to my survival further down the line, if not actually saved my life.

Bobby promised to be there to hold my hand as I went

in for surgery. I'd been told the operation would be more complicated but it had to be done. Less than a week before, as I sat in another hotel, at another work meeting, with another bouquet of beautiful flowers, I received a call from Bobby, sounding slightly distressed.

'Nat, I'm so, so sorry about this, baby... My uncle in Pakistan has passed away, I've got to fly out with Mum to the funeral. The funeral is tomorrow, so I'm going today.'

'Erm... OK, well, I guess you have to be there for your family. You are flying today?' came my reply, somewhat stunned.

'I have to, baby – I will miss the funeral otherwise. I don't want to go as I know I'm going to miss your op, but I'll be back as soon as I can. I could see if I could get a flight back in a couple of days...' he said as reassuringly as he could.

The op! We had fought the op battle together for so long, and he couldn't be there as promised. But I couldn't say anything: his late dad's brother had just died and he needed to support his mum and to pay his respects.

'You can't just abandon your mum after a couple of days, you go and be there. I wish you didn't have to go, but there's nothing that can be done about it. Just come home as soon as you can, within reason,' I told him.

'Of course, baby. I don't want to be away from you, I wanted to be there when you came round from the anaesthetic and now I won't be. I can't believe this, so sorry,' came his reply.

He flew that Tuesday. My operation was on the following Saturday. He missed the operation, as we knew would happen. He texted me to say he had a flight back on the following Tuesday.

The operation was as bad as predicted: I was in for double

the length of time of the first procedure and came around with a surgical drain coming out of each side of me. I was sore and in much greater need of pain relief. Bobby called the hospital on the day of the surgery to find out if I'd got out of theatre OK and regularly texted me for updates on how I was.

But the Tuesday soon came around and I lay in bed with Flight Tracker on my iPad to track his flight from Islamabad. I was excited to see it up in the sky and heading west back home. The flight had probably been up in the air for about an hour when a phone call from 'Bobby – Pakistan' rang on my mobile. I was confused, he should be enclosed in a metal tube up in the sky, somewhere near the Arab Emirates. With a degree of hesitation, I answered, praying it wasn't his mum deciding to have a rant at me – she was due to stay longer in Pakistan to see family whilst there. But it was Bobby.

'I'm not on the plane,' came his words.

No shit, Sherlock, I thought.

'My other uncle has fallen ill, we only heard about it as we drove to the airport this morning. So we have diverted to head up to the Indian border, to the small village where he lives.'

'What?' I said. It was still early morning UK time and my brain was fuzzy. 'You mean you've missed your flight because your uncle has fallen ill? Why do you have to be there?' I added, trying to assimilate the facts.

'Well, Mum needs me to travel with her and it's one of Dad's other brothers, and if he dies, I need to be here for his funeral too,' came the reply.

'But who are you with? Are either of your sisters or your brother going out there?' I asked, bemused.

'My other uncle and my aunt are driving us there, but

probably can't stay. I need to see if my uncle is OK. Sorry, but I won't be home when I said I would. My sisters can't make it, they've got family things to deal with, and neither can my brother...' he gabbled, half-defensively, half-distressed.

'Oh...' I bit back the tears. I wanted him home but I knew his family were important to him, especially his mother. Now he was in a car driving to the middle of nowhere. 'Well, keep me updated. When do you think you'll be able to get back to Islamabad for a flight?'

'I can't say, we haven't got our own transport and I have to see how ill he is. I'll keep you updated when I can. The telephone signal is bad up there.'

And with that the conversation ended. I was acutely aware that his mother was most likely sat next to him, so going off at him wasn't going to help. I was upset, but that's life – I learnt not to rely on others a long time ago. He didn't return for another week. I didn't hear much from him, and when I called, the phone rang out. He claimed it didn't ring his end, I'm still sceptical. It was my first experience of learning that when he went to Pakistan, I wasn't necessarily told the truth and he was always gone longer than he said. I'm sure his mum revelled in having her boy there by her side, and from what he told me, she took it as an opportunity to try and persuade him to leave me and not shame her any further. This was a theme that was to continue until the end of us as we knew it.

Meanwhile I recovered from the operation, with the drains coming out a week after surgery. I had spent the week carrying around a bag containing the drains, clutching it to me as I was connected by long plastic pipes to each port inside the bag.

Eventually, two weeks after he had flown out and with

limited contact, Bobby returned. Of course, I didn't question him too much – I didn't really have much reason to. Once back, he joined in with the hunt for a new house for the children and me. For some time I'd been thinking about moving from what was once my marital home with Ian – a fresh start. Mum and I had looked at countless houses and Bobby came on many of the viewings. We talked about the kind of house we would both like and soon the conversation turned towards him moving in officially. Bobby had been staying at the house more and more, so it seemed a natural step. The advent of a new house would be perfect timing for this, so as we viewed every new house, it held new meaning, new possibilities. Our first home together, our home for many years to come, to grow together as a family and, hopefully, one day bring our baby into. Bobby was still firmly fixed on this: family meant so much to him and he desperately wanted a child of his own.

It was over a lovely Sunday brunch out whilst my older girls were with their dad that Bobby and I talked seriously about when to start trying for a child and what our future lives would look like. He didn't want to be too much older before we started trying for a baby as he was already forty, soon to be forty-one, and we didn't know how long it would take. The conversations continued as Bobby whisked me away for a long weekend in beautiful Barcelona. Our plans were decided. I still had the coil in place from two years before, but I was having problems so we discussed having it removed and then using precautions until we knew the time was right. I made an appointment with my GP to have the coil removed. Two weeks later, it was done and I went back home to be greeted by a beaming Bobby. A step closer to his dream, he couldn't contain his happiness that his dream was becoming a reality. 'You make me so happy,' he said, enveloping me in his arms with the biggest hug.

The house hunting continued and we soon found a house both Bobby and I adored. The moment we stepped in, we gave each other surreptitious glances and nods: it had to be our house. It needed a fair amount of work, but it was perfect. After the viewing, buzzing with excitement and anticipation, we talked about our plans for the house, how we would extend it, have a massive shiny new kitchen and change the bathroom, redecorate throughout. We put an offer in straight away and after a bit of negotiation secured a deal. My house was already sold, so we were in a 'ready to go' position. Our excitement was sky-high as the reality of our first home hit us.

Friday, 17 July 2015: Bobby and I moved into our new home. The day was chaotic, the removal men were a nightmare, the chain nearly collapsed the day before, but we were in! As we pulled the door shut, we laughed, we hugged and jumped up and down. He was grinning like a Cheshire cat. We'd done it, our new future started here! I couldn't wait for all the happy memories that I knew were ahead...

Chapter 8

A New Life Emerges

THE DAY AFTER WE MOVED WAS EID. RAMADAN HAD COME
TO AN END AND THE CELEBRATIONS WERE IN FULL FLOW.
THE MAJORITY OF THE UK HAD ACTUALLY CELEBRATED EID
the day before, as British Muslims base their celebratory
date on the Saudi calendar, which had run a day ahead of
Pakistan. Although Bobby started fasting with the other
UK Muslims, therefore the day before Pakistan, he fasted
an extra day in order to celebrate Eid the same day as his
mother had decided she would celebrate. I understood he
wanted to celebrate it on the same day as his family, but I
still couldn't understand why he couldn't break his fast with
the other UK Muslims as he began fasting the same day as
them. One of Bobby's many quirks, it was also another clear
example of his mother having complete control over him!

Despite vehemently telling me he was an atheist, not
believing in any form of God and denouncing his Islamic
background, Bobby strictly followed the cultural traditions
of his Muslim background – he never drank, never ate pork,
only halal meat and observed Ramadan to the letter, setting

his alarm for when he could break his fast and eating a date before any other food. Indeed, he observed Ramadan so strictly that even when he was ill, he still fasted. That very same year he had been ill in bed with a fever, yet he refused water or anything that would cause him to break his fast despite conceding that you were allowed to break your fast if you were ill. For him it was almost an obsession and the long warm summer days didn't deter his strong will: nothing was going to get in the way of achieving his goal.

So, on 18 July, as per tradition on Eid, Bobby took his uncle and nephews (who were visiting from Pakistan) to the mosque to pray. It was one of the few times he ventured there. With Bobby out of the way, I continued cleaning and sorting. The house wasn't in the best of states, but our new home was full of promise and excitement.

We hadn't been long in the house when I had to go off on yet another managers' training meeting. I was away three days, and by the final evening in the hotel, I felt really sick and assumed I must have picked up something nasty from the endless shared buffets. On the last morning, I still felt ill, making a dash for the bathroom halfway through a session. The feeling started to wear off by lunchtime, but it niggled me – I recognised this nauseousness from before. When I checked my calendar, I was technically a few days late. With the move, my irregular cycle, etc., I hadn't thought much about it. My stomach lurched: Bobby and I had talked about a baby, I'd even started a course of folic acid and it was fair to say we hadn't been careful, but I'd only had the coil out a month and a half or so before. I kept this thought to myself, but took a detour to the chemist on the way home to pick up a digital test.

I'll do it first thing in the morning, I told myself, thinking

I was probably being over the top and my period would undoubtedly show in the next twelve hours. That evening, I mentioned it to Bobby and I could see the excitement in his eyes. We certainly hadn't planned for it to happen so quickly, hadn't thought it would, but he was like a kid on Christmas Eve. That night, we both woke regularly and looked at the clock. At 5am I rolled over towards him and he lay staring at me.

'OK, OK, let's get this test done. Neither of us is going to sleep until I pee on that stick!'

With a giggle we crept out of bed and into the bathroom. Luckily, we had passed the stage of embarrassment with each other and he stayed in with me whilst I carried out the test. I put it on the windowsill as we stood nervously, waiting for the result to come. As I flushed the loo, I saw the answer: 'Pregnant'. I didn't say anything to Bobby as the device was still 'processing' the result, coming up with how many weeks past conception I was. I held it to myself as we hugged. When the allowed time passed, I got the stick and handed it straight to him: 'Pregnant. Two to three weeks'.

His face was a picture: the biggest grin spread across his face and he grabbed me, lifting my feet from the ground in the process, and repeatedly whispering in my ear so as not to wake the kids, 'I love you!'

I pulled back from him, held his gaze and smiled. His deep big brown eyes stared back at me and the happiness radiated out.

'Congratulations, Daddy,' I told him.

'I've never been happier,' he whispered back, hugging me again.

After wrapping the test stick in tissue and putting it in a drawer to check later (we hadn't misread it or something?), we went back to bed. As I lay there, exhausted, Bobby still grinning in the darkness, my head spun slightly.

I'm really pregnant, I thought. *Christ, I didn't expect that yet!*

Don't get me wrong, I was happy. After all, it was something we'd talked about for hours and I knew it was a possibility, but actually pregnant was a different and scary thing. I knew how tough it was having a baby, I knew the strain it can put on relationships, and this was a relationship where the future grandmother refused to accept me: what would this mean for our baby?

I thought about what could happen, and over the coming weeks, my fears grew worse. Panicked slightly, I didn't know how to tell Bobby about how I was feeling – he was so ecstatic about becoming a dad for the first time.

Eventually, I hinted at some of my concerns and his face dropped.

'This is what we wanted, isn't it? It's what I want, and I thought you felt the same?'

'I do,' I reasoned. 'I'm just worried – I know how hard it is being a single mum of two and I *never* want to be a single mum of three, I couldn't cope with that.'

'That will never be an issue – I am with you for life, I swear. You are giving me the most precious gift I could ever ask for. I'm not going to leave you. You don't ever need to worry about being a single mum of three, you have me for life,' he replied calmly and reassuringly.

But he could tell by the way my hands twisted and I gazed down that I wasn't sure the pregnancy was the best idea, so he pulled me towards him and held me tight.

'I love you, Natalie. You are my world and you are the only person I have ever wanted a baby with. It is a privilege to become a father and I will cherish that alongside you, for life.'

As I looked up at him, I could sense that he meant every word so I nodded and blamed my hormones and tiredness for this slight flip out. I flipped a few more times since that day, but each time Bobby stood firm, reassuring. It was all he ever wanted and he couldn't be happier, he insisted. He repeatedly swore he was with me for life, would never leave me alone. Little did I know...

As my pregnancy progressed, in those early weeks I had an encounter with one of Bobby's sisters. It was the first time since I'd been with him that I'd come face to face with any of them. As I left M&S in the town centre, I caught sight of her. I could see she was heading my way, so I waited. She came out, slightly flustered, with her three children in tow and laden with bags.

'Shona!' I called out.

She stopped in her tracks and looked at me. We hadn't seen each other since our teenage years and I doubted she was going to remember me.

'It's Natalie, as in Bobby's Natalie. How are you?' My heart was thumping in my chest – as far as I was aware, none of the family particularly liked me because of my relationship with Bobby. They all wanted us apart, so I hadn't a clue where this was going to go.

After her initial gaping, she smiled, a wide smile.

'Oh, Natalie, lovely to meet you! Sorry, I'm weighed down with bags and children and my mind wasn't switched on. I'm also pregnant again. Only seven weeks, so early days, but already looking fatter and feeling tired,' came the warm response.

The news of her pregnancy struck a chord, but I couldn't

share my news. I hadn't told my girls and they were stood with me. Instead, I just smiled and congratulated her. We chatted for a while whilst the kids grew bored and agitated.

'We must arrange to meet up,' said Shona. 'Bring the kids over to ours with Bobby and they can play and we can get together.'

'I'd love that,' I replied, and I really meant it. It was my first glimmer of being accepted by Bobby's family, which with me being pregnant was even more important now. As we parted with a hug and promises that we would get together, I let out a deep breath, so glad I'd called out to her.

I texted Bobby straight away to tell him that I'd met Shona and how well it had gone. His reply came quickly, saying how pleased he was to hear that and we would sort something out. But I never did go round to see Shona and her family – Bobby always gave an excuse as to why we couldn't go there, ultimately because it would cause a family dispute and it was best not to antagonise his mother further.

The school summer holidays continued and not long after seeing Shona, Bobby and I took the girls away to Lisbon. I have always loved and felt an affinity towards the city. My family there are wonderful, kind, loving people. They welcomed and embraced us all, including Bobby, as part of the family. We had an amazing week, visiting historic sites, monuments, beaches and the amazing Oceanarium – one of the largest in Europe, I believe. As we looked around, we took a group family 'selfie' which I popped onto Facebook as my cover photo. It captured us all together, smiling, having fun and being a loving family unit. Little did I know that same photo would later haunt me in the press.

Bobby said it was the best holiday he'd ever been on.

Back home in the UK, we soon returned to the normal

school routine. Bobby's birthday was rapidly approaching. Having missed his fortieth the year before, I wanted to throw him a special party. We also wanted to have a housewarming, so we decided to combine the two and invite all our friends and family. Well, *my* family... Bobby said he wouldn't bother asking his as he knew the response. I pushed for him to still ask them all, especially Shona, but he said if his mum found out that either of his sisters had visited our house, she wouldn't speak to them again. I shrugged sadly and asked, 'Wouldn't it be worth just trying to build some bridges?'

He said he would think about it, but I knew this was just another way of saying no.

As we prepared for the party, Bobby and I thought about our upcoming twelve-week scan. We were both nervous about how the baby would be with our advancing ages, so we paid for a specialist scan and genetic test privately – something friends of mine had recommended. It involved a detailed ultrasound scan, a sample of blood from me and a DNA swab from Bobby's mouth. This would then allow the baby's DNA to be identified in my blood sample (by comparing Bobby's DNA and mine, then identifying the baby's small amount in my blood). Once the baby's DNA is identified, the scientists can then see if the chromosomes are all OK and eliminate the risk of Down syndrome, etc. The other advantage was that it meant we would know the sex too as they can obviously see that in the DNA. At the scan, they thought my bump was a boy. I hadn't thought about having a boy as I always had girls, but that was great – it meant Bobby could take him to football (he still played for the grammar school old boys' society every Saturday) and cricket. A couple of weeks later, and just before the party, we had a letter with the blood test results:

No chromosome abnormality
Paternity test confirmed
Gender: Female

Female? A girl? They got the scan wrong! Our twelve-week scan followed and confirmed everything seemed fine. Due date recorded as 30 March 2016.

Bobby was thrilled about the baby – his own little princess in the making, she was healthy and that was all he cared about. When it came to our house party, he exuded pride as all our friends congratulated him and talked about his upcoming fatherhood. With his friends around him, in his house, with his pregnant partner, excited about the developing baby in her tummy, he smiled and smiled, every bit like the cat who got the cream.

Chapter 9

First Family Christmas

I WAS NOW ABOUT FIFTEEN WEEKS PREGNANT. I HAD ASKED BOBBY ON MANY AN OCCASION IF HE HAD TOLD HIS MOTHER YET ABOUT THE BABY AND EACH TIME HE SAID HE WAS JUST 'waiting for the right time'. It couldn't be hidden forever. One evening as we stood in the kitchen, my exasperation burst through, I told Bobby to 'man up' and tell his mother. Without warning, he lost his temper and shouted at me, 'I've told my mother, OK?'

'What? When?' came my bewildered response.

'A couple of days ago. OK now?'

'And what was her response?' I asked coolly, knowing deep down the reply I would get.

'She was disgusted, she was angry. She said it was the worst news she had ever heard. She says I've shamed her and she can never forgive me. She would have nothing to do with it. She said she never wanted to see me again. There, you got the response, happy now?' his eyes flashed.

I stood there, dumbstruck. *Why had he kept it to himself?* He stood there staring at me, waiting for a response.

'How can she say that? How can she say it's the worst news she has ever heard? How can she be so disgusted? This is *her* grandchild. That's appalling to say that about the news of your very own grandchild. She has numerous mixed-race grandchildren already who she sees and loves, so why is this any different?'

I was on a roll now.

'Because I *am different* to my sisters, I *am different* to my brother. You *know* this. When it comes to my mother, there is no reason nor logic to her thoughts, it's just the way it is and we have to accept that,' he replied, slightly calmer.

I didn't know what to say; it was outrageous, it was unfair, it was madness. This was her precious eldest son, coming with news of a grandchild – *her* grandchild. From her most precious child.

'Do you think she will change her opinion? She's not seeing the baby unless she sees me. She has to accept both of us or no contact with the baby at all.' I'd had enough of his mother pulling all the strings.

Bobby's face betrayed a slight flash of concern, then he nodded. I hated what his mother was doing: she accepted both of Bobby's sisters' white, English, originally non-Muslim boyfriends, who were now their husbands, and welcomed their children yet I could not be accepted. *Our baby* could not be accepted.

'Would she meet me? Decide for herself what she thought of me as a person, not a religious based label?' I asked hopefully. I wanted to show her that I was actually a half-decent human being.

'No,' Bobby answered flatly. 'I've asked her to meet you, decide for herself about you, but she has said no, she doesn't want to meet you. She doesn't even want to talk to me again as I've disgraced her.'

'Well, that will last five minutes until another of your family pegs it and she wants an escort to Pakistan!' I muttered and left the room. There was no point continuing with the conversation. At least his mother now knew, which was a step forward.

A couple of weeks later, I was sat in traffic on her road and I spotted her standing on the driveway of her house alone. As the queue moved forward, I thought about pulling up to speak to her, show her my developing bump and ask outright why she couldn't accept me. But then I thought about Bobby: he wouldn't be happy with me putting his mother on the spot like that, so I never did face her. I wish to this day I had. It could have made so many things so very different, or maybe not.

As we reached the end of the year, Bobby and I discussed our plans for my maternity leave, especially money. I had paid for our move and I paid the mortgage and monthly household bills myself as Bobby's Mercedes car specialist repair business was still in 'set-up' phase and there wasn't much income at all. That meant my savings were pretty much gone and we relied heavily on my salary to live. He assured me from the outset that there should be a lump sum payment coming his way from the business by the end of the year, akin to a dividend being paid out. This would be a substantial sum, which he said he would transfer to me to pay the mortgage whilst I was on a significantly reduced maternity pay. Bobby was upbeat and assured me it could be nearly as much as £100,000 as business had been going well. I was surprised at such a large amount.

Whilst the conversation was positive, I broached the

subject of his family again, tentatively asking if we could visit Shona. He said that although she accepted our news and was happy for us, it was best to keep her out of the disagreement with his mother. It compromised her if we went over and would cause more family disputes, he felt. So I didn't push it any more. I then tentatively asked how his mother was with him.

'She's not talking to me properly, she is still angry with me. She hasn't changed her mind, I'm a disgrace to her,' he answered, sadly.

My heart sank: this was our future and his mother was doing her level best to destroy it all. I quickly changed the subject to the approaching Christmas festivities. Bobby had never celebrated Christmas properly before now. I love Christmas, always have. He and I had been discussing plans for a few weeks, all details right down to the halal chicken. He seemed really happy to be part of it all and hugged me tightly, telling me how much he loved me whilst little baby bump kicked in protest at being squished by her daddy.

It wasn't long before I was off again on yet another management course. I'd been having a few pregnancy-related worries so the gynaecologist asked me to come in after the course for repeat bloods and tests. Bobby texted regularly to check I was OK and I reassured him I was fine. I told him to stop being daft, worrying about me. Once more, flowers from him were in my room. I loved that he was so caring.

Exhaustion was starting to set in as I was now six months pregnant, dashing around with work and looking after two other children. I soon fell asleep fully clothed on my hotel bed with the TV on. When I woke, bleary-eyed, I had a number of texts from Bobby checking I was OK. I punched a reply, telling him I loved him and was going to get into bed properly. The next morning, I woke to a message saying how much he missed me and how he couldn't wait for me to get home that night. At this I smiled – I couldn't wait to see him again, happy to feel so loved and protected by a man I simply adored.

As I sat in the workshops that day, my phone flashed a message up from Bobby at 12.17pm, briefly asking me to call him as soon as possible.

I didn't actually notice the message until an hour later and I replied saying I was just in a lecture and was all OK? He replied he was fine, but I knew that was not the case. My heart sank; for some unknown reason I instinctively knew this would mean he had to leave the country again. I was in this exact hotel when he left last time, last minute. So, I asked him to message me what exactly was going on and the reply I dreaded soon came: 'I am fine. I hate to do this. I have been subpoenaed to appear in Pakistan for Thursday, along with my brother and Mum with regards to the land I own there. Spoken to my uncle and he says that if we don't turn up, we will be in contempt of court. Trying to get out of it.'

This was followed straight away, to tell me that he probably would have to go, even though he desperately wanted to be at home during Christmas.

I was dumbstruck: he was going to Pakistan – today? My reply came from the heart. I told him, 'You are NOT to miss Christmas. I'm serious, Bobby. I will be devastated if you miss next week. Seriously devastated.'

My hormones were flying. I was having tests at the hospital, I was six months' pregnant, and knowing what happened when he visited Pakistan, I was at risk of him not being there for Christmas either. Excusing myself from the room, I burst into tears in the toilets. I called him straight away.

He answered sheepishly. 'I don't want to go, baby. I really don't. I can't leave you whilst you are having tests at the hospital and I don't want to miss our first family Christmas. But I don't know what the consequences will be if I don't go.' There were tears in his voice, choking him slightly. My heart folded – I wanted him home so badly.

'But how can they expect you to appear in court on Thursday morning when they have just summoned you on a Tuesday and you live in the UK?' I asked.

He agreed and we discussed how it all came about. Bobby owned land jointly with his brother, Tom. It was passed to them from his father, but his father was previously married and had four daughters in Pakistan. They wanted a share of this land, although it was not in their names, so they occupied the prime piece of land and were now taking Bobby and his brother to court over the rights to it. It all seemed madness to me – I couldn't see why he had to be there with immediate effect.

But I knew he would go. I wanted to say goodbye to him in person at least so, as soon as the course finished, just after 2pm, I jumped in my car and drove like a woman possessed. I parked the car at Birmingham airport and, as best as I could – six months pregnant and in heels – I ran to Departures and up to Security. Bobby stood there waiting for me. We fell into each other's arms and I sobbed. He stroked my hair and reassured me he would be on a flight home the following week, the 22nd, so he would be home for Christmas. I nodded. Through tears, I waved him off through Security, both of us mouthing 'I love you' as he disappeared into the crowd. I had seen him for what was literally five or ten minutes. Wandering back to my car, tears rolled down my face. As I drove home, Bobby texted from the gate to tell me he loved me and that he missed me.

I replied from the heart once more, saying 'Going to miss you so much. Please swear to me that you'll be on that flight home on the 22nd.'

'I swear,' he replied.

I cried.

He texted to let me know he had arrived safely. The rest of the week we talked about my blood tests and his preparation for court. I was worried about what he was going through over there. Luckily, the court seemed to go well and he was pleased with how things were progressing. His plan was to get the land sold to give us a firmer financial background. Bobby had no savings and few assets, but the land was one. His brother also wanted it sold, but this dispute with their half-sisters was causing massive delays.

Happy 14 months! we texted each other on 18 December.

I told him how we all missed him and couldn't wait for him to be home.

On the Saturday, he texted 'Happy 61 weeks!'

Ever since we started going out, Bobby had texted me every Saturday with 'Happy x number of weeks!' It was like being a teenager in many ways but I loved it. It was similar to the cards full of words of love that he gave me every month to celebrate another monthly milestone.

In his text he also reassured me that he would be on the flight home on the Tuesday.

I awoke just after 5am Tuesday morning, courtesy of baby bump. My heart leapt: he was on his way home! With a smile on my face, I dropped off again. At 7am, my phone rang: *<Bobby Pakistan>*. He should have been on the flight.

Not again, please not again.

'I'm not on the flight. Don't go mad, I can't talk right now, I've been arrested,' he sounded stressed.

'WHAT?!' came my reply, my heart pounding.

'Don't worry, I'm getting help and being supported, my uncle's a lawyer. They are questioning me at the police station. I was arrested when I checked in. My half-sister has accused me of assaulting her after court,' he informed me, sounding calmer than I was.

'That is ridiculous! You wouldn't lay a hand on anyone. You've never even hit a bloke, let alone a woman. What the hell? Surely they can see she is being malicious, it's because of the land. She's manipulating the system,' I replied.

'I know it's exactly that. She's a bitch, but it will get sorted. My mum, Tom and uncle were with me the whole time after court, they can testify that I didn't go near her. I'm not on that flight, though,' he answered.

'That's not the issue now, don't worry about that,' I replied. 'I'm more worried about you being in a police station for something you haven't done!'

'It will be OK, baby, I swear. I'll get it sorted, I promise, and sort another flight. I've got to go now. I love you so much and sorry.'

'I love you too and you don't need to apologise.'

But he was gone.

My head span. I sat down on the bed and rubbed my belly. I couldn't believe it – he wasn't on the flight, but in a police station being questioned about an assault that clearly didn't happen. I pulled myself together, I had to get ready to take the kids to school.

The rest of the day was spent in a blur. I didn't get an update from Bobby until 5.30pm UK time (10.30pm Pakistan).

He had been allowed home but had to go back again the next day. My head span, but I tried to keep calm. It was ridiculous. He spent three days being questioned, until Thursday, 24 December, Christmas Eve when he was cleared of the charge and free to leave.

Relieved it was at last all over, we both looked up flights but the police still had his passport and Pakistani ID card so we would have to wait. I could have screamed with the frustration of it all.

I then got a text which gave me some hope at last: he had a flight reserved with a travel agent in Islamabad, leaving Lahore on Boxing Day, landing in Manchester that afternoon. I would go and collect him. He said he would have to go to the travel agent early on the morning of the flight, collect the ticket and then his uncle would drive him to Lahore. He might be missing Christmas Day itself, but I didn't care, I was getting him home soon. He added that he would also go to the airport Christmas Day morning and see if he could get a standby seat.

And so I ploughed on with Christmas Day preparations to make Christmas the best it could be for the kids. I sent photos to Bobby to keep him part of the celebrations despite being thousands of miles away. The girls had a fabulous Christmas morning and we saved Bobby's presents for him. He soon broke the news that he had been at the airport but the flight was full and no chance of standby, so he would travel back tomorrow.

Boxing Day arrived and I remembered excitedly that Bobby would soon be on a flight back home. The excitement was soon to be dashed though as a text from <Bobby Pakistan> came through, telling me the travel agent had never shown up and he didn't have a ticket to travel. He swore numerous times through the message, using language he didn't normally put down in text, and said he would travel to the airport to see if he could get on a standby flight. But he didn't. He texted me later, 5.30pm UK time, or 10.30pm Pakistan time, to say he had been at the airport all day but couldn't get on a flight. I sighed. It wasn't until later that evening that I heard from him again – it would have been the early hours of the morning in Pakistan. He told me how he had had a three-hour row with his family about me. His mother had apparently been at the centre of the argument and many angry words exchanged. He told me his family were happy for us and how they had all turned on his mother.

He then phoned me: 'I'm sorry, baby, but I need to stay here longer. The family row has been awful and Mum isn't speaking to me. I need to spend time here with her, trying to work things out. I may stand a better chance of talking her round with the support of my uncle and aunt – they are really pleased for me and don't mind you are not Muslim. They have even offered to host our wedding here at their house. Mum now feels isolated though and I can't leave her like this. Give me a few more days and I will return. It will be the best for us, long run.'

It looked like Bobby was going to be away for the entire Christmas holiday. As I came off the phone and cried, I realised I was always going to have his mother to battle against as she refused to accept me. What was it going to be like when our baby came, I wondered. What division would she try and cause then? I pushed these worries to the back of my head: his mother wasn't going to change overnight and I had to accept that.

Bobby stayed there until New Year's Eve. At 14.15 on 31

January 2015, sixteen days since he had flown out, Bobby's plane actually touched down. The girls and I watched it land and we were buzzing with excitement. They had made 'Welcome Home Bobby' signs and we stood in Arrivals, waiting for him to come through. As we spotted his head emerging through the crowds, we bounced up and down and the kids called his name. I threw my arms around his neck. Kisses and hugs all round. We took a group selfie in the arrivals hall, capturing the joy of having him back, all crowded together with Bobby's hand instinctively and protectively resting on my baby bump.

When we walked through the door, the girls pulled out his presents, still sat wrapped up under the tree. Bobby opened his case and pulled out presents for us that he had bought in Pakistan. It was perfect – later than expected, but it didn't matter now.

We all got changed and set off for a party. It was time to welcome in a new year, an exciting year, one where, in Bobby's own words, 'You will bring our child into the world and the year you become my wife'.

The year 2016 was going to be one to remember. Little did I know for all the wrong reasons, though.

Chapter 10

The Big Four-O

JANUARY 2016, THE DAWN OF AN EXCITING YEAR AHEAD. I WAS COMING UP TO SEVEN MONTHS PREGNANT.

EARLY 2016 SAW THE ARRIVAL OF BOBBY'S BROTHER'S baby boy. Tom had been excluded from the family by their mother as he had married a Sikh girl, whom she didn't approve of. All hopes she would come round once the baby was born were soon dashed, which affected Bobby as it was almost like a test case.

Bobby's mother returned from Pakistan at the end of January. As we rolled out of bed, he looked at his phone and cursed.

'I'm really sorry, baby, I have to go and pick Mum up from the airport today.'

'But I thought she wasn't speaking to you and wanted nothing more to do with you. I thought that when you left Pakistan, she hadn't even said goodbye to you as she was so mad and, in your words, disgusted by you, never wanting to look at you again? Can't one of your sisters or your brother-in-laws collect her as she's actually talking to them?' I asked, sighing inwardly.

'No, I said I'd do it and she's texted me to check, so I am. It gives me a chance to try and talk her around on the journey back,' he insisted,

'Well, that didn't work out when you stayed on in Pakistan, what the hell is going to be different now?' I said, incredulous at his mother's gall.

'Well, I have to keep trying, don't I?' soothed Bobby, drawing me into a hug. 'I just have my duties and expectations. You know this. I won't be long, I promise. She lands at 11am – I can pick her up, drop her home and come straight back.'

He set off and when he sheepishly returned at about 6.15pm, he flew at me, saying he knew he was in trouble with me, but he had also been in trouble with his mother and youngest sister, Shazan, for leaving them to come home to me! Our plans for the day to use the precious little time we had together to shop for nursery furniture for our impending bundle of joy were binned because of his mother. Inside, I was livid, but I knew there was no point exploding – it was part of my life that I didn't particularly like, but I knew that was how it was.

As we approached February, the dawn of my Big Four-O came upon us. Bobby had intimated on many occasions that potentially on my fortieth birthday an official engagement would be forthcoming. Despite the general dread most of us feel approaching such milestones in age, there was an underlying excitement that the next step in our life was soon to be taken.

Bobby had asked me many times to be his wife, both in person and in texts. He looked up pictures of different engagement rings, asking me what I liked. We had checked out a few wedding venues and had chosen the place we wanted to have our reception, even talking to the owner about what we wanted. Life felt really good – at last it seemed to all be coming together.

The weekend before my birthday, Bobby whisked me off to London. He had booked a boutique hotel and, to my surprise, got us into a West End show. After the show, we arrived at the hotel and as we entered the room, flowers and chocolates were laid out for me, with 'Happy Birthday' messages on each. That evening, he took me to the swanky Bluebird restaurant in Chelsea and as we sat opposite each other, he told me how much he loved me and couldn't be happier. In between courses he sidled round the table to sit next to me and we sat hugging and kissing like a pair of teenagers. I even managed to get a selfie of the two of us, the love and happiness as he looked at me evident.

I hoped that night there might be a proposal – everything was perfectly in place, but it never came. I'll admit I was a little bit disappointed but, in the scheme of things, it didn't matter. Money was an issue with him at the moment, so it could wait. We were happy, we were together and soon to be parents to our much-anticipated baby daughter. It had been the perfect weekend.

The morning of my birthday started out exactly as you would hope for: presents, a balloon and a cake with my face staring back at me (!) were presented to me in bed. The kids bounced around in excitement – my family were coming down and we were all going out for lunch. Although it was a Monday, I kept both kids at home. You're forty only once and I wanted them to be part of the day's celebrations. We met my mum and sisters at a lovely pub and after the suitable humiliation of being sang to at the table (led by Bobby), we headed home for more presents and cake! In the evening, my dad and his wife came over for further festivities. It was perfect – I had spent the day with all the key people in my life around me and we had had fun and laughter.

The card Bobby sent me said it all:

> *Dear Natalie*
> *Happy 40th birthday!*
> *I love you with all my heart. You are my world, my life, my everything.*
> *Can't wait for the day that you are my wife.*
> *Love Bobby*

As he gave me the card, he told me my present was still on order – a Rolex watch, which he was getting inscribed. I told him he shouldn't have spent so much money, that we needed to save all the money we could get, especially as there was *still* no money coming in from the business. He told me not to worry – it was all in hand.

I did worry, though. I was due to finish work on 26 February and after a short amount of annual leave I had left to take, my pay would be dramatically cut. I knew we didn't have enough savings to live off and the cash was crucial. But Bobby maintained it was coming and not to stress.

In the following weeks, the nursery decorating was finished and the furniture arrived. The baby car seat we had ordered also arrived. Bobby had insisted on buying the most expensive car seat and base in the shop! I told him we didn't really need to go that far and the next model down would be more than safe enough. But he insisted, as he said in his words, there was no price that could be put on the safety of our child and she was to have the best to keep her safe.

The furniture obviously all needed constructing and no sooner had all the boxes arrived than Bobby set about building it. One evening, coming home from work, I found him putting the last parts together. The next day I got out all the toys we had bought for our little lady and put them in the nursery, including the one he had specially chosen and paid for, so she would have something from her daddy right from the start. He also bought a gorgeous babygro with embroidered pink elephants on it, which I laid out on the changing table. His eyes swam with tears when he saw it.

'What's wrong?' I asked, concerned.

'I'm just really happy. It's all real, isn't it? We'll soon have our baby girl and I couldn't be happier. Thank you for giving me everything I have ever wanted,' he sniffed.

I hugged him hard as 'Sofia' – the name we had decided on (suggested by my friend Suhail) for baby bump – squirmed in my belly.

As the end of February approached, the lack of money became part of daily conversation between Bobby and I. Elaborate stories eluding to the accountant having embezzled the funds started to emerge. It developed into him and his business partner chasing the accountant, literally, down to his house to demand the money off him. All lies, as I was to find out much later. But at that time I believed it and was sure we would work it out somehow regardless.

Soon it was my final week. I couldn't believe I was actually finishing work! I'd gone full pelt to the end. I think in many ways I was in denial that I was actually finishing to have a baby. For some unknown reason, I had an uneasiness about my upcoming maternity leave. I couldn't put my finger on it, I just knew it didn't quite feel the same this time.

Thursday, 25 February – Bobby and I had our first real almighty argument. He texted to say he was helping with childcare for his sister Shona as she had been taken into our local hospital with some pains. That evening, whilst returning from Emily's martial arts, round the corner from Bobby's mother's house, I spotted Bobby's car still sat on his mum's driveway, with his mum's car and sisters' and brother-in-laws' too. It reminded me that I wasn't part of that family unit, despite the large bump on the front of me, and I felt sad. I got the children home, bathed and settled into bed before coming downstairs. Bobby still wasn't home. It had been a couple of hours since I'd driven past and was pushing 8pm. I hadn't eaten as I was waiting for him – I couldn't understand where he was. He had said he hoped to be home well before 6pm, but not a word. I texted to find out where he was, asking what time he would be home. He said for me to crack on with my dinner as he had eaten and he'd be home when he could be.

I broke into tears. He had only been saying that week how his mother still refused to have anything to do with him and he was going to leave her to it. Yet he had been there for hours with her and eaten, without even letting me know, despite me sitting home waiting for him. Tiredness, hunger and hormones got the better of me and I texted to say he might as well stay there and not bother coming back that night. He reacted straight away and before I knew it, we were in a massive text argument, where all the resentment about his mother, her quite frankly outrageous and hypocritical opinion (as she had both of her British white non-practising son-in-laws sat in her house) and lack of money to support me came pouring out. I felt let down, isolated and, quite frankly, I'd had enough. In no uncertain terms I told him to stay at his mother's that night and I was locking the house up. I did lock the door, leaving the key in it and bolting it shut. Even if he came home, he wasn't coming in – I was taking a stand over this damn woman, who was hell-bent on doing what she could to split us up. He eventually came home and sat parked up on the drive, texting to ask me to let him in. But I didn't – I told him to go back to his mother's. She pulled all the strings so he may as well react. I went to bed, leaving him sat out there. Just after 10pm, I heard the back door open. Bugger, I'd forgotten he had the back-door key on his set of keys! He came into the bedroom and informed me that he was sleeping downstairs.

'Fine,' I mumbled from under the duvet.

The next morning, I awoke to a text from him apologising for being 'an arse' and telling me he loved me.

I wandered downstairs, squashed onto the sofa with him and we hugged and kissed, both of us apologising for our behaviour the night before.

'I love you so much, Natalie. You mean the world to me and this little madam,' he said, stroking my belly.

'I know you do, and I love you so much too. We'll work through all these things, they don't count in the big picture. We will get through the challenges, I promise,' I replied.

'I know we will. I love you and thank you for being "you",' he replied and squeezed me tight into him.

The rest of the day was filled with our usual loved-up messages, all memories of the night before forgotten. Bobby was confident he would get some of the money that day, which cheered us both up.

The morning was Friday, 26 February, my last day at work. I had tons of admin to finish, handover documents to finalise to pass on to my maternity cover so they could pick up where I left, yet 'Sofia' obviously hadn't got the memo that she had to wait at least until tomorrow before trying to make an appearance. Backache started to kick in – maybe it was my position sitting at my laptop, I thought at first – then period-type cramps began. And a very slight bleed. OK, so even I couldn't ignore this.

I called Bobby.

'Please call the midwife straight away. I'm serious, Nat – I don't want either of you in danger,' he urged.

'OK, OK, I will in just a bit – I'm just finishing something up,' I replied, trying to calm him down.

With promises that I would call the midwife forthwith, we exchanged 'I love yous' and hung up. I carried on with a bit more paperwork, but the pain didn't go away and the cramps developed.

Bugger! Sofia, couldn't you have just waited a bit longer? I told the baby bump. I picked up my mobile and called the midwife. She instructed me to head straight to Good Hope and said she would call ahead to let them know I was heading to the assessment unit. I texted Bobby an update. He replied that he was caught up with a customer and then meeting the accountant as he hoped to get some cash off him, but if I could get Mum to go with me, he would catch us up as soon as he could. I phoned Mum and asked if she could come over. Luckily, Ian had already collected the girls from school and they were staying with him that night so that pressure was off. When Mum arrived, I was just finishing my final emails, putting my 'out of office' on and closing the laptop.

'I just need to call my boss before we leave to let him know I've finished up,' I told Mum as she came in the door. I dialled my boss and he told me off for not having gone to the hospital before, but he knew I just wanted to finish my work off properly. I rang off and Mum and I grabbed our coats to walk down. If I was in early labour, it would help things along and it was a pain in the backside to park there anyway, I figured. I texted Bobby to tell him we were setting off.

It didn't take long before we arrived – it was about 4.30pm so the roads and car parks were quite busy. I was glad we had walked down! We headed to the fourth-floor maternity assessment ward and I was shown into the waiting room. As Mum and I sat and waited for the midwife to appear, a familiar figure appeared outside the door, chatting to a midwife, overnight bag slung over her shoulder and bump clearly visible: Shona. I automatically went to call out to her, but then stopped myself – she was talking for a start and I didn't really know how she would be with me. After all, we hadn't spoken since that day outside M&S, months before. As I debated it in my head, my fate was chosen for she set off out the door and was gone. I'd missed her. She hadn't looked into the waiting room, so she wouldn't have seen me. Afterwards, I told Mum who I'd seen and texted Bobby, telling him I thought I'd seen Shona leaving.

Half an hour later, I got a reply from him, telling me there was £20,000 in the safe, and that he loved me.

And when I asked him whether he'd be having it, or the business, he told me I would be.

At last, I thought, *we have some money behind us!*

Bobby arrived at the hospital at about 6.30pm. He had stopped to pick up some bits and pieces for me, he said. I was strapped to a monitor when he arrived. The tightenings had turned into contractions and they were sending me down to the labour ward. I'd waited for him to arrive before going down. Taking a deep breath, hand in hand, we walked down to the labour ward. *It could really be happening!* I hadn't even finished packing my hospital bag or buying all we needed. On arrival, a midwife welcomed us and showed me to a delivery room. I was shown the gas and air and strapped up to a monitor again.

'It looks like this little one isn't waiting for their due date,' she smiled. 'How many weeks are you?'

'Thirty-five weeks and two days,' I replied.

Early, but manageable.

Bobby spent most of the night on the labour ward and although the contractions were still there, it seemed Sofia wasn't going to appear that night. They were going to leave me to sleep in the delivery suite because of the premature baby risk, but I sent Bobby home to get some decent sleep – after all, if this really was it, he needed as much sleep now as he could get. He popped home to grab some more things for me, dropped them off and then headed home to bed.

The next day, I woke to my Saturday 'anniversary' text.

I texted back that the contractions were kicking off again and more examinations were to follow, along with a steroid injection to develop Sofia's lungs. Bobby made his way back to the hospital and by lunchtime I was allowed back to the ward to be monitored carefully. The rest of the day passed with regular monitoring and after sending Bobby home for the night, the midwives started to get concerned about Sofia's heart rate – with every contraction, it dipped. As a midwife stood with me, watching what was happening, she grew concerned as Sofia's heart rate didn't recover after a particular bad tightening. She got me to shift position, still not a good response. With a swift movement, she lunged past my bed and hit the alarm bell. Before I knew it, midwives were running into the room, double-checking the monitor, and then throwing all they could onto the bed and unlocking the wheels before running the bed with me petrified on it down the corridor to the lifts.

'Straight to labour ward! Let them know we're coming, foetal heart rate not recovering!' they shouted to the woman on the desk.

I fumbled for my phone and called Bobby: 'Baby, it's me.' I tried my best to sound calm, but the tears were starting to come. 'They're running me down to labour ward on the bed as baby's heart isn't recovering from my contractions. Please come quickly now, they are talking about a possible emergency c-section.'

Poor Bobby was confused and slightly bleary as he was in bed. The girls had stayed another night with Ian with me in hospital, so he threw his clothes on and dashed down to the hospital. He came running into the delivery room as I was surrounded by a plethora of medical professionals. Panicked, he asked for an update, but they were concentrating on the job in hand, so he got a very broken response. He desperately tried to get through to hold my hand, but was stopped by a midwife as they tried to insert a canula in the back of it. Wide-eyed, I stared at him – I was scared, this wasn't how things were supposed to happen. An obstetrician assessed me and told us to wait: Sofia was recovering OK again now. They kept me in the room for a while longer and decided they could hold off the emergency c-section for the moment, but if it got bad again then I would be straight in (I didn't want a c-section, I wanted to give birth to her naturally as I had with the other two).

When everything calmed down enough, they let me back on the ward. I was kept in until the next day. They said

I might be in early labour but I was to be allowed home that night if my readings stabilised. Bobby and I spent the afternoon curled up together on my hospital bed, my head resting on his chest as I read and he watched the rugby on TV. It had all been a bit of a scare, but it was calmer now.

That evening, I was back home and the next day the school run routine was to start again. I was instructed to rest as best I could, not easy with two other children. I was just getting the girls ready for school when Emily puked. Bobby took Isabel to school for me and he later popped home to collect Isabel from school, so I could stay home with a sick Emily. Afterwards he had to return to work, but when he came home he confided in me that he had cried at work.

'What about?' I asked him, concerned. His car repair business was a completely male-dominated territory, so I was surprised at this admission.

'I was so scared I was going to lose you and baby bump this weekend, it got me really upset at work,' he replied.

I hugged him and told him it would take more than that to get rid of us.

The next morning, we were woken in the early hours by a crying Isabel.

'What's wrong, sweetie?' I asked, concerned at her little face, wild hair sweeping across her face, tears staining her cheeks and clutching her favourite snuggle toy, which she has slept with since a baby. She broke into further sobs and came running around the bed to me. I prised myself up as a sleepy Bob stirred and asked what was up.

'It's OK, Isabel appears to have had a nightmare. I'm just going to take her back to her bed,' I reassured him and, hugging Isabel to me, I walked her back to her room.

'What's all the tears for, little miss?' I soothed as I tucked her back under her duvet and sat on the edge of the bed.

'I had a nasty dream... really nasty...About you and baby bump...'

Fresh sobs poured out of her.

'What, baby? It can't be that bad! Remember, it's just a naughty nightmare,' I reassured her as she clung to me and the large protruding bump of her growing little sister.

'It was horrible, Mummy! Jason came up to you in the street and killed you and baby bump. You were just outside in the street and he killed you both!' She was full-on sobbing at this point.

'Ah, baby, that's not going to happen! Jason isn't going to come near Mummy or baby bump. We are both safe, I promise you. Don't worry about that, he certainly wouldn't try and kill us!' I reassured her.

I sat with her for a bit, stroking her hair whilst she settled to sleep before returning to our bedroom.

'Is she OK? What upset her so much?' Bobby asked groggily.

'She's fine now, but she was really upset as she had a nightmare that baby bump and I were killed in the street by Jason. She was so convinced it was real, it was horrible for her,' I explained.

At this Bobby seemed to stir out of his slumber and propped himself up.

'She dreamt *what*? That's ridiculous! Why would she dream that?' He sounded almost annoyed by Isabel's nightmare.

'I don't know, poor kid worries about me after all Jason did – although I thought she was over that. Anyway, she's asleep now so it will all be OK,' I responded, not quite sure why he was annoyed. 'Let's just get some sleep in. This little madam keeps me awake enough!' I said, rubbing my belly and rolling over.

The next night, Bobby had a meeting at The Old Boys' Society to discuss their upcoming annual dinner planned for the following Saturday. Again, he said he got all emotional, telling the boys what had happened to me at the weekend. He seemed so worried about losing me and baby bump, I hugged him hard to reassure him we were fine.

On the Wednesday, Bobby texted to say the money would be in my account by the end of the week. He had done a transfer from his account, where £20,000 had been paid into from the safe to my account. I had checked for the last couple of days, but no money as yet. Later that afternoon, I had my routine midwife appointment. I had to take Emily with me as she was still off school, so she sat in the waiting room book in hand and iPod on. My midwife and I did my birth plan: I wanted the birth to be as natural as it could be with just gas and air. I told her I was looking to do some hypnobirthing to help me control the pain better too and be more relaxed. She asked about cutting the cord, to which I replied, Bobby would do that. After I left, I texted Bobby to reassure him all was OK, but he was still on edge. I told him I had put him down as the person to cut the cord, to which he replied that it'd be his honour.

'I wanted you to do it. It's such a special moment. Definitely Daddy's job,' I told him.

This conversation happened at about 4pm. It would be weeks later when I would learn what exactly he was doing at the same time as sending those messages.

The next day, at long last, Emily was back to school and I could have a simpler day, although I still had to take Isabel to the Birmingham Children's Hospital for an appointment – she is a diagnosed coeliac. I also had a few things to sort, not least this hypnobirthing. It wasn't cheap as we were doing it one to one with an instructor, but Bobby insisted on paying for it – he felt it was important we did it together to make the labour the best experience possible.

Bobby texted later that evening to say he was just dropping a car off and would then be home. He even texted to tell me when he was on his way home with lots of kisses! When he got in, he broke the news that he had to write a last-minute speech for the Old Boys' Society dinner – their main speaker had dropped out and they needed someone to fill in.

Once the kids were settled in bed, we pulled out my iPad and I looked up various quotes and facts he could use. Bobby seemed fairly laid-back about it all and just lay on the sofa, his head in my lap. He was so relaxed in fact that he couldn't be bothered to get his phone from the kitchen – unusual for him – but he asked to borrow my phone to look something up. I handed him my iPhone without a second thought. We knew each other's passwords, etc., and just shared everything. He lay scrolling through my phone as I scoured the internet. Occasionally our daughter kicked her daddy in the head when he squashed her too much, to which he rubbed my bump and kissed it back, saying, 'OK, OK, I get the hint not to squish you!'

I smiled; we were relaxed and snuggled together. We both knew it wouldn't be long before Sofia would arrive and so we just enjoyed every moment we had left together as a couple.

Chapter 11

The Day Life Changed Forever

HERE, WE PICK UP FROM WHERE WE LEFT THE STORY EARLIER: FRIDAY, 4 MARCH 2016, THE DAY LIFE CHANGED FOREVER.

AS YOU WILL REMEMBER, I WAS EIGHT MONTHS PREGNANT at this point. The day had started with a rude awakening, courtesy of my alarm and the advances of Bobby, whose amour I batted away with a smile. Seizing my ID documents that he needed for the bank, he dashed out of the house after kissing us all goodbye. It had been arranged that I would meet him later that day, potentially after his bank appointment, to sort out the troublesome money. I have replayed that morning repeatedly in my mind: did I miss something? Was he just pretending? He must have been, as his plan was already in place. Why was he trying to make love to a woman who, less than nine hours later, he would attempt to murder in cold blood? Could anyone really be that detached, that callous? Seemingly so.

To me, it was a normal day. Never would I have imagined what was to unfold in the next eight hours, that neither he nor I would return to the house later that day and our home would become part of a wider crime scene.

After shooing the children out the door for the daily school run, I watched my eldest in her school play. Ian and I sat smiling alongside the other parents. I was proud of both my girls – I would/will always do my best never to let them down. The thought of ever being apart from them was one I couldn't begin to comprehend and something I never thought I would have to do.

After waving the girls goodbye at school, not knowing I wasn't going to be returning later as planned, I headed for the gym. Throughout the morning, Bobby was in constant contact by text and when I left the gym to do the usual weekly supermarket shop, we spoke on the phone about dinner and weekend matters. The bank appointment had apparently been moved to the afternoon and I had asked Mum to collect the girls, so I could support Bobby at the bank as he asked me to go with him.

Once home, a final call came from Bobby to say the appointment had been pushed back further – to 3.30pm – and we discussed how I was getting to Sutton. He insisted on picking me up, ignoring my preference to walk in and meet him there to save him dashing around. He then asked the fateful question about which way I would walk if I did, which I found strange at the time and joked that he sounded like a stalker. Obviously annoyed, he told me he was picking me up regardless. As the clock approached 3pm and, determined that I would leave if he hadn't arrived, I abandoned all cake-making ideas and with ingredients strewn across the worktops, made for the front door.

As I pulled on my brown leather jacket, the very one I had worn on our first date, I headed across the road and took my mobile phone out from the pocket. Recalling Bobby's number on my phone, I strode towards the traffic light junction. It didn't take him long to answer: he was stuck in traffic on the other side of Birmingham. I said that I'd left home as I hadn't heard from him so assumed he had got caught up and would meet him when he got into Sutton. His voice sounded completely normal and he was happy enough that I was making my own way in and he would call me when he parked up. He ended the conversation with 'I love you', a sentiment I reciprocated before hanging up.

This is another conversation I have replayed in my head time and time again. Was there a hint in his voice? Did he sound tense, edgy, even angry? Perhaps agitated or unfriendly? Not at all – he was normal Bobby. He even apologised for not calling me to tell me he was running late. There was nothing in his voice to betray what must have really been going on in his head and that's still one of the hardest things to accept. There was no warning, no hint of anything being wrong. He was *my* Bobby, the man I loved with all my heart. The man who was about to be father to our baby.

Our baby, the baby he was soon to try to murder alongside me.

It was about 3pm, and the rain poured down. I pulled my umbrella out of my handbag and walked on with my head down. As the rain came down harder and faster, I considered turning back – the bump was getting soaked and it was freezing cold. I could nip back and get the car and drive in. But then Bobby and I would both have our cars in Sutton and that would be a waste. Also, I was all the way down the hill and would have to trudge back up it.

Nah, push on, my head told me.

So I walked quickly, head down. At the top of the road, I prepared to cross over to Trinity Hill, where the memorial to the murdered Nicola Dixon stands as a stark reminder of its grim history. Dark trees overhang the top pedestrianised part that cuts down behind Holy Trinity Church. I hesitated – I was early and could walk around the front of the church, skipping Trinity Hill completely. But the rain still came down and the cold bit through my top and jacket. It was nearly 3.10pm on that Friday afternoon and a woman emerged from the top of the hill, carrying her shopping bags.

Just walk down it, for pity's sake, I told myself. *Jeez, what's the worst that could happen?* And off I strode. A decision that sealed my fate, as did the decision to leave the house less than twenty minutes before.

So I set off down the darkened tree-lined alleyway and it wasn't long before I heard heavy fast footsteps behind me. My heart quickened and turning slightly, I glanced over my shoulder. A man was catching up from behind me. He wore scruffy jeans and a dark hooded top, the hood pulled firmly over his head, which was bent down. A sense of foreboding filled me, a sixth sense, telling me I was in danger. I looked ahead: I could see the town centre, there was also a guy walking up the hill: dark jacket and hat, striding up the hill towards me, probably on his way home from work. The pedestrianised section I was on was soon ending and the opening out into the dead-end part of Trinity Hill merely a footstep away. The road part had cars parked on it and was lined with buildings, the first building being the white painted Christadelphian Hall.

Don't be silly, you'll be fine. Just keep walking, get out in the open and by that white building, you'll be fine. No one would try anything here. There's a guy walking towards you, for pity's sake. You'll be safe.

The self-talk we all do in our heads to reassure ourselves in times of perceived danger was in overdrive. I quickened my step and made it to the white building, but I knew the hooded man was behind me, he had caught up with me. I stepped to my left, making it clear I knew he was there, that I wanted him to pass me.

Just please pass me, I thought, *allow my heart to calm down.*

But then it happened. An arm reached around me and grabbed me hard and fast. His rough gloves brushed my face as he pounced on me. My umbrella fell to the ground and I screamed. He held me fast as I struggled; he was over my right shoulder and his left arm went over me, gripping me tight across the body, pulling me into him.

I'm being mugged! my head screamed.

My handbag was on my right side, so this was the logical explanation.

'Get OFF me!' I shouted out. My fingers grappled at his arm to prise it off me, his arm drew tighter and his rough gloved hand cupped my right breast.

Was this a sexual attack, some pervert who got off on pregnant women? No, please, I'm pregnant, my baby...

Then I saw it: in his right hand he drew out a large carving knife. I stared at the blade in disbelief and within a second, he brought it down on me, plunging it into my chest. The blade sliced through my top and deep into my chest. As he pulled it out, I remember seeing flesh and blood through my ripped top.

I'm being stabbed, what the fuck is happening? I'm actually being stabbed!

Fear coursed through me. This was worse than anything I could ever have imagined. The knife came down again and again repeatedly – he wasn't stopping and he wasn't letting go. Throughout the whole attack, he didn't speak a word.

My scream came from a place I couldn't recall, an ethereal, deep-seated place of fear. My face contorted with fear as I cried out to the man in the dark coat and hat that I had seen walking up the hill: '*Help me! Please help me. Please, please, help me!*'

I saw him look up in disbelief, his mind processing what was unfolding before him. He then started running towards us.

'Get off her!' he shouted and threw himself on the attacker.

Another man, who must have been walking down the hill behind us, then jumped on the attacker from behind and we all fell to the pavement.

The knife continued to slash away at me as the attacker clung to me, not letting me escape. He was determined that I was his target, it seemed.

What had I done to this man?

'Why me?' I screamed. 'What have I done to you? Why are you stabbing me? Please stop!'

But he wasn't stopping. I lost count of how many times the knife struck me. Meanwhile, the two men wrestled with him. I remember their deep voices shouting for help: no one else was coming. I had to get away – I had my baby, I had to protect her. My precious bump needed me to get out of there, *but how*? I struggled more, thrashing about on the pavement as his grip remained tight on me and the knife blows kept coming. One of the men then managed to grab his arm with the knife and hold it back on the pavement, preventing the incessant blows for a moment and distracting the attacker. It was just enough for him to lose grip of me temporarily. Without a second thought I prised myself free of the mass of bodies and blood and stumbled to my feet. I didn't look back, but I did look down: I was pouring with blood.

This really isn't good, my head told me.

My hand rested on my bump, the side of my wrist had been slashed open through my leather jacket and it seemed as if blood oozed from every part of me. I stumbled onwards, screaming for help. Ahead, I could see the busy town centre but I just knew I couldn't make it there, my legs were giving way under me. The Baptist Church gates were approaching, there were cars parked.

If I can just get there, there must be someone in the offices who can get help.

'Help! Someone, please help me. Please... help!'

My legs buckled and I went crashing to the ground. The severe loss of blood and the fact that I was eight months pregnant had overcome my adrenaline surge. I passed out cold, but soon came round and pushed my upper body off the pavement. My bump, my precious bump... God knows what damage was done to her! I found myself near a brick pillar. Sliding towards it, I propped myself against it and my eyes came into focus on the men I'd left up the hill as my arm protectively gripped around my bump. The hooded man was now standing and walking down towards me – he had broken free of the others. But wait, I saw his face: it was Bobby, *my* Bobby.

My heart skipped a beat, a short spurt of excitement ran through me. *It's Bobby, he's come to save me*, I thought. *How does he know I'm here? I'll be OK now, Bobby has found me.* My mind trailed off as I saw the knife in his gloved hand and my head became confused. *But he's the man who stabbed me... What...? I don't understand, it can't be Bobby. It looks like him, though.*

But this man was fatter than my Bobby, his top stuck out. *It couldn't be him, I was being stupid. But it looked like him.*

He drew up in front of me and held the knife to my face, the tip pressed into the side of my nose.

'Please, just leave me alone. Please...' I begged.

One blow, two blows... I lost count. I thought he had cut my face but he was punching me in the right eye – trying to knock me out, I assume. Whether or not he was temporarily successful, I still don't know. The next thing I remember is him holding my left arm down on the pavement. Taking the knife, he deliberately sliced deep down my wrist towards my fingers and through to almost the centre of my palm. Blood spurted out; he had sliced open my main artery, split it in two. He then took the knife and repeatedly stabbed me in the belly. I felt it slice through my distended abdomen, my baby bump. It felt like I was being repeatedly punched, as my body grew numb, but I knew the blade was still piercing me deeply.

'*Not our baby*!' I screamed. '*Please, not the baby*!'

The knife cut through my bump. He had killed her, I was sure. And I knew at this point that he wasn't going to stop until I was dead too.

'PLEASE DON'T KILL ME, PLEASE! I HAVE TWO CHILDREN, I'M A MUM ALREADY. PLEASE, PLEASE DON'T! I HAVE TWO SMALL CHILDREN,' I begged him. But he knew I had kids – he had kissed them goodbye that morning. No response, just the sound of his exertions as he stuck the knife in. He remained focused on what he had to do.

As I continued to beg, I was aware that someone was kicking him. People were screaming for help, but he wasn't stopping. He grappled at the scarf I had wound around my neck.

My throat, he was going for my throat. This is it, he's going for the final slice. I can't get up, oh my God, I can't get up! I can't get away, I can't stop him! Help me!

As he fumbled to get the blade onto my neck, I screamed more and more.

'NO, NO, NO! DON'T DO THIS! NO, DON'T KILL ME!'

But my begging had no effect on him. His first attempt of cutting my throat was thwarted as a guy kicked him so hard, it knocked his hand off me. He changed stance and came at me from behind. My arms reached up, desperately trying to fight him off. His fingers grappled with my scarf once more.

This was it, I knew I couldn't survive this...

Then he was gone, snatched from me.

A young man who had appeared from nowhere, it seemed, tore him from me. The force pulled me over onto my side on the pavement. Once more, I pushed myself up to seating, leaning against the pillar. But the attacker got himself to his feet once more, adjusted his clothes, picked up the knife and headed back towards me. Like a horror film, it was never-ending. I held my hand up to protect myself, just as the thundering feet of three police officers approached, rounding the corner, stopping him in his tracks as he held the knife over me, ready to strike again. Dropping the knife, he threw himself face down onto the pavement – his time was up.

'It's over, mate,' said a deep male police officer voice.

Relief flooded through me.

At last it was over, properly over.

Much later I learnt that the attack had lasted in total about nine minutes, a very long time when you are being attacked incessantly.

Two police officers jumped on him, as a female police officer faced me. I could see in her eyes it was bad, but she did her best to smile and look calm.

'Hi, my name is Cassie. I'm a police officer, I've come to help you. What is your name?' she asked.

'Natalie... Natalie Queiroz,' I replied.

'OK, Natalie, I need you to do something for me. Don't look down but press your hand on the top of your bump, I'll guide your hand,' she told me levelly.

Of course, after being told *not* to look down, the first thing anyone does is exactly that.

'What the hell is that?' I asked as my hand touched this white spongy stuff.

'It's your intestine, Natalie, and we need to keep them covered. Keep your hand over them, I will need to press on your chest. We also need to get this tied around your arm.'

I felt a tight band around the top of my arm. It was so tight, a tourniquet. My wrist was pumping out blood through the split artery and they were desperately trying to stem the flow as best they could. Once my arm was elevated, Cassie pressed firmly down on my chest. I could see in the corner of my eye the feet of my attacker lying pinned by the police officers, his dirty trainers just a couple of feet away from my blood-stained boots.

The officers spoke to each other as they worked on me whilst others arrested him. Sirens filled the air. To this day, the sound of sirens takes me back to that point: propped against that cold brick pillar, my bottom on the wet, cold stone pavement. They asked me where I lived and I managed to slur out my address.

Cassie noticed me glancing in the direction of my attacker.

'Do you know who that is, Natalie?' she asked.

'I think it's my partner, Bobby... but it can't be...' I replied groggily.

'It is,' she said.

It really was. How? Why? How the hell could it be? My world spun. I felt everything draining out of me, slipping away. I looked forwards and the colour and detail in the world drained away, everything went white. Cassie's face, despite being so close to mine, lost all detail: she was a black outline on this bright white canvas in front of my eyes.

'I can't see you!' I panicked. 'I can't see anything, everything has gone white. I don't feel good, I can't see anything,' I told her.

'Stay with me, Natalie,' she urged. 'Keep talking, don't stop talking to me. Natalie, keep focused on me and keep talking.'

'I don't think I can,' I slurred.

The fight was getting too much for me. I couldn't believe it, it hit me like a train. There was a real chance I could die here. I suddenly realised that it wasn't enough staying alive until he stopped, he wanted to terminate me with those last blows but I was still fighting. But life was slipping away, bit by bit, with every extra spurt of blood loss.

I can't die here! I thought. *Not here, not on the pavement. This wasn't how it was supposed to be!* I was almost indignant. *I've got Emily and Isabel, they need me. I can't die, what would happen to them? I can't leave them!*

Fear coursed through me afresh. I couldn't leave my kids, but I felt like I couldn't hang on either.

I heard Cassie shouting for someone to get me a drink. Full sugar cola from the nearby McDonald's. There was some debate as to whether I should be drinking any fluid as I would need to go straight into surgery but Cassie overrode this and said I needed fluids and sugar now. I remember them holding the cup near my mouth as I took sips of it – I felt awful, but I couldn't let go. I don't know how many times I drifted in and out of consciousness. It felt as though I was awake for all of it, but I'm not so sure looking back.

'An Air Ambulance is coming in for you, Natalie. You just keep hanging in there,' Cassie told me. The land ambulance still hadn't arrived and every police officer on scene pulled First Aid packs from their cars to stem the bleed. Police cars swamped the area. There had been shift change when the 999 call came in, but both shifts turned out for me. Another station also sent out CID officers.

Cassie kept talking to me. I became fixated on the fact my handbag was on the pavement up the hill. I kept telling her that if I was going in an ambulance she needed to get my bag as it was lying on the hill. My phone was in it and my purse. And my house keys. She kept reassuring me it was fine and she would sort it out. But I remember thinking no one was going to collect it.

Why not? It couldn't be left there!

Little did I know that the area was being treated as a murder scene and no one was allowed on the hill as they taped off the area and called in Forensics.

The land ambulance arrived and they got me in there to assess me whilst we waited for the Air Ambulance. I was so cold, I desperately wanted to get off the pavement. Cassie came with me and continued to hold my hand whilst the paramedics cut my clothes off me. Before I knew it, they were off. As they removed my bra, a pool of blood spilled out. Blood was everywhere and the paramedics worked hard to get a line into me to get fluids in. They checked my blood pressure and it was barely above what was needed to survive – and I was eight months pregnant. They had to act fast or I was going to die there and then. My body was slowly shutting down from the shock and as a result, my veins started to disappear. Attempt after attempt to get a canula in, to tap into that vital vein. With each attempt, they uttered the immortal words, 'Sharp scratch, Natalie!'

In the end I just replied, 'You really don't have to say that, I've just been stabbed lots of times!' and a small smile crossed my lips. I was told afterwards they couldn't believe I had tried to crack a joke whilst hanging onto my life by a thread.

The loud rotary blades of the Air Ambulance thundered overhead. They were trying to land. We were in the town centre, it was a busy Friday afternoon. Not an easy task. Hearing the blades rotating before they touched down seemed to go on for ages. I remember thinking,
Please just get it down and get me to hospital now. Tired of the fight, I could barely breathe.

A tall man in a bright red/orange jumpsuit entered the back of the ambulance. He was surprised that I was still conscious, not in cardiac arrest.

'Hi Natalie, my name is Ravi and I'm a doctor off the Air Ambulance. We're going to get you straight off to hospital now,' he told me calmly and firmly.

I nodded a response.

Ravi and the paramedic with him, Steve, talked to the ambulance crew and they drove the ambulance the short way off the hill and round to where the helicopter had landed: right in the middle of the road junction, on a slope. To minimise the time I would be outside, they reversed the ambulance up to the helicopter. After transferring me onto a stretcher, they lifted me out of the land ambulance. As they lifted me down they enlisted the help of surrounding police officers to lift me up onto the sliding platform coming out of the helicopter. Police officers surrounded me and shouted to the large crowd, which had now gathered, to stop filming on their phones as they transferred me.

As they lifted me onto the sliding platform, Ravi spoke to me. I opened my eyes wide and looked up at him. One of the community support officers who lifted me said later that I looked at him like a child would look at an adult, with totally trusting eyes. He was struck by how a grown woman could look so small, so scared, yet so trusting of another human being. To me, Ravi was my lifeline. He and the Air Ambulance crew were all I had to cling to until they flew me to the hospital. As I listened to his instructions about what exactly they were going to do, I knew I just needed to stay still and calm.

They were keeping me propped up because of the bump. Once in the helicopter, the monitors beeped in front of me. Steve and Ravi both spoke to reassure me as another crew member – Richard – negotiated the tight lift out of the centre. Breathing was becoming increasingly difficult and at one point, I knocked Ravi's leg to tell him I couldn't breathe. I pulled at the oxygen mask covering my mouth and nose as it felt like it was smothering me. Ravi replaced it and told me I must keep it on. I told him I couldn't breathe, but he just kept reassuring me that I would be alright.

As I lay still and silent in the helicopter I didn't dare move, every breath was a struggle. I was scared, so scared I would die. In my head I kept repeating, *I can't die. I've got Emily and Isabel, I can't die*, over and over again. I had to focus on staying alive.

When I glanced out of the side of the helicopter the weather was awful. We were heading for the Queen Elizabeth Hospital in Birmingham, a major trauma centre which deals with the military – soldiers flown back from war zones with horrific life-changing injuries.

'Natalie, can you feel your baby move?' Dr Ravi's voice cut through my thoughts.

'No... No, I can't,' I replied.

It suddenly struck me that I hadn't felt her move through the entire attack. I knew he had stabbed me in the stomach. My head wouldn't let me even think about her, it was too horrific. I couldn't contemplate if she was alive or dead.

It wasn't long before we came to land. I generally hate flying but there was no way around this one! We touched down, the side of the helicopter was opened and as I was pulled out on the stretcher, the cold hit me once more.

The helipad for the QE Hospital is on top of a multistorey car park opposite the A&E department – you have to go in a lift down to the bottom, then be wheeled across the road to A&E. As we entered the lift, it crossed my mind how I had been in those very lifts many times in the past when I used this exact same car park for work many years ago when it was open to patients and visitors. The ride was bumpy across the road; a man in a high-vis jacket held up the traffic as they bumped me across the zebra crossing.

As the automatic double doors to the hospital swung open, the pace picked up. The team were now running down the corridor, wheeling me at a fast pace as the overhead lights flashed.

'Straight to theatre!' I heard them call.

They wheeled me into a room. Later, I learnt that they had cleared three resuscitation bays for me – they were not even certain I would make it down the corridor from A&E to theatre. The resuscitation room was full of doctors and nurses – thirty in total, I have since discovered. Karen, the paramedic on the air desk who coordinated the whole rescue, had been in constant contact with the helicopter. Using their information on my injuries and her medical knowledge, she ensured every speciality needed was there waiting for me. No one needed to be bleeped when I arrived, all were on standby. It was scary and confusing in the room, yet comforting too.

'Hi, Natalie, I'm Colonel Kaye,' said a voice to my left.

'I can't breathe,' I uttered. I felt suffocated, drowning.

'We will be sorting that out for you any moment, don't worry. I'll be leading your care. We need to take you straight into theatre for surgery, Natalie, and then get your baby out. We have doctors here for that and to put you back together again.' Calm and in control, he turned to speak to Dr Ravi about what had happened and what they had done so far.

An obstetrician introduced herself and said she would be delivering my baby. She told me she would be putting in a catheter now.

Now? I thought. *What the...?*

Yep, she was putting it in now whilst I was still awake.

'Right, Natalie,' Colonel Kaye turned his attention back to me, 'I'm going to knock you out now. You won't come round until at least tomorrow or the next day as we need your body to recover, OK?'

As he spoke those words, he plunged down the syringe full of anaesthetic.

Thank God, I thought, *someone else can take over this fight.*

Then it all went dark.

Chapter 12

'Hello' From the Other Side

OK, I MAY HAVE JUST STOLEN A LYRIC FROM A WELL-KNOWN TOTTENHAM-BORN ARTIST, BUT MY STORY DIVERGES SLIGHTLY HERE FROM MY PERSPECTIVE. THE LIFE-CHANGING event that unfolded on Friday, 4 March of course had a profound effect on all those around me: my children, mother, siblings, friends and even my ex-husband. So, what was happening whilst I was fighting for my life, how did they get to hear about it all and what did they go through?

The best starting point for this is with my mother. If you remember, Mum agreed to pick up the kids from school that very Friday afternoon as I'd asked if she could help me whilst I met Bobby at the bank. Being the amazing mum that she is, she of course said yes. At just after 2pm she received my text saying the bank appointment had been put back to 3.30pm so not to worry if we were a bit later back than expected, to which she replied 'OK'. From her perspective, the day was like any other.

The school run had its challenges that afternoon as the children were particularly stroppy coming out, so Mum told them that as they were being grumpy, they weren't having their usual Friday 'Jen's Sweet Shop' visit, which was met with more moaning and pouting. Ignoring their protests, she shuffled them into the car to drive across Sutton to my house. Luckily, they didn't go through the town centre, which was mostly closed off and teeming with police cars, cutting down the back streets instead. As they sat in a queue of cars at a set of traffic lights, just down the road from the top of Trinity Hill, they saw the distinctive red Midlands Air Ambulance helicopter lifting up into the sky. Obviously, it's not a usual sight in the town centre and they talked about it, with Mum telling the kids how the Air Ambulance only came for very sick people, so there must have been a serious accident or something. They watched and listened to the loud rhythmic beating of the rotor blades as it lifted and flew off, not knowing that they were in fact watching myself and baby bump being air-lifted from the scene of a vicious crime. The memory of this moment has always stuck with them. In Isabel's words, 'It had Mummy and baby bump really hurt in it and almost going to die'. My heart contracts every time I see her little sad face recall the memory.

Once through the traffic, Mum pulled her car onto the driveway and bustled the children towards the house, searching for her keys to unlock the door. The door swung open and they ran in. A strange sight then greeted my mother's eye just as she was about to step into the house: a police van had pulled across the driveway and two officers stepped out.

'Does Babur Raja live here?' one of them asked her directly.

'Yes, he does...'

'Well, can we ask who you are, please?' he said, breaking her reply.

'I'm Natalie's mum, Natalie who owns this house, Bobby's partner. I've just collected her kids from school and brought them back. Why?' she asked, confused but wondering if they were hunting Bobby. Her instant reaction was that maybe they were looking for him in connection to all these strange goings-ons with the money and his business.

Was he caught up in a fraud?

'Can we come in, please? We need to tell you something.' The tone of the police officer changed slightly.

Mum nodded and invited them in. The children, freaked out by the sight of two police officers entering the house, turned tail and ran upstairs to Emily's bedroom. The police officers took Mum into the front room, pushing the worn wooden door closed behind them. Facing her, they took a deep breath.

'There's been an incident in Sutton, I'm afraid Natalie's been stabbed,' one of them relayed formally but with empathy too.

What? Mum's head span. *Stabbed? Natalie? Surely she got caught in the crossfire of some other incident? It can't be that bad, can it?* Mum's head filled with questions, but nothing came out of her mouth.

'We need to get you to hospital. Is there anyone who can look after the children for you?' the officer continued, looking at Mum's bewildered face.

'Erm, her sister, her eldest sister Jane. I'll call her now,' came her first words as she searched for her mobile in her handbag.

Meanwhile, the children stayed upstairs, clutching each other, curled up by the radiator, knowing instinctively that something serious was happening and that it involved Mummy. They heard Nanny fumbling in her bag downstairs in the hallway, looking for her phone, but didn't dare move, pinned to the floor and each other.

Mum found her phone and in a daze walked back into the lounge. Scrolling down her phone book list, she found Jane and dialled. The phone rang just a couple of times before my niece Louise answered.

'Hi Nan, Mum's driving.'

'Er, OK, can you tell her something has happened to Aunty Nat and I need to get to the hospital, but I've got Emily and Isabel. Could she come down and collect them?' said Mum, trying her best to sound calm.

Louise relayed the information to Jane, who said that was OK but asked what had happened.

'Natalie's been caught up in some incident in Sutton and has been stabbed. I need to get to the hospital. The police are here at the moment,' Mum replied.

I don't know to this day what that news must have done to my sister, who was driving, nor my niece who was relaying the messages to her mum. But it was agreed that Jane would come straight away. Luckily, she had just picked up both my niece and nephew (Ben) from their respective schools and they were in the car near the A38, so would head straight down. Mum said it would probably be best if Jane had them overnight, not knowing how long she might be at the hospital. Jane agreed straight away and set off for the A38, calling her husband, Andy, who was working in a clinic at the hospital at the time. I believe that as soon as Andy was told, he left the hospital. They took his patient list off him, passed it to his junior doctor team and shoved him to the door. He got into his car and set off for the journey down to the QE in Birmingham.

'She's on her way down.'

'How long will she be?' asked the officer, looking concerned.

'Oh, about half an hour. She's coming from Derby but she's just about to get on the A38–' Mum began.

'We haven't got that long to wait,' the police officer cut in. 'I need to take you now. My colleague, Nicky, can stay here with the children until your daughter arrives.'

The urgency and seriousness of the situation started to seep through to Mum. She nodded 'OK' at him and took herself up the stairs to find Emily and Isabel. Their little faces stared at their nanny, terrified, as she entered the room.

'Girls, listen carefully to Nanny! Mummy has been hurt in an accident in Sutton and I need to go with this policeman to see Mummy in hospital,' she began as calmly and reassuringly as she could muster. Isabel let out a whimper – it was like her nightmare from earlier that week was coming true.

'This lovely police lady – Nicky – is going to stay with both of you until Aunty Jane, Louise and Ben get here. They are on their way from Derby. Aunty Jane will then take you back to her house and you can have a sleepover there,' Mum continued as the children's faces crumpled to tears.

'What's happened to Mummy? Where is she? Why is she in hospital?' they asked through sobs.

'Mummy will be fine, she has just got a bit hurt and so they have taken her to hospital, but she will be fine. I just need to go and see her. You stay strong for Mummy and Nicky will look after you until Aunty Jane is here,' Mum repeated, most likely to reassure herself more than anything that everything was going to be fine.

The girls kept crying and Mum hugged them tight and told them they would be OK.

Nicky stepped forward and said, 'It's OK, I'll look after them. You better get going.'

Mum prised herself from her grandchildren and, in a daze, headed downstairs to the waiting officer.

'You'd better get your bag and phone and we need to set off,' he said firmly but kindly.

She nodded, got her things and followed him out to the police van.

Nicky encouraged the girls to come downstairs to choose a DVD. They carried a photo of me that was in Emily's bedroom, clutching it to them as a reminder of my face and if I looked fine in the picture, I must still be fine surely? As Mum shut the door, they led Nicky to see their vast DVD collection. Once a film was eventually chosen, after much debate and not much focus understandably from the kids, they all went into the front room to put it on. The girls huddled together whilst Nicky sat in an adjacent chair, bolt upright, surveying the scene in front of her.

Mum meanwhile walked to the police van still parked across the drive. As she stepped inside, the officer made a comment about heading to the QE.

'The QE?' Mum exclaimed, thinking they were heading to our local hospital. 'Why the QE?'

'Because that's where they have airlifted her to,' he replied.

'Airlifted?' Mum's head took another spin. 'The Air Ambulance I saw earlier was for Natalie? How serious is she?' she asked, incredulous.

Both now sat in the vehicle and the engine was started up.

'It's life-critical, I'm afraid. She has been severely injured, that's why I need to get you to the hospital as fast as I can,' the officer replied.

Mum sat back in her seat, absorbing all this.

Stabbed? Life-critical? Airlifted? The QE?

Her mind could barely process it all, so she stared ahead at the heavy queuing traffic.

Not far into the journey, the officer became unsettled.

'This is taking too long,' he muttered. 'I'm going to radio through to request blue lights.'

With that, he radioed through to Control.

'I've got the mother of the stab victim in the vehicle with me, trying to get from Sutton Coldfield to the QE. Traffic is heavy. Request to use blue lights as patient in critical condition.'

The request was accepted and on went the blue lights. They weaved their way through the heavy Friday afternoon traffic and as with everything for Mum at that precise moment, it all became a blur. Once they had arrived at the QE and parked up outside A&E, straight away Mum was taken in.

'She's in theatre,' came the update. 'She needed immediate surgery. She was able to talk when she arrived, which is good, but her injuries are life-threatening. We can put you in the relatives' room to wait for news. Have you contacted anyone to come and be here with you?'

The staff looked at Mum with kindness and concern.

'I've only called my one daughter to come and have Natalie's children for me – I was looking after them when this happened. I need to phone her other sister and my ex-husband, her dad. I'll do that now,' Mum replied.

The police officer insisted on staying with her whilst she made the calls and waited for the others to arrive. Her first call was to my middle sister, Mand. Unfortunately, as Mand was at work, Mum struggled to get hold of her and ended up calling her partner. After a number of calls he managed to get hold of her to tell her the basics: that I had been stabbed and was in the QE, having emergency surgery. As luck would have it, Mand was working late in Birmingham centre that day, so she packed up straight away and jumped in her car. Driving up the main Bristol Road to the hospital, her radio kicked in with the breaking news on Radio 2: 'A heavily pregnant woman in Sutton Coldfield has been repeatedly stabbed in a town centre attack and is in a critical condition...'

Critical condition... the words swam in her head. Up until then she hadn't thought that her little sister might actually die. But there it was, an attack so severe it hit the national news headlines. Mand has since told me that she doesn't really remember the drive from that point to parking her car. She recalls abandoning the vehicle in one of the main car parks and scrabbling towards A&E, dreading the news. As she entered the busy A&E department, she disregarded all the queues to the check-in desks and headed straight for the front.

'My little sister has been brought here. She was stabbed and I believe my mum is here, I've come to be with her,' she garbled anxiously at the woman behind the desk. All the staff in the department were aware of the severity of the case and took my sister straight through to the relatives' room, where my mum sat, talking incessantly, in shock at what was unfolding.

The next phone call, to my dad, didn't last too long: he was away in London with his wife, Jill, looking after my step-brother's children and couldn't get away till the morning. He asked my mum to keep him updated. That did hurt me when I learnt about it.

Her final call was to my ex-husband Ian, who wasn't on shift that day so was going out with a woman in Birmingham. He was on the train when Mum called. I'm not sure what exactly was said in the conversation, but she relayed the key facts that I'd been stabbed and was in a critical condition in theatre and the children were safe with Jane, who was taking them to Derby for the night. It must have been a surreal moment for Ian, going out on a date and your ex mother-in-law calls you to say your heavily pregnant ex-wife has been stabbed repeatedly and is now lying in theatre in a major trauma centre.

It would put a dampener on any date, I would guess.

Ian returned to his flat, jumped in his car and came straight to the QE to find out what was happening. As he entered the relatives' room, he noticed that Bobby wasn't there.

'So, where's her partner?' he asked the police officer who was still there.

'I can't say at this stage but he's not here,' came the reply.

My family were not told that day what had happened to Bobby or why he was not there, but they pieced together he must have something to do with it, especially because the officer had first asked if 'Babur Raja' lived at the address, rather than asking about me. None of them could believe it, though.

Not Bobby... Surely not Bobby?

My brother-in-law Andy soon joined them as they all sat waiting for news. It didn't take long before an update came.

'The baby has been delivered... A little girl. She did need resuscitating, but she is alive. She has been put into a coma and has been transferred to the Neonatal Intensive Care unit at the Women's Hospital. She is in a serious condition.'

Birmingham Women's Hospital sits on the same site as

the QE. It's a fantastic place dedicated to gynaecology and maternity with specialist care facilities. My baby daughter was in the best place. She had a massive fight ahead of her and was far from being out of the woods, but had already proved herself to be a fighter. They just still had to see if her mum would also pull through surgery.

I was in surgery for over five hours, then taken for a specialist scan. Andy, being a consultant himself, went to get an update from Colonel Kaye, the surgeon leading my care. He found out they had repaired a lot of my injuries. Some still had to be done, but they had stitched up all the critical parts. I had lost an extensive amount of blood and had to have that replaced. Now I was being kept in a coma to allow my body to recover, but once they got me back into Critical Care and settled, my family would be permitted to see me. I was attached to lots of machines and was being ventilated, Colonel Kaye warned.

At some point around 10.30pm, my family were given the news that they could go in and see me. As they walked towards me they were faced with my body lying motionless, tubes coming out of me, lines going into me, monitors and bleeping machines surrounding my bed. My face was sheet-white and a ventilator was doing my breathing for me as drains either side of my chest took away blood-stained fluid from the knife-damaged areas. It's fair to say I wasn't looking my best, but I was still alive. I had to get through the next couple of days, but like my baby daughter, my body hadn't given in and kept the fight up – there was too much to fight for.

My family stayed and spoke to me, reassuring me that they were there with me and I was safe. After about half an hour, they left me to recover. As they exited Critical

Care, they decided that they really needed to go over to the Women's Hospital to see my newborn daughter. After all, her mummy was lying in a coma in another hospital and her daddy was who knows where. Also, they didn't know for sure if either of us would pull through the night.

All four made their way across the hospital grounds to the Women's Hospital. The air was bitingly cold. It had snowed earlier and although that had disappeared as fast as it had arrived, the cold hung in the air. Stepping inside the warm, brightly lit entrance to the hospital, they looked around to see where to go and a passing ward sister asked if she could help. They explained they were trying to see the baby and the nurse made it clear that it was categorically stated no one was to see her.

Mand pleaded with her, 'Please let us see her, it's really important to us and to her mum that we tell her she is loved.'

The nurse nodded tearfully. She knew what had happened and promised to do what she could. My family were ushered into a spare delivery suite to wait whilst she made calls. The doctors in the hospital all stuck with protocol – it was such a sensitive case that everyone was protecting my little one. But the nurse wasn't going to give up. In the end she went to the very top, calling the CEO of the hospital, waking her up. It was the only way she could get permission for my mum and sister, which she managed after an hour of persistence. It is with massive gratitude that I type this. I don't know who the nurse was that night, but whoever she is, and I hope she may read this, *Thank you*. Thank you for not letting my daughter be alone, with none of her family seeing her on her first night in this world. I know why the rules were put in place, but as that nurse understood, she was my baby, in a serious condition and she didn't have her mummy or daddy with her. Born in the worst possible circumstances, almost murdered by her own father before she saw the light of day. The pain that still causes in me is deep-seated and I don't think it is something I will ever come to terms with.

As Mand and Mum approached the little plastic cot, they saw her for the first time. Relatively small, 5lb 4oz at birth, she was unconscious, with tubes coming out of her and monitors attached to her scalp to record brain activity. She wore just a nappy as they cooled her body by 3°C to preserve her brain. She'd been severely starved of oxygen as my blood pressure was so low, she hadn't received enough oxygen after the stabbing and on delivery, pale, floppy and lifeless, she wasn't breathing at all. It took five attempts to resuscitate her. My baby, the precious child her daddy had wanted so badly, was now fighting for her life at the hands of his actions and for what reason?

As they stood by her cot and spoke to her, they stroked her little hands. They told her she had a strong mummy, who loved her very much. A mummy who would always protect her, love her and care for her. They told her about her amazing older sisters and how they would adore her, repeatedly telling her how much she was loved already by a family who adored her. Her mummy was poorly in another hospital, so that was why I wasn't there but I would be dreaming of her. Even though she was unconscious, it still means the absolute world to me that my mum and Mand were there with her that night, talking to her, reassuring her. Her daddy – who should have been there – was in a police cell, arrested for the attempted murder of her and her mummy. Bobby, the man who swore to love and protect me for life, had done this and now two people were fighting for their lives.

Exhausted, my family left the hospital at some point after midnight. Andy and Ian made their way back to Derby, whilst Mum and Mand returned to Mum's house, all trying to process the last seven hours.

Once home, Mum checked her phone. There was a message from my friend Anita offering her support. She and the rest of my lovely friends all had their own stories too. As the news hit national headlines early that Friday evening, 'Pregnant forty-year-old woman stabbed multiple times in Sutton Coldfield town centre. Baby delivered. Mother still in a critical condition', they all started to wonder. Most of them tried calling my mobile, sending WhatsApp messages. My answer machine kicked in time and time again, the messages left unread.

What about Facebook? Natalie surely will put an update on there to reassure people it's not her, they thought.

Nope, nothing on Facebook.

What about Bobby's Facebook? They're probably in the hospital. Nat's probably in labour after last weekend. We'll see a joyous announcement any time soon.

But nothing. Messages were also sent to Bobby's phone, Bobby's Facebook messenger. No reply. Silence. There was a growing sense of dread.

One of my closest friends, Wayne, had his wife Jo call him about the news. He had only half-listened to the news, but she had heard it and her sixth sense told her it was me. She told Wayne to call me, but when he failed to get a response, she begged him to pop round to mine to check. As he pulled onto the driveway, he saw a light on in the house and my car on the drive.

Ah, see, it's all ok. She's there, he thought to himself as he wandered up the drive. He rang the bell. No answer. Rang again.

Er, OK, this is weird, he thought to himself. *It's the girls' teatime, she would be in making them dinner.*

As he turned to walk down the driveway he was met by a police car pulling up at the house. There was something else they had to check.

'Who are you, sir?' they asked Wayne as he sauntered up the drive.

'I'm a mate of Natalie's. I heard the news and wanted to check she was OK. Please tell me it's not her who's been attacked,' he said, slightly worried now.

'We're sorry, but yes, it is her. We can't tell you any more than that,' he was told.

'But… What…? Who did it to her, for fuck's sake?' he asked.

'We can't tell you that, sir. She's in a very serious condition. I'm afraid we can't say any more than that.'

And with that, Wayne was left to take in the news before shakily dialling Jo back,

'It *is* Nat! I've been to her house and the police are here. It's her!'

Jo's heart sank as she whispered, 'I just knew it.'

Thinking about who else might be trying to get hold of me, and knowing how close Anita and I are, he called her straight away. She answered chirpily.

'You don't know, do you? You've not heard the news?' he asked.

'What news? I've just left work,' she replied.

'Are you driving? Can you pull over? I need to tell you something,' he said as calmly as he could.

Anita's head span.

As the news filtered out that it was me, the pregnant woman who got attacked, no one imagined that it could possibly be Bobby.

Annabel hadn't got a mobile phone signal that Friday evening and hadn't heard it was me. Her sister Helen called the landline and asked if she had seen the news and if she had heard from me. Annabel passed it off that it couldn't possibly be – that was until she switched on the BBC News the following morning. The BBC had filmed at the scene as forensics investigated and there, sat on the hill, was my large orange handbag. Annabel had gone on at me for ages to swap that bag – it was old and I used it all the time. As she watched them pan around the crime scene, my bag sat there in the street.

'That bloody bag!' Her hand flew to her face and she turned to her son, stood with her: 'Oh my God, it *is* Nat! It really is… That's her bag!'

Slowly, my friends got in contact with each other through various media, all in shock and total disbelief. Still, nobody knew it was Bobby who had carried out the attack. On the Saturday afternoon, his closest friends from school days tried in vain to get hold of him: they had learnt it was me who had been attacked and they assumed he was in the hospital with me or the baby. They even went down to Sutton Coldfield police station to report him missing, worried he had been hurt in the attack and lay injured somewhere, where no one could find him. After all, they had known him for thirty years – no way could he had been involved.

Except he was. He was sat in a police interview room somewhere behind the very desk where they were reporting him missing.

On the Saturday morning, the police told my family officially that it was Bobby who had carried out the attack. They arrived early at Mum's house to interview her and Mand. Mum and Mand were taken into separate rooms and interviewed. After all, Mum was one of the last people to have been in contact with me. They also wanted to build a picture of Bobby and my relationship, but they were stumped: it had always seemed so happy, some money worries at the end and pressure from his mother, but nothing to justify this in the slightest.

The police weren't the only visitors to Mum's door that day either. Press swamped the street. They were knocking on Mum's door, those of her neighbours and my friends (after scrolling names on my Facebook), trying to get an interview, a piece about the family. But they all stayed quiet; no one broke my trust or confidence. Indeed, the press were sent away from many a door that weekend.

Sunday morning: Bobby's name was given out officially. My very good friend and colleague, Vish, had been trying desperately to get hold of me. I always replied quickly to his WhatsApp messages, but I hadn't even read them. As he sat with his family, having lunch out for Mother's Day, the news broke: Babur Karamat Raja named as the man who attacked the pregnant woman in Sutton Coldfield. His skin went cold, his stomach lurched.

It was Nat, and Bobby had done it!

Vish called my senior managers to break the news. That night, my work issued a formal statement and formulated a company-wide email, telling employees what had happened, confirming it was me and instructing that no one should speak to the press. I will be forever grateful for the steps they took to protect me right from the start.

It was Monday when my name was formally released. Photos taken from my Facebook and LinkedIn profile adorned the front of every newspaper.

Officially named and photographed.

Ian had innocently taken the children into Sainsbury's that day to get some food, only to be met by a sea of newspapers and my face staring back at them. He soon hurried them out, but they have never forgotten it.

There was also a photo of Bobby and I together, the girls' faces pixellated out. It was taken at the Oceanarium in Lisbon the summer before. The happy family photo I once used as a cover photo on Facebook forever more serving as a reminder of the day I was named the pregnant forty-year-old almost murdered on the streets of Sutton Coldfield.

Chapter 13

'What the ****
is Going On?'

BEEP, BEEP, BEEP, BEEP... RHYTHMIC, PULSING, ELECTRONIC NOISE. SLIGHT MOVE OF MY HEAD... MOUTH OPEN, TUBE DOWN MY THROAT... SLOWLY BEING PULLED OUT. GAGGING. Head groggy, eyes slowly focusing.

What the **** is going on?

'Natalie, hi, Natalie... Do you know where you are?'

A voice came from somewhere, I'm not even sure where.

'Erm...'

What?! What the hell is happening? The attack... The helicopter... The baby? Bobby?...

'The QE... I think I'm in the QE...' I slurred, my eyes not wanting to open properly.

'That's right, Natalie. You are in the QE. You were brought here yesterday after you were badly attacked in the street. Do you remember that?'

I nodded.

Stabbed... I was stabbed, my head was telling me. *They think it was Bobby – was it? Surely that wasn't true?*

'You have a little baby daughter, Natalie. She is alive, in Intensive Care at the Women's Hospital – a true little fighter.'

I smiled and nodded to show I'd heard them.

The baby survived? How? I thought the knife would have killed her. Our baby, Bobby's daughter, is here. Born alive... My little girl.

I think I must have drifted off again, stirring out of the blackness some time later. As my eyes opened and adjusted to the light, I saw many people near my bed, looking at me in concern. I couldn't move my body. Tubes and wires seemed to be coming out of me or be attached to every part of my body. I felt numb, alone.

Bobby... he can't have gone? He can't have done this, surely?

I needed him, I wanted him. Where was he?

That question was soon to be answered as the police visited my bed later that day. Soon, it became apparent who the man sat near the end of my bed was, too: I was having twenty-four-hour police guard for at least the next few days – standard procedure in a case like this. As DI Ian Ingram and his colleagues came in and introduced themselves, a sense of empathy radiated from them.

'Where's Bobby?' was my first question.

'Natalie, we need to ask you what you can remember about yesterday. Do you remember who attacked you?'

'I was attacked in Sutton... as I walked down Trinity Hill. I was stabbed... lots of times.'

Had it all really happened?

'And I think I remember being told it was my partner Bobby, but I can't fully remember...'

Every part of me was wishing they would tell me I was

wrong but, deep down, I knew I had remembered it correctly, plus he wasn't with me.

'Yes, Natalie, you were attacked in the street yesterday by a man with a knife. That man was indeed your partner, Babur Raja – Bobby. He's under arrest at Sutton Coldfield police station, currently being questioned.'

Tears streamed down my face as I lay back on the pillow, coursing past my earlobes and landing on the white linen behind my head. The officers looked at me with concern, knowing this was almost certainly beyond anyone's ability to take in, especially after coming out of a coma following a violent attack.

'Natalie, I'm really sorry but we need to take a statement from you about the attack. It's really important that we do so sooner rather than later. Anything at all you can remember may be key in this. I know it's difficult and if you don't feel well, just tell us,' an officer informed me.

Feel unwell? I'm in Critical Care, unable to move, attached to monitors, drains, oxygen, drips, catheters. I've been stabbed lots of times by the man I adore. Don't think I feel that perky now, if I'm honest...

My head betrayed my thoughts and nodded. They had to do it, that much I understood, and so I numbly pushed on through this surreal world I had woken up into. I went through my account of the previous day in as much detail as I could recall whilst an officer scribbled it all down on official statement sheets.

How is this happening? This surely can't be real? my head screamed.

The statement was to be used in court at a much later date. As we finished, or I drifted off to sleep (I'm not entirely sure which), I was presented with a pen and asked to sign what I had just gone through. I went to move my left arm, but it was heavy – encased in bandages and plaster.

Of course, he slit open my wrist on my left hand. Is the hand OK? I wondered.

I put my right hand up to my bandaged limb and stared at the exposed fingertips. That was the moment when I realised the damage to my hand was serious – I couldn't feel it at all. I tried to wiggle the tips of my fingers. Nothing, it was dead. Completely dead.

Is my hand still intact? Am I going to lose it?

My head swam with questions. The gravitas of my whole situation was sinking in me, like the *Titanic* into the icy waters. I was drowning with it too, it was almost all too much to bear.

'I want to speak to him.'

I turned to face the officers. They stared at me in sympathy, knowing I was struggling to understand exactly what had happened.

'You won't be able to have any contact with him at all, Natalie. Not until the investigation and trial is completely over,' an officer replied kindly.

But he's my partner, the father of my baby! I should be able to speak to him at least! Why on earth did he do this, just why?

Fresh tears streamed down my face. The police went off, saying they would return. They thanked me and the doctors. I then saw my family for the first time. Everyone was acting as if things weren't that bad, but their faces told me everything I needed to know. I wasn't totally 'out of the woods' and I pushed down the rising fear that I could still die. Then my thoughts turned to my baby: how was she? Was she out of the woods herself?

'Have you seen her?' I asked croakily, my eyes searching theirs to see if there was anything they were hiding from me.

'Yeah, we've seen her. We've just been with her now whilst you were with the police,' Mum replied, smiling, holding back the tears. 'We even got to see her last night so she wasn't alone.'

'What's she like?' I wanted to know. Then it came bursting out: 'Does she look like him?'

There was a noticeable pause around the bed.

'She's absolutely beautiful, Nat. Perfect little girl,' said Mum, smiling again.

'Who does she look like, Mum?'

I noticed she had swerved that part.

'She does look a bit like him, I won't lie to you. But she's so tiny and her own person,' she added.

More tears came like a wave over me. *My daughter, the baby Bobby and I chose to have, the baby he so wanted – but he wasn't here.*

I couldn't ask any more questions so I settled my head to one side and dropped off to sleep again. High volumes of morphine and a cocktail of other drugs flowed through my bloodstream, taking the edge off the physical and emotional pain.

Life was more than I could bear. I had woken up in a true nightmare, a hellhole. How on earth could I pull through this? But I didn't have any answers, I was numb.

As I stirred again, my hand reached for my belly. I was laid flat on my back and in my hazy state, I suddenly thought, *Don't lie on your back, you could cut vital blood supplies off to the baby.* But as my right hand rested on my tender, dissected and jelly-like stomach, I remembered

I was no longer pregnant: she was born, but not with me. That hurt a lot.

Panic then set in. *Where were my other two? How were they? What had been said to Emily and Isabel?* I looked around for my family – gone for a leg stretch as who knows how long I had dropped off for.

Nurses came over every fifteen to twenty minutes to check my stats, smiling at me, comforting me, as my terrified, tear-filled eyes stared back at them. Nobody could really give me any clear update about my baby, there wasn't much to report back on: she was in a coma, her body cooled, and no one knew what extent of oxygen starvation she had endured nor what effect that would have on her in the long term.

As soon as my family came back onto the unit, after strict security checks as to who they all were, my first question was about Emily and Isabel.

'Where are the girls?' I asked, panicked.

'With Jane, and they are fine, we promise. They're at their Aunty Jane's, building teepees with Louise and Ben, having a great time.' Mum smiled once more, but her smiles were hollow.

'But how were they told? Who told them? When? Were they OK?' Question after question... I needed to know how my babies were. Now they were all I had left in the world, I felt. My three girls... Everything else was a barren bombsite.

Mum proceeded to fill me in on the story of how it unfolded at my house. My head could barely register all this information and I had to be told more than once. As I thought about the sheer terror my poor girls must have gone through, my stomach flipped. I knew this would affect them for life and it made me feel physically sick; I was lying here and I couldn't even hold them and reassure them. A decision was made that the girls shouldn't see me in the state I was in, it would really traumatise them. Critical Care are wary of kids being on the ward due to the risk of infection, plus, it just isn't a place for children (with all the machines and the very sick people). I had to speak to them, though, to reassure them I was OK.

My dad had been by my side since the morning, having travelled up from London. He too had gone off to see the little one in Intensive Care whilst I slipped in and out of consciousness. As he sat by my bedside, he asked if I had a name for her, saying they had asked over at the Women's Hospital.

'Sofia,' I croaked. 'We had chosen the name Sofia already, she was always going to be called that. With an "f" rather than a "ph".'

Bobby and I had always referred to her as Sofia.

'OK, I'll let them know.' My dad nodded and when he next went over, I believe he told them. At first they misheard him and on the little pink card above her cot they wrote 'Sophie' before it was crossed out and replaced with 'Sofia'.

On his way over to her bedside, Dad fumbled in his jacket pocket and felt a small plastic bag. Working with engines and little parts coming in small plastic bags, plus having a mind not quite in tune or focus with the chaos unfolding around him, he screwed up the bag and chucked it in the nearest bin – the last thing he needed to be doing was carting around rubbish. It wasn't until much later that it dawned on him what was in the bag. When Dad arrived at the hospital, I was still in a coma. I'd been wearing a pair of beautiful solid gold earrings, given to me by Annabel for my fortieth, when I was flown in. They had of course removed these and put them in a small plastic bag, which they had handed to Dad to look after, but he forgot. My precious gold earrings have almost certainly been incinerated somewhere or maybe they're lying in a landfill!

It was the next day before I managed to speak to my 'big girls' briefly on the phone as someone helped me with my mobile. It was Mother's Day, the morning I had been discussing with Bobby on the phone just hours before the attack. I should have been lying in my own bed, having smoked salmon and scrambled eggs, made by my two older girls and partner. Instead, I was lying all alone in Intensive Care, drips keeping me going, a side serving of oxygen blasted through a mask. No children by my side and no partner. Despite people visiting me and doctors and nurses being at my bedside non-stop, I can honestly say I have never felt so alone. That feeling of loneliness was one I was not going to lose for a very, very long time. All-encompassing isolation from everyone and the world around me. Tears streamed down my face again as I stared up at the ceiling. When I glanced to the side, the police officer on guard was still sat there.

Poor guy must be bored senseless, I thought.

It wasn't long before Mum and Mand appeared. My auntie and uncle from Wales had also arrived with them, but were waiting outside as visitor numbers by my bedside were severely restricted. They ended up staying the whole week – supporting my mum, coming in every day to the QE, yet hardly getting to spend any time with me. They swore they didn't mind. They waited in the coffee shop and restaurant purely as support to Mum and I. Such unquestioning love and support, it's something I will never forget.

As Mand walked towards me, I noticed she was clutching something in her hand: it was photos she had printed off of Sofia! I pored over them, taking in every detail. She looked so tiny! Tubes and wires covered her bare skin, with only a nappy on her as they tried to keep her body cool.

She was perfect, an absolutely beautiful miracle. How did she survive? My fighter, my Sofia.

Sofia...

The name didn't seem right now. Sofia was the name Bobby and I chose, the name he had been part of. He had lost all right to have a part of her now. I couldn't keep that name. She needed a new one, thought of and chosen by me.

Leah. Leah Queiroz.

Her name card had yet another name crossed out as the line scored through Sofia, eradicating all trace of it from the records. Sofia was gone, the baby Bobby wanted was no longer. In effect, he had killed off Sofia. My baby girl, Leah, *was* here, though.

Later that day, the midwifery team came over from the Women's Hospital once more – after all, I had given birth and needed checking over. They felt my abdomen and discussed feeding. Leah had a tube going down her nose to feed her, into her tiny stomach. Sucking and swallowing were well outside her capabilities. However, as with any new mum and despite the trauma, my chest would soon be producing milk to feed my offspring and they wanted to know what my thoughts were.

'We were wondering if you wanted to breastfeed Natalie? Obviously, you'd have to express now, but it will set you up for later,' they asked, smiling at me, unsure of my reaction.

Breast feed? Have they seen the state of my chest?

Sliced to pieces, there were large bandages covering

stitches, which held together the eleven-plus wounds in my chest alone. Even my nipple had been stabbed. That was in addition to the risk of any silicone floating around in there, left over from my removed shredded implants and the multitude of drugs coursing my veins, entering my breast milk no doubt. But I found myself saying, 'Well, I guess I could try expressing some.'

WHAT? my brain was screaming at me. *WHAT ON EARTH ARE YOU THINKING, WOMAN?*

Aside from the above reasons, you had to add to the mix I was essentially one-handed, with one arm in a huge splint. Not the easiest thing to manoeuvre a small pre-term baby around on an extensively damaged and painful chest. This thought process was soon unnecessary anyway as one of the midwives proceeded to show me how I could hand express and it was immediately clear this was an absolute no-go! I was relieved that box had been ticked – at least it had been tried, but couldn't work.

Aside from the awkward breastfeeding conversation, they also came laden with a little card, photos of Leah and a gift box, put together by a charity who make up boxes for mums of premature babies, with premature baby clothes, premature baby nappies, creams, etc. It's the small things like this which can really lift you – an incredibly thoughtful gesture which makes a huge difference to new mums. The card was a Mother's Day card from my little one, the only mark that day of it being Mothers' Day. The card and gift I had bought my mum were left lying in the wardrobe back home – understandably, none of us thought to exchange cards or gifts. The photos of Leah were propped on my bedside table alongside the ones my sister had got and framed for me. My heart ached as I looked at my daughter, this little person, *my* little person, who I didn't even know yet.

Mother's Day was to pass that year without me seeing any of my three children.

That afternoon I had a visitor to my bed, a doctor I instantly recognised. He smiled as he approached the bed and greeted me.

'Hi Natalie, I just came to see how you're doing. I'm guessing you probably don't remember me.'

'I do, you're off the Air Ambulance. You were with me when I was airlifted,' I replied, with greater clarity than I had had all day. Dr Ravi was extremely shocked that I had remembered him – he said most people don't. After praising me for having stayed so calm in the helicopter despite being so desperately injured, he told me he would pop by again to see me and he was really pleased I was still fighting on. It's funny how when life is so chaotic, our minds focus on the smaller things. I put it down to the fact our brains can only process the small stuff, the bite-size chunks. Thinking about the attack and who actually did it was too much, too painful to even contemplate – my brain just couldn't go there. But I could remember the face of the guy talking to me in the helicopter.

Monday – Day Four if you include the day of the attack as Day One – and I was relieved that I had made it this far. I went off for more surgery. My right bicep had been completely cut open by the knife and still hadn't been put back together. I caught a glimpse of it as they took off the dressings: it was something akin to an anatomy book diagram. That needed repair, as did my hand. The main nerve to the hand had been severed, along with the tendons to my thumb and little finger when he cut my wrist open.

In the life-saving surgery on the Friday, the surgeons had stemmed the bleeding and repaired the artery, but the detailed work had been left until now. The bonus of being quite as dosed up on strong drugs as I was meant that I don't actually remember going for the surgery at all. Little did I know this was the beginning of a long journey with my hand, an injury that was to stay with me for life.

Later that day, post-surgery and lying in Critical Care, I remember feeling a strange bubbling sensation in my left-hand side. Every time I took a breath in, I could feel the skin bubbling away. I knew something wasn't right, so my hand fumbled for my buzzer. The nurse came straight away and as she glanced up at my stats, she bleeped for support: an immediate mobile X-ray at my bed and a respiratory doctor.

My left lung had collapsed. I knew I didn't feel great and my oxygen stats were starting to plummet. The cause of the collapse? Whilst I was having my left hand operated on, the surgical team accidentally knocked my drain out. It had come out of my body enough that the perforated holes along it were outside the body, so every time I took a breath in, it was letting air in around the lung, causing it to collapse. I was quickly wheeled round to a side room, where they told me they would have to reinsert the drain whilst I was conscious. They injected a local anaesthetic to my already heavily sedated body, but even with all the drugs circulating my system, I can testify that it hurt when they pushed it back in!

It was quite a wide tube and as they pushed it deep into my left side, I winced with pain. Another chest X-ray was requested, which showed my lung nicely reinflating, so in a matter of four days, both lungs had collapsed. It was fair to say my chest had 'gone through the mill'! The complications caused further delay in being able to be wheeled over to see Leah. The medical team were not happy for me to be wheeled over to the other hospital as I was still in a critical condition and both lungs were still being drained. I had to wait until I was drain-free.

Another day passed without seeing or holding my baby. The silence, the pain, the heartache was overwhelming. I had to stop myself sinking.

Don't sink, Natalie, Don't give in now, keep fighting...

Chapter 14

First Cuddles

CRITICAL CARE WASN'T A RESTFUL PLACE OF RECOVERY FOR ME. SO MANY DIFFERENT TEAMS WERE CONSTANTLY COMING IN TO SEE ME AND AS ONE TEAM OF DOCTORS left, another arrived – I think mainly to marvel at the fact that I had survived. One absolutely lovely Critical Care nurse, Andrea, put her foot firmly down in the end. Grabbing the leading edges of my curtains, she whipped them soundly shut around my bed, encasing me in silence inside. She then wheeled the drugs trolley across the join in the curtains and stood there, her own barricade. She wanted me to sleep. I was exhausted – the recovery, the pain and the emotional destruction were taking their toll and she was adamant I was going to have time out, come what may. My own personal guard, she was constantly shooing people away and instructing them to 'Let the girl rest, for pity's sake!' It makes me smile now, thinking back to her.

Family came in to see me and a couple of friends, my colleague, Vish, being one of the first and few to see me in those early days. Lots of people were desperate to come but visiting was restricted, so the few who did see me spent a lot of time keeping others updated on the basics. I had no means of communication and my family purposely kept me away from any media. I was aware that the amount of coverage on my story was widespread across news channels, newspapers and radio. It had even gone international. But I didn't want to hear or know about any of it.

On the Monday, whilst I was in surgery, Bobby, having been charged on the Sunday with my attempted murder as well as four other charges, including attempted child destruction of Leah, attempted murder of John Mitchell, grievous bodily assault of Anthony (Tony) Smith and carrying a knife in public appeared in Birmingham Magistrates' Court. John Mitchell, the first man to come to my rescue, had been stabbed in the hand by Bobby in the ensuing frenzy. Anthony (Tony) Smith was the gentleman coming down Trinity Hill who jumped on Bobby's back to bring him down. Both were exceptionally brave and incredible men. According to press reports, Bobby appeared in Birmingham Magistrates' Court in a grey jogging top and trousers to say his name and for the charges to be read. He wasn't asked to plead as the judge said it was a matter for a higher court than themselves, so it was being passed straight up to Birmingham Crown Court. Meanwhile he was taken to HMP Birmingham to be held on remand.

Our lives were diverging rapidly in the blink of an eye. A man I once curled up with in bed at night, woke up next to and lived with on a day-to-day basis was now being shipped off to prison for what was always going to be a substantial stretch of time as I lay drugged up in a Critical Care bed, with only memories of the life I had lost and fears of the life ahead. How all that had changed in a matter of days was baffling.

As I reached the Tuesday my desperation to see my baby daughter reached new heights. My emotional state was in pieces, not only because of the barren destruction caused by Bobby, but now being Day Five (post-attack), the baby blues were setting in. I was still attached to various monitors and the chest drains were still taking fluid away from both of my lungs. I also had a slight squint – my eye wouldn't open properly on the one side – and the eyeball seemed to be tilted slightly inwards on the one side. An ophthalmologist was bleeped and examined my eye. The squint was caused by Bobby punching me in the face repeatedly through the attack and to this day, when I get tired, that same eye starts to close more than the other one.

I knew with all my injuries, there was no way they were going to let me go and visit Leah until I was at least free of the chest shackles. With both of us in Critical Care but in separate hospitals, both kept alive by various machines, it seemed almost impossible. But my sense of fight kicked in as I knew I had to see her: Leah needed her mummy and, one way or another, I had to get over to the Neonatal Intensive Care Unit (NICU) in which she lay, unconscious. I spent the day nagging any nurse or doctor who came near about whether I could have the chest drains out. Though I was still not quite ready for them to be removed, they sensed my desperation to see Leah and agreed that I could have a chest X-ray to review my progress later that afternoon. If the lungs were clear enough, they would remove them and I could be taken over to see her with a portable oxygen cylinder.

As the afternoon progressed, I harassed them as much as they 'harassed' me with various checks and visits. Everyone knew how much I wanted to see my daughter and they all sympathised. Mid-afternoon, a portable chest X-ray machine was brought once more to my bed and more images taken. Then the waiting began: 5.30pm came and a slightly weary-looking chest consultant came to my bed. Good news, the X-rays signalled I could have the drains out, so I was wheeled back to the side room (where the one was replaced) to have them removed. I didn't notice the discomfort of them being pulled out or the small stitch that had to be put in each side to close up the gaping holes left by the drains, I was too busy focusing on the fact that I was a step closer to seeing my baby girl. As I was wheeled back to my hospital bay, my excitement was soon dashed as I was told it was too late to go over and see her. It was left to one of the Critical Care nurse team to break the news.

'Really sorry, Natalie. It's just too late to get you transported over there today. Hospital transport has now stopped, it finished at 6pm. And you need official transport as we are taking you out of one hospital and to another. I know you'll be disappointed, but we'll have to wait until tomorrow morning now.'

Five days of anguish, which had been building since the moment the knife struck, erupted like a volcano.

'NO! Please!' I blurted out as fresh tears streamed down my face. 'My baby was delivered five days ago and I haven't laid eyes on her yet. She hasn't got her daddy. I can't wait another day, I HAVE to see her now. Please! I've waited all day for this X-ray and to get these drains out. I know the delay was nobody's fault, but I've managed to get them out now and you all said if I was free of the drains, I could see her. Please, I'm begging you. I want to see my daughter today, I've been through enough!'

Motherly instincts had kicked in, in full force and I

wanted to be with my baby. I did mumble an apology after my outburst. The nurse stared hard at me – it was the most fuss or noise I had made since being admitted.

'Let me go and talk to the team to see what can happen. I think they will stick hard and fast with the decision, but let me go and discuss it with them,' she replied evenly.

So, off she went and I turned to my family – my sister Jane was there with my mum.

'Sorry about my outburst,' I mumbled, tears streaming down my face, 'but I really, really need to see her and I've waited so long. Everyone else seems to have seen her and I just want to go too.'

They nodded back at me. Of course they wanted me to see Leah for myself, but we all knew I had to be careful as I was still so ill. About ten minutes later, the nurse appeared with blankets and a wheelchair.

'Right, Natalie, myself and a colleague are going to take you. We've had to get special permission as this isn't standard procedure, but we all understand you need to see your little girl. We will have to push you in this wheelchair over there. Do you have anything warm you can put over your surgical gown? We will wrap you in blankets too and take this portable oxygen cylinder with us. We all totally feel for you, you have been through so much,' she beamed.

I borrowed my sister's warm fleece and the blankets were stacked on the bed ready for my movement. Manoeuvring out of bed was the next challenge – I hadn't been on my feet since the attack. Tentatively, I swung my legs around as someone took each side of me and lifted.

Head rush...

And down into the seat of the wheelchair: I was in! Slightly flopped in, but full of anticipation: I was going to see my baby daughter. I took a deep breath as the nurses pushed me out of my bay and out the doors to the corridor. It was all very surreal, my head turned to look at everything we passed: the world was still continuing, people bustled in and out of the hospital, rushing in from the dark outside with its biting cold to the bright entrance lobby, clean, warm and strangely welcoming. Some glanced at me as I was wheeled past whilst they clutched magazines, bags of sweets, drinks to give to their relatives, reminding them there is another world outside.

It struck me how their lives were perhaps just the same as the previous week. Their world continued, their plans from a few months ago most likely still playing out or being prepared for. But I didn't fit into this mould any more: my normality, my reality, was gone, blown out of the water. I was an outsider, continuing as normal. I didn't know where I belonged in this world, I couldn't even think about it. For now, my world was this bubble in the QE Hospital in Birmingham and I could not think past that – every moment just had to be dealt with as it came.

After wrapping the blankets tightly around me, the nurse pushed me out into the cold air, my family following alongside. The slope between the two hospital sites is on a relatively steep upward incline. The poor nurses had to push hard to get up the hill in the cold and dark. Their devotion, empathy and care for me, their patient, was second to none. All the staff at the QE will always be held in the highest regard in my eyes, such a wonderful hospital team.

At last they pushed me through the automatic door into the Birmingham Women's Hospital and through the warm lobby. It was here that another deep-set fear and integral grief engulfed me. Wandering around were couples, hand in hand, women lumbering along with large bumps, rubbing their stomachs and their lower backs, whilst their partners watched anxiously, knowing that their new arrival would be here soon enough. Their exciting new lives about to start… together. The life I'd been robbed of. I closed my eyes and hung my head – I couldn't bear it, tears pricked my eyes. This moment was the mark of the start of my innate fear of pregnant women. Since before I had Isabel, I had always wanted to retrain as a midwife, it was my dream. Now that too was gone. So much ruined and forever changed.

The nurses pushed on, sensing the difficult emotions I was experiencing on seeing this sea of heavily pregnant women around me. The corridor down to NICU seemed so long. Pictures of smiling midwives with new mothers clutching their newborns lined the walls. My heart cracked a little more but I focused on what was at the end of that corridor and my heart raced: I just wanted to be in the unit.

The nurses buzzed the door and soon we were in the stifling heat of NICU. Blankets and fleece were stripped off. They told the staff who I was and smiles radiated out at me, laden with sympathy and good wishes. Then they pushed me down to the room where my precious daughter lay. In through the double doors we went. She was lying in her cot, eyes closed, wires and tubes coming out of her. My eyes filled with tears. So small, so precious, she was truly real. I was wheeled to her side and my hand reached out to stroke her.

My girl, my baby.

'Hey Leah, it's Mummy. I've waited such a long time for this. I'm here with you now, baby. I love you. Mummy loves you so much.'

Tears streamed down my face but I carried on talking

to her. Watching the rise and fall of her tiny chest as the ventilator kept her breathing. Monitors bleeped and alarms rang out. It was a scary environment: all the babies were so small and so precious. And so poorly.

'I wish I could explain to you why we are both here like this, but I can't. Your daddy really wanted you but he's done such a bad thing. I don't know why he's done it, I really don't. But you're a fighter, you never gave in and you can't now. Mummy is here now by your side to help you fight on. We are in this together, we will be fine. I'm here to protect you for life. I love you so much.'

I told her again and again how much I loved her. She couldn't hear me, let alone understand me, but I hoped the sound of my voice would penetrate through her unconscious state and comfort her somehow. After all, she had spent eight months inside me, hearing my voice reverberate around her. However, no true physical contact could happen as she was too ill to be taken out of her cot and held. It would take until the Thursday before she could be extubated, her ventilator taken off her, and I would have the chance to hold her.

The nurses wheeled me back to the QE. Emotionally exhausted, I needed to be back in bed. I thanked them profusely. It was a moment so precious to me. As I shut my eyes as I lay back on my bed in Critical Care, the image of Leah's tiny body, a living miracle, flashed before my eyes.

Thursday eventually came and turned into an extremely significant day. First, I was assessed as being stable enough to be moved up to the major trauma ward. To keep me away from the main patients and allow a focused assessment of me, I was allocated a side room. I had spent most of the week in Critical Care and although far from recovered, the intensity of my care could now step down a grade. I kept myself predominantly enclosed in the side room and visitors kept streaming through the door, medical and family/friends alike. It was this day that I met David, one of the chaplains, for the very first time. A kind and caring man who listened so well, he brought me a cross made of soft wood, which warms as you clutch it. Small enough to fit in the palm of my hand, I took it to bed with me night after night. It was also a source of comfort at times during the day when my thoughts threatened to overwhelm me.

I carry it with me to this day.

I also got to meet Anna, a clinical psychologist at the QE, for the first time. Anna.

She was lovely from the moment I met her. I would never have been able to envisage what a key part she would play in my recovery over an extended period of time. She was to become my rock, a great source of guidance and formed an integral part of my rebuild and recovery; the person who helped keep me alive and encouraged me to keep going in those truly dark days still to come.

That afternoon the police forensic photographer also came. She had to take photos of all my injuries. At this stage I hadn't seen them myself. I was covered in dressings and bandages, surgical tape seemed to hold me together. A young male healthcare assistant was assigned the task of stripping me carefully of all my dressings. I watched his face as the injuries saw the light of day. He kept a calm expression but occasionally the widening of his eyes and a muffled sharp intake of breath told me how bad it was. Once clear of all the dressings, I stood in front of the plain wall in my room as rulers were placed alongside the stab wounds to measure them. *Snap, snap, snap!* Numerous photos taken as I stood there numbly. I wanted to see them all properly for myself, so I asked the photographer to take some for me on a phone left for my use. She duly obliged and snapped a few at the end. It was all functional and I pushed all thoughts from my head as I stood motionless, staring at a long lens black camera pointing at my naked torso. Humiliation, hurt and pain hung in the air, filling the room.

The photographer was as efficient as she could be, and once finished, she packed her bag quickly and thanked me for my cooperation, wishing me luck in my life ahead. As she left the room to inform the staff I was ready to have the dressings put back on, I wandered into my bathroom. Taking a deep breath, I turned to face the mirror: the scars were extensive and so ugly. Huge tears welled up in my eyes and fell like a heavy rainstorm. Forever changed, I could barely look at my own body. All my life I'd struggled to become comfortable with my body to the point I was when I was with Bobby and now it became once more a point of pure hatred for me. It needed covering up for life. As a nurse came back in, I hastily wiped my face but she saw my swollen puffy eyes and gave me the biggest empathetic smile.

'Oh, Natalie, I'm so, so sorry! What you have been through and are going through is beyond comprehension.'

Too numb to speak, I just nodded, then walked to the bed and lay down as she dressed all the wounds again.

The pinnacle of that day came later that afternoon. This time my family wheeled me over to NICU to see Leah. When I got there, she was off the ventilator. They had tried the day before but she became distressed and they had to quickly ventilate her again. This time she was breathing on her own! Another step forward. As I sat in my wheelchair, smiling proudly at her, they told me the news I'd been waiting for.

'You can hold her today, Natalie. Get yourself comfortable in that big chair and we will pass her to you.'

As a smiling nurse handed me this tiny bundle, still attached to lots of monitors with tubes coming out of her nose, arms, etc., my heart melted. She slept soundly in my arms. My pale face, mottled with bruising and a slightly swollen eye, looked down on her.

'I love you so much,' I whispered again and again, planting kisses on the top of her tiny head. They then manoeuvred her to pop down my top, so we were skin to skin and she nestled in amongst my bandages and dressings. My chest was of course painful, but none of that mattered or was even felt as she snuggled into me, her mummy.

Her mummy, who would protect her and love her unconditionally for life.

Chapter 15

Sisters

FRIDAY, 11 MARCH, A WHOLE WEEK AFTER THE ATTACK. FROM THE MOMENT I WOKE UP, I CHECKED THE TIME AND REPLAYED THE WHOLE DAY IN MY HEAD, HOUR BY HOUR. Every detail, from when he left the house to our texts – when I received them/what I replied – and our phone calls. I recalled his voice, what we talked about… there was nothing in his voice I could identify that would have betrayed what he was thinking or planning to do. I have re-run those conversations so many times in my head, exhausted the memory of them.

As we approached 3pm, I became increasingly unsettled. All my family were around me, almost like an unspoken vigil. Together, we thought about the events of the week before. Just one week before, but in so many ways a life that was already more than a lifetime ago and a life now so alien, I couldn't comprehend it.

The flashbacks came thick and fast. My heart pounded as I recalled hearing those steps, heavy and fast behind me. *Thud, Thud, Thud…* I knew I was in danger, but there was nothing I could do. *Should I have run?* It would probably have made no difference. He was catching up so quickly, I was in wedge-heeled boots, heavily pregnant and going down a steep hill in the rain. *Could I have fought harder? Did I succumb too quickly?* Four men came to my aid and they struggled with him. I was eight months pregnant and very quickly heavily wounded by stab wounds to the chest. I did fight hard – after all, I got away for a moment – but sense doesn't always heed intelligent and logical thought. *How could I have changed that day?* I know now nothing could have changed what happened but you can't help but have those pockets of time, those fleeting moments, when you just wish a time machine would let you go back and change things. But that won't happen. I knew I had to accept this life course already set out for me. Bobby was in prison, I was severely injured and our daughter had a huge fight ahead of her and so much to take on board later in life.

Between 3 and 4.30pm, the clock ticked by slowly – the airlift, the touchdown, then into theatre. And my memories of the day terminate there. Just as I got to the end of the timeline, I knew I must prepare myself for my precious girls. It was the very first time I was going to see them – I had spoken to them so many times but not been able to see them. They were also going to meet their baby sister for the first time. I was nervous: how would they react to me and Leah when they saw us?

The day had been such a long, emotionally draining one. As always, the ward staff did their best to support me – Marie particularly sticks in my mind as someone who checked on me regularly. The support continued that morning as they came in to update me on how Leah was doing, over in NICU. It made me reflect on how I felt so separate from her at times. I was petrified about the moment I would have to take on full-time parenting alone. All I could see ahead of me was loneliness. I was convinced that I would never have a partner again. I couldn't see myself letting anyone in again, trusting someone, let alone anyone finding my scarred body remotely attractive.

I was sentenced for life by what he'd done to me.

As 5pm approached, Ian arrived with the girls straight from school. Emily and Isabel appeared at the door, their small faces uncertain, but relief flooded across us all as they came rushing in, arms outstretched and shouting 'Mummy!' at the tops of their voices. I clutched them to me, enveloping them as best I could with my splinted left arm and painful chest and stomach. As I pressed my face into the tops of their heads, I inhaled their familiar smell. The rush inside of me from holding my babies again was overwhelming.

My girls, my very reason for fighting on this far.

Tears swam in my eyes. It was incredible to be there holding them. The last time I had seen them was a whole week ago as I waved them goodbye at the end of Emily's assembly. Since then life had changed beyond all recognition, but the love I felt for my girls swelled up inside of me like a hot-air balloon. The trauma for that moment no longer mattered as I had what was truly important in my arms. Isabel clung to me like a limpet, not wanting to let go in case I slipped away again. Once untangled from me, they produced amazing huge cards made at school. Each of their classes had made me a beautifully decorated card with paper flowers on the front and buttons forming the centres. Inside the one from Isabel's class, each child had written a message: 'Get well soon' and 'Hope you get better soon'. Isabel had made her own card stuck to the back, with a drawing of Leah and me and the words,

To Mummy, I hope you get better. I can't wait to see Leah. Love from Isabel xxxxxxxxxxxxxxxxxxxxxxxx xxxxxxxxxxxxxxxxxxxxxxxxxxxxxxxxxxxxx

Those cards meant the world to me. They are placed carefully in a wardrobe in my bedroom, showering the room with glitter whenever they are pulled out to be looked at and admired again. All of these experiences sharpen your gratefulness for the small things in life. They make you realise it really is worth the fight and so many people do care. Always take in every small positive detail in life when everything else is in turmoil. Take those things and store them as the precious moments they are, to draw upon when everything else looks bleak.

As I pored over the cards and all the messages, Emily and Isabel started to explore my room, taking in the incredible view. After pointing out the Birmingham Women's Hospital which stood opposite, I explained that was where their little sister was and how she was waiting for big hugs from them. At this the girls jumped up and down in anticipation, begging we go over to the hospital to see her.

I started to pull all my stuff together, determined to walk it if I could, although I wasn't sure I would make it all the way. We arranged for a wheelchair so I could do parts sat in the chair and then when I could, I would walk short distances so the girls could see Mummy was on her way to being her normal self. I wanted to put on a front of normality with the kids as much as I could – they needed to see I was OK, even when inside I felt like I was rapidly sinking and fighting against the tide.

Just as we were about to set off, Ian passed me an old iPhone of his. Luckily Ian's clear, methodical head and caring heart counted for a lot, as he did his best to make sense of it all and consider the practicalities of how best to support me. He sorted out a temporary pay-as-you-go SIM card (synchronised with my contacts, email and music) and had put it in his old handset so I would have contact with the outside world. My emails started to download. As I was pushed towards the Women's Hospital, Emily and Isabel skipping alongside me, I scanned through the emails rapidly pinging through. Then my heart stopped...

UNREAD MESSAGE *<Friday, 4 March Time 14.41. Bobby Raja>*

An email from Bobby, sent less than half an hour before he started stabbing me.

What the f***?

It was like a message from beyond the grave. I froze. By now we had arrived in the lobby of the Women's Hospital, a point I had said I wanted to walk from. Ian glanced at my pale face.

'You OK?' he murmured as he bent down to give me a hand stepping up and out of the chair.

'There's an email from Bobby. Unread, sent just before the attack...' I mumbled, stunned and confused.

'Well, don't read it now. It has waited this long and you have three little girls to focus on,' he urged, seeing how affected I was.

Nodding, I tucked the phone away. Ian was right – Bobby was not going to ruin this moment, I had to focus on what was important, my girls. Somewhat unsteadily, I walked with Emily and Isabel towards Leah's room. She had had to be put back on the ventilator after I'd seen her and held her the day before as her airways were quite swollen and she had not been able to cope with breathing on her own. Being the fighter she was, she was completely free at last this Friday afternoon – one week on and already showing progress. Emily and Isabel stepped towards the plastic box holding their baby sister tentatively. Isabel soon became very scared by it all. She started pulling on Ian's hand, saying, 'Daddy, I feel sick, I'm going to be sick. I want to go, I'm going to be sick. I need to go NOW!' Understandably, it was all too overwhelming. She was six years old and the heat, the bleeping machines and the tiny precious bundle of her sister lying with tubes and wires still coming out of her.

We did our best to calm her down, but she was adamant she wanted to leave. Of course, we couldn't force her to stay and we certainly didn't want to cause more distress: she had to face this in her own way and in her own time. The whole situation had been foisted upon the girls as it was and they had to process it their way. As parents, all Ian and I could do was support them as best we could. We decided that Ian should take Isabel back to the coffee area near the lobby to get her a drink and something to eat to help calm her down. After kissing and hugging her, off she dashed with Ian. I knew he would talk to her gently and do his best to calm her fears. The whole time Emily stood quietly by the cot staring at her sister, taking in every detail.

'You can talk to her if you want,' I said, turning to stand with her.

'But can she hear me? She's got her eyes closed.'

'Come on, who can't hear you, Miss?' I laughed.

'Oi!' Emily shouted and playfully pushed me as she giggled. And that was that, the tension was broken. Emily soon started talking her little sister's ears off – it was so lovely to watch her chatting away.

One of the paediatric specialists came in and Emily proudly announced she was Leah's big sister. She smiled back at Emily and asked if she would like to hold her little sister. Emily's face flashed uncertainty.

'But she's soooo small! Will it be safe?' she asked.

The nurse reassured her it would all be fine, that Emily could sit in the comfy chair by the cot, have a big cushion on her lap and then, with Mummy's help, she could hold her. Just as Emily settled herself in the chair, the door opened and a sheepish-looking Isabel came in, clinging to Ian's hand.

'Come in, baby, Emily's going to hold Leah. The nurse is coming to help get her out of her cot for her. You can have a hold too after, if you want,' I said with a smile and held my arms out to her for another hug.

She rushed over and tucked herself under my arm as she watched Emily hold Leah for the first time. As soon as she saw the big smile creep across Emily's face, she was hooked. She loved her little sister, she wasn't scared and she wanted to hold her too! Isabel soon took her turn after. Photos of the proud sisters holding the precious bundle that was their little sister were taken. I still look at those photos and they make me both smile and cry – they look so little, so innocent. Yet only a week before those photos were taken, they almost had their mummy brutally snatched away from them. They nearly lost the precious little bundle they were both proudly holding too.

After much cuddling and passing their little sister like a parcel at a party, the girls realised that it must be getting late.

'Oh, we've got to go to a party, we're doing a sleepover!' Emily announced.

It was the birthday of one of Emily's school friends and, as a treat, the mum had invited a group of friends over. Isabel was also invited as the birthday girl's little sister was a friend in her class. The girls starting nagging Ian that it was time to go.

'Go on, it's fine,' I said.

Ian insisted on wheeling me back to the hospital, to help my mum, and then after lots of hugs and kisses with my precious babies, he and the girls went off in a whirl of excitement. I believe they arrived at the sleepover in a fairly dazed state. The birthday girl's parents were amazing and kept the girls happy and occupied. Again, another glimmer of human kindness, another precious moment to tuck away and draw upon.

Back in my room, I took a deep breath and opened the email from Bobby. My stomach lurched. As I have said it was written less than half an hour before he began stabbing me. He must have been changed into the clothes he wore as a disguise, or getting changed when he wrote it.

It was just three kissing emoji faces.

It was a reply to an email I had forwarded to him earlier that very morning. The one-to-one hypnobirthing session, which was £150, had been paid for by Bobby just the day before the attack. Faye, who ran the session, had sent an email confirmation on the morning of Friday, 4 March, advising she had received payment and instructing us on what we needed to bring to the session. I had forwarded it to Bob to thank him for paying, laughing at the thought of the two of us on a yoga mat, and to tell him I loved him. It was sent just hours before the man I loved attempted to kill me and our baby. None of it made sense. To this day, I never understood why he sent that email when he did. Maybe it was part of his cover-up – after all, he had planned to get away with it all. I guess it's another thing I will never know.

That Saturday was my final day in Major Trauma – the team had decided it was time I joined Leah full-time. They waited for confirmation that a side-room bed had become free in the Transitional Care ward, over at the Women's Hospital. I'd been earmarked for this as they knew the emotional trauma was much too high to cope on a bay with other new mums. I also needed extra support and attention, which they could give me there.

As I waited for confirmation, the doctors visited once more. It was time to face up to a fear I had: due to the stabbing, I was to have an HIV test. It was an early sensitivity test as a full accurate result would need to wait for a test three months down the line, but this would give a fair indication. My sensors went into overdrive, my head telling me I couldn't possibly be that unlucky to have contracted HIV as well. But the way my life was going, I just didn't know. So, a nurse with a needle and syringe soon came along and a blood sample was taken. I would get the results in a couple of days and for now I just had to try and forget about it all. Besides I was becoming numb to everything anyway.

I was soon distracted from these thoughts as a nurse came into the room.

'We've secured you a side room today on Transitional Care. You will be with your daughter by this evening. I know it feels quick, but you will be supported and if we don't take this room, it could be gone,' she said smiling before checking that I was OK to move on.

I nodded dumbly, though my heart and stomach lurched. I didn't feel ready for this yet. This was a massive step and the responsibility of being a brand-new mum was about to smack me in the face. I knew what to expect – after all, I already had two kids – but the fear of it all and how I would bond with Leah completely engulfed me like a tsunami wave.

Birmingham Women's Hospital

LATE AFTERNOON SATURDAY, THE BIG MOVE BEGAN. FOR SOMEONE WHO HAD BEEN FLOWN INTO THE HOSPITAL JUST OVER A WEEK BEFORE WITH NO BELONGINGS ON HER, I sure had accumulated a lot! As I left the Major Trauma ward, quite a few of the staff came by to say goodbye and wish me luck with my road ahead. I'm sure I looked like a rabbit caught in the headlights, the security of this vast building was being stripped away. I knew I had to do it, but I could barely look after myself, and still had help at times with bathing and dressing. Yet here I was about to be put in charge of this baby girl of mine. My heart raced at the thought and my stomach repeatedly lurched.

I had to wait for the official hospital transport to transfer me between hospitals. A driver arrived with a wheelchair. As I was pulled backwards down the corridor I saw my security slowly diminishing as the doors swung shut on the ward. This was it, no going back. Mum, Ian and the kids all went ahead with my belongings. I was wheeled through the bright, warm hospital entrance lobby and out into the biting cold to a minibus, where I was wheeled up a ramp. Already there were three male patients inside. I was parked up and the brake applied. The air was gushing in, damp and cold.

'OK, are you alright there? I'm going to fetch one last patient,' the driver said. Silently nodded, not daring to speak as tears were threatening to come spilling down my cheeks. On my nod, he grabbed the handle of the wide door and slid it shut. *Clunk!* I was sat in the back with three complete strangers. My heart raced, I was petrified. It was my first real taste of Post-Traumatic Stress Disorder (PTSD), which was to play such a huge part in my life later. My eyes darted to the side to watch what the guys were doing. I shrunk further down into the wheelchair and mentally begged the driver to soon return – I don't think my shoulders relaxed back down until I was out of the transport at the Women's Hospital. The whole way over, I'd been petrified that one of the men (innocent fellow patients!) would jump me. I didn't say a word to anyone, though. I hated being so scared and hoped beyond hope that the fear would change, at the very least diminish slightly. But I was to learn this was to stay with me for a long, long time.

I met my family in the lobby area and was wheeled to the lift to take me to the Transitional Care ward. At the door I was greeted by a smiling midwife, who ushered us into the side room. She introduced herself and her colleague. They took the nature of my case very seriously indeed and were particularly conscious of the never-ending press attention and general safety of both Leah and I. After initial discussions about phone calls, who was allowed in to see me, etc., there was a knock at the door and in swung a midwife, pushing a little plastic box on wheels.

Leah! She was here, my baby girl had arrived. This was it, Mummy time!

I went over to meet them at the door and smiled as I saw Leah's tiny face, her eyes tightly shut and arm up by her head as she poked out from the blanket. Emily and Isabel came running over to see their little sister, who was now decidedly less scary without the tubes coming out of her.

My little miracle, I marvelled as I stared at her. *How has she got this far, tube-free after just eight days?*

I wheeled the cot proudly to my bedside. She slept on soundly, completely unaware of the magnitude of this next step in our lives. It was now down to me to protect her for the rest of her life.

Just as we all fussed around the little person asleep in her cot, the midwives came in to announce I had my first visitors. My sister Jane, brother-in-law Andy and my niece and nephew Louise and Ben came in. It was the first time I had seen the children and they looked almost shy as they entered the room.

Jane nudged Louise's arm and said, 'Go on, go see your Aunty Nat, you've been worried about her all week.' And with that, Louise walked towards me. She was nearly as tall as me now, a teenager and young woman in the making all mixed into one. I caught a glint in her eye, a tear glistened; I put my arms out and hugged her so hard. She clasped onto me and we both wept into each other's shoulder. Tears streamed down my cheeks. Everyone had kept themselves pretty well together up to this point, I guess it was a relief at long last the emotional barrier had been burst through.

'Hey! No one gets rid of Aunty Nat that easily,' I murmured and laughed.

Louise smiled and we wiped our tears away. She made

her way to the cot as I then grabbed Ben and hugged him too. It wasn't long before they all wanted a share of my little bundle and she was passed around as she slept soundly in their arms. We had always been a close-knit family, but this strengthened us even further.

Soon my room began to resemble an impromptu party. We pulled the curtain across the door and the midwives were happy that I had temporarily got far too many visitors in the room. Andy had made a lemon drizzle cake. Large slices were cut and passed round on bits of hand towel. I nibbled at a corner, my appetite non-existent. In the last week, I had barely eaten and that continued in the weeks ahead. My face was drawn, my eyes sunk and lost. I was constantly nauseous and small amounts of food made me feel sick. It was fair to say my baby weight soon dropped off me. As I looked around the room, my family chatting away, it was like a temporary normality had almost descended over the room for that short period. I wanted life to be normal, I wanted to be part of this normality. But I couldn't be – I was a spectator of events as they happened around me.

After about an hour or so, the midwife came in and made subtle noises about time being up. Ian gathered my older girls together, Jane and Andy picked up the numerous bags they had brought and Mum picked up her handbag.

'You going to be alright, love?' She looked at me with concern.

'Yep,' I nodded, tears threatening to spill out again. Mum could see right through me and knew I didn't mean yes at all, but I couldn't answer any other way with everyone there.

'I can stay for longer, if you want?' she offered.

'No, Mum, you need to get home and rest. Plus, it's dark out there and I don't want you walking back to your car on your own. I'll be fine, I swear. I'm tired so I'll chill before madam needs her next feed,' I answered.

Not at all convinced, my fake smiling insisting it would be OK, they slowly made their way out of the room. There were big hugs from Emily and Isabel before they shuffled towards the door. Then the door swung shut behind them and I was all alone with Leah. The silence echoed around me and tears started to spill down my cheeks.

How the fuck am I going to do this? I thought as I glanced over at the cot. But Leah started to stir and, as if by magic, a midwife came into the room.

'Time for Leah's feed, we'll get a bottle ready for you,' she told me with a smile.

'OK, yeah, great. Thank you,' I said, nodding dumbly at her. Time to crack on.

The next couple of days brought extreme challenges. Leah was only just getting used to a bottle as she had been fed through a tube going down her nose into her stomach. Her sucking reflex was weak, as was her swallowing and gag reflex. She had tiny bottles of milk with only a few millilitres of feed in them. Each one seemed to take forever and she would frequently drop off to sleep in the middle of a feed. The midwives were fantastic in their support of me and would come and help on the really challenging times. I was also struggling with the fact my entire left arm (my dominant hand) from elbow to fingertips was in a splint and as good as useless – changing nappies, trying to bathe and dress Leah were all difficult. My mum and sisters visited the hospital every day to support me and Ian had moved into my house to look after our two girls to minimise disruption for them. But obviously nothing was normal, it was a whole new world for everyone.

Social Services were the next to visit the house. As Bobby had lived with us up to the moment he plunged a knife into me, it was technically classed as a domestic incident. Hence our home had to be assessed to see how the kids were. So, whilst I was stuck in a hospital bed, a social worker visited. To this day the kids talk about 'the lady who went through our cupboards and even checked what was in the fridge'. She came to the hospital too to see me. Her first visit had been before she went to the house, whilst I was still in Major Trauma. She wanted to go and see Leah then, but Leah was still in Intensive Care. Once we were on the Transitional Ward, she visited again and at last got to meet Little Miss for herself and assess me with her.

It wasn't too long before the social worker and a couple of staff at the hospital asked how I was bonding with Leah. In the circumstances, plus the fact that Leah was Bobby's daughter, I guess it was only natural that they would ask. I loved her with all my heart, but I hated the life I'd been left with. Each morning, I woke and openly cried. I would periodically weep throughout the day and as I lay on my starched white pillow at night, tears streamed silently down my face. At times the pain was more than I could bear – I hated the destruction I was facing and it overwhelmed me completely. Dark thoughts entered my head regularly. I would say to Mum, my sisters and closest friends how I wished I had never survived, how I wished I had never put up a fight, as then I wouldn't have to face this now. Everyone understood I was doing my best coping with all this as well as managing a newborn. Bonding, therefore, was of course hard.

The hospital did talk to me about whether I was considering adoption. I knew it would be a way to keep my child safe as Bobby and his family wouldn't know where she was. But as I held her tight and looked into her little face, love engulfed me and I knew that I could never give her up. I would spend my life looking for her and her sisters would be distraught. It wasn't an option, even if I felt it might have been the best way to keep her protected from Bobby for life.

As each morning dawned, I pulled myself out of bed, weary despite excellent support from the midwives on the unit (especially Linda, who took Leah each night after her late evening feed for the night feeds so I could sleep). As I opened my eyes to a new day, forcing myself to carry on, as I had to, I would play music on my iPhone. I needed a bit of sanity and normality and as music was something I usually had around me each morning, I played certain tunes to Leah. Bob Marley's 'Three Little Birds' and Eric Clapton's 'Layla' soon became favourites.

On one visit, Mand appeared with a notebook and a pen. I did raise my eyebrows as she handed them to me – I was left-handed and therefore couldn't write following the attack. But, as she pointed out, my right hand worked and I could scrawl something. So, I started to write some 'To Do' items that had come into my head and then notes on what was happening to me on the unit, what I remembered from the attack, my thoughts and my feelings. It started to become a journal, a fairly illegible journal but nonetheless somewhere I could reflect on what had been happening and empty my exhausted brain. Tears sometimes spilled as I wrote, other times my thoughts flowed, but each day I managed to write something with my right hand. The journal soon filled and was later used as the basis of the chapters in this book.

During my time on the ward, Ian visited regularly with the girls. On one visit, a paediatric doctor asked to speak to me so I left Ian watching over the kids and made my way to an office on the ward.

'Now you know how serious Leah's condition was when she was delivered, don't you?' he asked, watching for my response.

'Yes, I know she had to be resuscitated and then put in a coma,' I replied, not knowing where this conversation was heading.

'I was one of the doctors working when the call came through that you were being flown in. When we were bleeped, we were told to expect a dead baby. Your baby girl was pale, floppy and unresponsive when she was delivered and we gave her five rescue breaths before she came round. We then ventilated her, which took five minutes after she was born. She therefore suffered a significant degree of oxygen starvation, which will have had some effect on the brain. Initially, she had no gag or swallow reflex, as I think you have already been told. She had a brain scan at the Children's Hospital a week after the attack and the MRI scan done there confirmed there was swelling all over the white matter of the brain, along with several micro haemorrhages – small bleeds – across the brain. The swelling signifies damage to the brain. We don't know yet what long-term effect this will have on her. She will be closely monitored going forward, but you do need to prepare yourself that she may have challenges ahead. There is absolutely no prediction of what extent the damage will be, it could be as severe as Cerebral palsy or as mild as dyslexia when she is older...'

Cerebral palsy?

Tears streamed down my face as I tried to process this latest blow. My child might have severe learning difficulties or severe mobility problems, even both. I knew she had been affected, but this was the first time it was explained to me in black and white. My head span some more and the doctor paused and looked at me.

'There is nothing you can do at the moment as we have no way of knowing what this will mean for her, long term. But we have to prepare you for the fact that she was severely compromised just before she was delivered because of the attack and we won't know how much until time as passed further on. Sorry I cannot give you better news or more detail, but that puts you up to where we are with Leah. You obviously missed the doctors coming when she was in Intensive Care because you were in Intensive Care yourself, otherwise this would have been relayed to you a lot earlier.'

I looked at him helplessly through my tears and stifled sobs and nodded. It was like the gravitas of the whole situation sunk harder and deeper with every day. Nothing was getting better, it seemed – if anything, the outlook appeared bleaker the more I could see it.

I walked out and went to the bathroom to rinse my face to remove any signs of crying before I returned to the side room. As I walked back in, I found Emily and Isabel prancing about, Leah sleeping and Ian staring at me, instantly guessing something was wrong. I shook my head slightly; luckily, he knew me well enough to know that I didn't want to talk. He nodded back and I could see genuine concern in his eyes. After he took the girls home, my mum and sister Jane arrived and I was able to let it all out. I sobbed loudly, my body shaking and shoulders heaving, just about able to spit out all that had been said and they hugged me tightly.

'We'll get through it, Nat,' Jane comforted me. 'Whatever

help she needs, you have all of us and we will support you and her. We'll give her all the love, care and specialist support she needs.'

I nodded, knowing every word was meant, but this wasn't how it was supposed to be. Leah was absolutely fine before he attacked me. She wasn't supposed to be 'damaged' and certainly not by her own father. The magnitude of it all grew and grew. I couldn't snap, I didn't dare let that happen as I knew it would be a monumental break, but I felt parts of my resolve cracking and the enormity of the life ahead started to loom up and face me full-on.

Aside from looking after Leah, which in itself was so hard, the major police investigation continued. My family liaison officers, Ruth and Louise (Lou), were in contact most days. They were always kind and empathetic, explaining everything that was happening and what was needed to be done next. Inevitably, more interviews had to be undertaken and this time on camera as I was unable to be interviewed in a police station.

The first day, I hadn't fully expected the cameras and was still in my pyjamas when they arrived. I quickly dashed off to the shower and washed myself down as best I could (my dressings were still on and they needed to be kept dry) and dressed. Pale, tear-stained and drawn, I sat in a big armchair near the window as Ruth sat opposite me with a list of questions (the midwives took Leah out whilst they filmed). The interviews took me through every step before, during and after the attack. I re-lived how our relationship was up to the day of the attack, our conversations on the day itself and details of the day. Two sessions of these interviews were done on separate days. They were exhausting and I looked and sounded every bit as broken as I felt. The ongoing nightmare I'd been plunged into on Friday, 4 March was never-ending, it seemed.

On one of their visits, Ruth and Lou brought my handbag back – the very handbag I thought was going to be stolen at the start of the attack. If only that was all it had been about. Forensics had finished with it and here it was, returned to me in a brown reinforced paper bag with 'Biohazard' warning stickers all over it. With the packet wedged between my knees and with a shaking hand, I tore the top off the brown wrapping and pulled out the familiar orange bag. It was splattered with blood and through the leather shoulder strap was a clear slash, right the way through the double-thickness leather – even the bag hadn't escaped stab wounds, it appeared. My stomach turned as I examined this relic of my former life. Even though it was an inanimate object, it was something that had been through that day too. I sat and stared at it on the floor of my hospital room as more tears streamed down my face. The bag reminded me of the violence of that day, the violence replayed again and again like a broken record in my head.

When they brought the bag back, they did say that Cassie, the police officer who had kept me alive and conscious as best she could on the pavement, wanted to come in and see me. Of course, I instantly agreed to this – I really wanted to see her to thank her. The day they brought her in, there were instant tears, an eruption of emotion came from us both. We hugged as I sobbed on her shoulder. I introduced her to Leah and she was speechless. No one had thought that Leah could possibly have survived.

Cassie will always, as will everyone from that day, hold a very special place in my heart.

So, the week played on. More visitors, more tears and,

amazingly, some laughs, the latter when Paul McManus visited me. A very good friend for many years as well as an amazing boss and work colleague, he came and sat with me in my room to chat just as one of the midwives came bustling through the door, waving an anal suppository in the air (my bathroom visits had been limited, to put it mildly). The look of sheer horror on Paul's face when he thought it was actually going to be inserted whilst he was there still makes me chuckle to this day – I've never seen him so uncomfortable.

But all the laughs were few and far between. Generally, I kept myself in my room with the curtain across the firmly closed door as I couldn't bear seeing couples doting over their newborns – it was too harsh a reminder of what I'd lost.

Somehow I had to prevent myself from focusing on that, so I starting to consider all practical steps I could take. The car Bobby had borrowed from his work still sat on my drive. I needed it moved before I got home so I plucked up the courage to phone Bobby's garage.

'Good morning, Haden.'

Pause.

'Er, hello… Is that Nivad?' I asked nervously.

'Yep, speaking, how can I help you?' he replied.

'Hi, Nivad, it's Natalie… Bobby's Natalie…'

Stunned silence greeted me and then a sharp intake of breath down the line.

'Oh, blimey! Natalie, how are you? We are so, *so* sorry. We cannot believe it. He was here at work that morning – normal, smiling and joking. We are lost for words, just so sorry. Are you OK? How is the baby?' said a clearly shocked Nivad.

'I'm as well as can be expected. Very badly injured, completely destroyed and trying to make sense of it all. The baby has just come out of Intensive Care, we don't know what her long-term prognosis is yet,' I replied, not knowing what to tell him.

'Oh, Natalie, we are so sorry. He was really looking forward to the baby being born, we only talked about it that morning. And he was always saying how much he loved you,' Nivad continued.

Tears welled and a surge of emotions, sickness and hurt filled me once more.

But then why kill me? Why do his best to kill me if he loved me so much and wanted the baby so much?

I just couldn't vocalise my thoughts out loud, afraid I wouldn't stop crying if I did.

'I don't understand, Nivad, I really don't. I thought everything was fine. I have no idea why he did it. He has destroyed everything, though. And I've got to continue on whilst he sits in HMP Birmingham, locked up,' I replied.

It just didn't make sense.

'I saw him last weekend,' Nivad cut through my thoughts. 'I visited the prison with his mum and brother-in-law – he asked us to come in...'

'What?'

He had seen him, actually seen him?

'What was he like?' I asked, shocked that someone had visited him already.

'He was quiet. He said he doesn't know what happened, he doesn't know why he did it – he can't explain it. He didn't really say much else about it, the rest of the time was spent discussing practical matters, things that needed sorting,' Nivad finished.

'I don't know what to say, Nivad. He *must* know why he did it, he's the only one who could explain it.'

Tears were flowing freely down my cheeks now. This all hurt too much – I needed to sort out what I'd called for and get off the phone.

'I guess I'll probably never get a proper reason unless the police uncover one. I too need to sort some things out, hence me calling you.'

I went on to give Nivad my dad's phone number so they could arrange to meet at my house, then Dad would help them get the car on their truck and taken away. After Nivad wished me well, I rang off, then let out a huge sigh. That was ridiculously hard, but a good first step and something for me to take pride in – I was so glad I hadn't lost control.

As more days passed, more cards and gifts arrived at the hospital. Some were from total strangers. One person sent an absolutely beautiful white dress: heavy material, embroidered, patterned with light blue cherubs and small animals, with a pretty dark gold trim along the top edge and a lovely bow and matching knickers. If that person is reading this, I want to say a sincere and huge thank-you for that beautiful dress. Leah wore it many times and I always wanted to thank you personally and never could.

Strangers reaching out just proved to me once more that there are good people in the world.

As the week wore on, final health checks and tests were done as discussions about my discharge started to crop up. I had made it clear I was desperate to get back to my children at home. My HIV result had come back clean. I was then told that I needed to inject myself with a blood-thinning drug for the next few weeks to prevent clots from the surgery, etc. As the midwife demonstrated how to inject it, she used their frequently used term:

'Natalie, you just need to grab and stab…'

Pause.

'Oh gosh, I'm so sorry! That was a really bad use of words with you, wasn't it? Sorry, it's what I'm used to saying to all patients when training them to use it.'

She looked mortified, but I just giggled and told her not to worry. I did have to reassure her a few times and show her I really did see the funny side before she relaxed, though.

As I started to think about life ahead, I decided to start putting my 'mask' on to face the outside world. I asked for my make-up bag to be brought in and my body lotion with fake tan. My sisters joked that I was obviously getting better, but the truth was I just wanted to hide the real me away. I wanted to apply my mask, paint my face, make it look as though I was better than I was. The body cream would add colour to my skin and tone down the bright red scars that stood out like red streaks across a sheet of white paper. There was no vanity in this, it was all about disguise: I had to apply a different face as the broken, empty, pale one was not planning on changing itself in a long time. I had to pretend, create a charade.

Two weeks on from the attack, I repeatedly asked if I could go home. I was still on a huge number of medications, including high-dose morphine, but I so wanted to get out and home to my other children – I needed to be with them. It took a fair amount of begging and persuasion. The medics wanted me to stay another weekend, but I insisted.

Friday, 18 March, 7.30pm: just over two weeks from being flown in to the QE, I was discharged. Wobbly and with no idea how I would take those next steps, petrified of facing all those demons back home and moving on, I dressed Leah in her 'going home' outfit. The original suit was far too large, so I made do with a newly donated baby jacket and blankets over her. Ian came to collect me – he had put Leah's car seat into his car and driven over to get us. There were many deep breaths as he went back and forth, loading the car with my vast array of belongings, and then it was time to leave. A carrier bag of drugs was handed to me and a list of numbers I could call if I needed support in any way. As I hugged them all goodbye, tears filled my eyes, but I had to do it – I had to go home. Walking alongside my ex-husband in silence as he carried Leah in her car seat, the car seat Bobby had chosen. This was the third time Ian and I had left a hospital with a baby, yet a world away from before and certainly a situation I would never have predicted just over two weeks earlier. Once in the car he glanced over to me, smiled reassuringly and nodded,

'Let's get you home.' And with that he started the engine.

Welcome to a new world, Leah Queiroz. We just need to work out together how we do this.

Chapter 17

Welcome Home?

AS IAN'S CAR DREW UP, MY STOMACH LURCHED AND CHEST TIGHTENED. *MY HOUSE...* I WAS NOT SURE I COULD REFER TO IT AS *MY HOME* ANYMORE, NOT SURE IT COULD EVER BE home again to me. Bobby's car was gone, but aside that, it looked as it had when I left that Friday afternoon.

A different life ago, not a fortnight ago.

Ian helped carry Leah indoors. She was sound asleep in her car seat, totally unaware that she had left the comfort of the hospital. Mum and Mand waited in the kitchen for me, whilst a very excited Emily and Isabel bounded up and down the hallway as their little sister and Mum had at long last come home. After initial hugs and love, Ian chased our two girls upstairs to bed, saying they had us for life so they could sleep now until tomorrow.

I don't think anything could have prepared me for the horrific personal pain I faced walking back into the house. Leaving Leah asleep with Mum and Mand, I wandered around in a daze, taking everything in. The house was completely topsy-turvy – cupboards, drawers and wardrobes looked like I'd been burgled as the police had turned over every single one in their search for evidence. Then there was *his* wardrobe and *his* drawers. His belongings sat in drawers, his clothes hung lifeless on their hangers. My heart twisted. I breathed in his scent from his tops. It felt like he was still here, like he could walk in home any moment. But I knew he wouldn't. It was like a bereavement – the Bobby I knew and loved was dead.

Slamming the wardrobe door shut, doing my best to seal off all memory of him, I went back downstairs, overwhelmed. It was so much to take in.

Was it the right decision to push to come out of hospital so early?

But it was done, so ruminating wasn't going to help. As I pottered and messed with things downstairs, putting things back in places I felt they should be, my mum and sister looked on, asking if I needed any help with anything. I shook my head vehemently: this was my house, yet I felt a stranger in it.

'We should get Leah into her bed,' Mum reminded me gently. I nodded. She was still asleep. I carried her upstairs and laid her in her Moses basket, prepared by my family and already waiting my return, next to my bed.

This was real, horribly real. This little girl has no daddy here and I'm the only parent she'll ever have. And I don't know how the fuck I'm going to do this.

Tears spilled down my cheeks. It was all far too much. I flopped on my bed and watched my daughter sleep. I hugged my pillow and buried my head in it as the tears came out of me in muffled sobs.

'Come downstairs.' Mum had entered the room behind me when I wasn't looking. She took my hand and led me downstairs. I was agitated as I walked back down, I had to put everything straight. *So much to do, I had to crack on with it all.* Before I knew it, I was pulling things out of cupboards, putting them in places they should have been in as my family watched on helplessly. I was desperate to gain some form of control.

Ian reappeared in the kitchen and was the first to question me calmly with a hint of concern: 'What are you doing, Nat? Just sit in the lounge and relax. You've just got out of hospital, for pity's sake!'

'No!' I rounded to face the three of them, all looking uncertainly at me. 'The house is an absolute bloody mess. Everything is out of place and I need to get it back straight as I obviously can't rely on you lot to keep it in order!'

'That's not very fair, Nat...' Mum began.

'Well, tough! Nothing is fair, that's fucking life!' Tears poured down my cheeks. After slamming the kitchen cupboard shut, I stormed out of the kitchen. I was completely out of order, but my emotions took over. I threw myself onto the sofa, the very sofa I had been sat on just over two weeks before with Bobby lying on my lap, talking to my bump as I stroked his hair. I felt like I could explode inside. Mand followed me tentatively into the front room.

'I just want to be left alone, totally alone. I don't want to see anybody, I just want to be with my kids, working out what the fuck I'm going to do next,' I told her, sobbing as I said it.

She sat quietly next to me as I cried and cried.

My family knew it was going to be difficult for me to come back to the house I had left that Friday, the house I lived in with Bobby. But no one really knew how to deal with me. *I* didn't know how to deal with me, nobody could.

They all just showed love and patience. Amazing, right from Day One, they let me rant, scream, cry and took none of it personally.

Every day, my phone bleeped constantly as more and more people got hold of my new number. It was out of love and concern, people were asking how I was and what they could do to help, but it was like a constant tidal wave. I was getting in the region of forty to fifty texts per day. Mum told me just to ignore them, that people would understand, but I couldn't, I felt I should answer everyone. But every answer would lead to further texts. It was overwhelming and she threatened on more than one occasion to take my phone off me.

The only saving grace was that the incessant messages temporarily distracted me from the blackness in my head. With the new dawn each day, I stared out of my window to the outside world carrying on as normal and realised I was still in this hell and it was never going away. But I forced myself out of bed, looked after all three of my children, obviously Leah needing even more care than the others (as she did throughout each night, sleep was the obligatory minimum as I was of course still looking after a newborn), and got myself showered, dressed and hair/make-up done. I felt vacant and unable to see any way out of this, but I had to pretend to the kids as much as humanly possible that everything was OK.

Mum moved in with me from the day I was home and for the first two weeks, Ian stayed in the spare room as well. They took the girls to school every morning for me. I was unable to drive so it was impossible for me to do the school run. Also, I had to prepare myself for facing all the parents. Once they left with the eldest two and I had Leah settled for her morning nap, I would turn on my music (usually *The Best of Bob Marley*), step in the shower and not just cry, but howl in emotional pain. I craved my morning shower as I could let the tears flow freely as the water poured down my face. It was as if I could pretend I wasn't crying as much as the tears became diluted in the shower flow. I did my best never to cry in front of the older girls as I felt they were going through enough without seeing their mum crying. They knew I cried, my pale, gaunt face and puffy eyes told them that without me actually doing so in front of them, so my time in the shower was my release valve and I needed it, like an addict. Sometimes I would have to prop myself against the wall as I would cry so hard, I could barely stand up. My heart was torn in two. I didn't understand how I was in this mess so I reviewed and scrutinised every aspect of my relationship with Bobby. No answers came to me. My world as I knew it was destroyed and somehow I had to rebuild it, but I was spent, emotionally and physically.

In those early weeks I didn't dare be left alone – the very thought of it scared me. I had a cupboard full of enough powerful medications from the hospital and my own GP to finish myself off in one sitting. Sometimes I looked at them and my hand would hover near the boxes, but my head would scream, *Don't you dare give in! Don't let him win. Your kids need you, all three of them. Pull yourself together, you have to get through this. There is no other choice!*

Ultimately, I couldn't do this to my children – it wasn't a realistic option. But I still didn't want to fully test the theory that I wouldn't actually do it, so I made sure I was never left alone in the house.

There was one particular evening when it all got far too much, though. Friday, 25 March, one week after being home, I couldn't take it anymore. It was pitch black outside and exceptionally cold. The children had just had their dinner and the pressure of the whole situation got too much. I walked out the house, taking just my phone and bank card, and walked for miles in the dark with no regard for my own safety, not knowing where I was going or what I was going to do. I wanted it all to end. After walking to a cashpoint, I drew out over £100 – enough to pay for a hotel room to hide in whilst I decided what to do. And I thought that if I did not use my bank card to pay for the room, I couldn't be easily found. But as I walked further, I suddenly came to my senses.

What was I doing?

I was cold and alone – and not in a particularly safe state or place. My mobile phone battery had died and I started to feel scared. I had to get back. I thought about getting a cab but, numbly, I turned around and started walking back through dark streets, under railway bridges and deserted areas. The closer I got to home, the more I came to my senses and the fear crept in. I was scared, really scared, so I started to jog home.

When I eventually got back, exhausted and cold, the kids were crying, petrified as to where Mummy had gone, and my poor mother was beside herself. I held the children tight and we all wept. I apologised repeatedly; I knew I couldn't go through with anything that would hurt them and I never did walk out like that again, but my self-preservation was something I toyed with for months to come as suicidal thoughts ran through my head.

I was missing Bobby more than I could describe to anyone. In many ways it was the most illogical thing to miss the man who had tried to kill my daughter and me, but my heart didn't think that way – I couldn't connect the man on the hill that afternoon with the one I loved and lived with. I asked the police if I could send photos of Leah to him. I wanted him to face her and I guess I was craving a connection which I knew deep down was long gone, but I couldn't accept at this stage. The police said a categorical 'no'. It was to be left up to the barrister to decide and that would not be until we got to plea hearing on 13 April – which I was waiting for confirmation that I could attend. It was not 'conventional' for the victim to attend such hearings, but I was determined to see him when he entered his plea.

As each day passed, I knew I had more hurdles to overcome, not least facing parents at school. Isabel wanted me to come to school to collect her so I chose the morning of Emily's Easter production for my first return to the school. I waited at Mum's house, just walking distance from the school, to delay my arrival until after the school-run crowds had gone. Everyone had taken their seats when I wheeled the pram quietly into the back of the school hall. Ian was already sitting with Mum near the front and they turned to see me. Pale, lost and using every scrap of energy to hold it together, I stood there. A few of the mums I knew turned to see what Ian and Mum were looking at and their mouths dropped open when they saw me. No one had expected me there so soon.

I stood for the whole performance. Emily caught sight of me towards the end and her face was a mixture of pleasure and tears that I was there. Some of the mums standing near the back came and hugged me as the performance played out. At the end of the performance, the children were given permission to say a quick hello to their parents. Emily broke free from the group and was off the stage in a blink of an eye, running down to see me. She clung to me and tears fell silently down her cheeks. As I held onto her tightly, tears trickled down my own cheeks. It was a momentous occasion for us both.

The other school mums then started to head towards me. Sensing I might be overwhelmed, Ian dashed across the hall and stood close to me to check I was OK. I nodded slightly to silently say, *It's OK, I've got this.* But he remained there just to make sure. Hugs were in abundance and some of the mums cried. It was a sea of emotion which I knew would be emotionally draining, but had to be done.

That afternoon, I faced the school again and walked to collect Emily and Isabel with Leah in the pram. I was nervous as I approached and I didn't make it past the car park entrance before I was swamped. People who hadn't seen me earlier that day stared in disbelief that I was there. There were more hugs and tears shed, all of us trying to pull it together before the kids came out of class.

Isabel was so excited to see her mummy standing there in the throng of parents. It was another step towards what we recognised as the normality of life. I cracked a smile, a real smile to see her excitement. In those early days, each step that resembled normal life was another tick in my mental checklist and another thing to smile about, if just for a few minutes. The school run stayed an overwhelming experience for quite a while. Soon the children started to struggle with the attention as conversations revolved around the attack and the sympathetic glances and comments didn't escape them. I could see the pain it caused them so I talked to the school and penned an email, thanking everyone for their love, thoughts, best wishes, cards and gifts. But I then addressed the discussion at the school gate, requesting that people didn't talk to me about the attack in front of the kids. I explained how it was affecting them hearing it talked about. The email was sent to every parent and they all took note. No one was upset or offended, everyone understood. Another tick in the checklist of actions, a bit of control gained and the kids' normality adjusted again.

There was one part of 'normality' for my children though, and a source of upset, that I couldn't change – and that was my body. From the day I got home they struggled seeing my scars. Isabel would hide if she caught a glimpse of my chest and stomach. The trauma of seeing them was clear. She cried and sometimes screamed if she caught sight of them as I changed my clothes or dressed in the morning. I did my best to cover myself, to not let her see. The scars were ugly, deforming and scary. I couldn't bear them and for a small child seeing her mummy like that was too much.

Before I had the stitches out in my wrist and hand we did our best to make them less scary. The stitches stuck out on either side of the scar and looked like bristles or insect legs so we referred to them as the 'caterpillars'. Now Isabel could look at them a bit more without flinching so hard. But it would take time to adjust to this and for her to accept that the scars were here to stay.

Life carried on. The majority of my time was spent at the QE, attending appointments, sometimes visiting three to four times a week. As I was unable to drive, I relied on Mum taking me everywhere. And wherever we went, so did the little one. It wasn't the way anyone would envisage their maternity leave starting. Along the way people did their best though as they saw Mum, Leah and I about so regularly. The staff in the hand unit were amazing!

It was at their clinic that I had my many stitches taken

out. No mean feat in itself. I don't know how many stitches exactly I had – after all, it wasn't just my hand, but my chest, stomach, arm, etc. – there was plenty to keep them busy. As I took deep breaths each stitch was removed with a small hooked cutting tool. My hand had to be left as parts were splitting open. A little infected hole had opened up in the side of my wrist. Antibiotic creams were prescribed and I was advised on how best to deal with it. Red and swollen, with a small pit developing in the middle of the wound, it wasn't pretty!

My recovery was fully supported by everyone at the hospital so I will always say the NHS are wonderful because of the people who make it. Plus, as each week unfolded I saw more and more examples of the kindness in people, for which I'm forever grateful.

Hospital appointments at Birmingham Women's Hospital were also a regular for Leah. Dread still filled me each time I approached the hospital, seeing pregnant women supported by their partner. But I had to go there, head down and striding to clinic. One of those first baby clinic visits, when the midwife weighing Leah looked at her notes and realised who I was, still makes me chuckle.

'Oh, you are the lady that terrible attack happened to! How are you?' she asked, concerned.

'I'm alive, got a lot to be thankful for. There's a long road still ahead but I'm glad to be here, as well as being glad she's still here with us too,' I replied, nodding at Leah kicking around in the weighing scales.

'You were airlifted, weren't you, into the QE?' she persisted.

'Yes, I was. Leah was delivered over there before being transferred back to Intensive Care here. If it wasn't for that helicopter we would probably be dead,' I went on.

'Ah, wow! How was it in the Air Ambulance? I've always wanted to go in one,' she asked excitedly.

Erm, I was half-dead, fighting desperately for my life. I wasn't exactly thinking about the excitement of the helicopter trip...

I was slightly bemused, bearing in mind the circumstances in which I was airlifted, but I gave a stoic reply as only a Brit could do.

'Well, it was bumpy getting in, view wasn't great either!' I replied, deadpan.

Above left: Bobby and I huddled up together in Trafalgar Square in January 2015 – our first trip to the capital city, and all loved up.

Above right: Bobby and me in Cascais, near Lisbon, Portugal. Our first family holiday abroad with my children. We had not long found out I was pregnant!

Below left: Celebrating my fortieth birthday. Bobby took me to a beautiful restaurant in Chelsea for dinner, and we stayed in a gorgeous hotel in Kensington. Just over three weeks before the attack.

Below right: Sunday, 28 February 2016 – Bobby snuck onto my hospital bed. We snuggled together to watch TV whilst I was admitted for premature labour – taken just five days before the attack.

Above left: Bobby getting back to his feet after being ripped off me by eighteen-year-old Callum Gibson. Blood is clearly visible over his gloves and jeans, as he calmly adjusts the rucksack under his top.

Above right: Bobby advancing upon me for a third time. I am just off-shot, slumped on the pavement. The broken knife is in his hand and a bin bag is sticking out of his back pocket.

Below left: The sleeve of my blood-soaked leather jacker after the attack. The place where the knife had sliced right through it, and through my wrist below, is clearly visible.

Below right: The remains of my top, littered with stab holes and stained dark from the profuse blood loss.

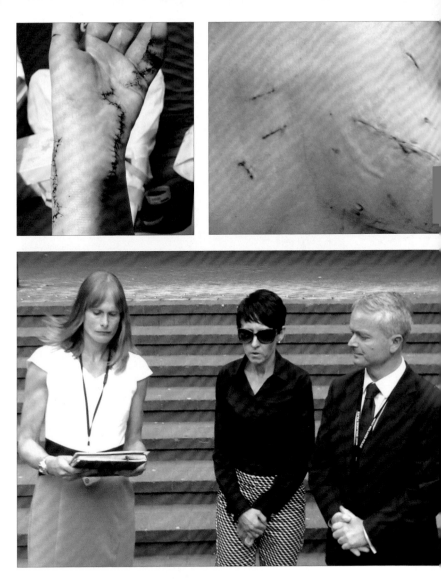

Above left: My left hand one week after the attack. The scar slices down my wrist to the centre of my palm, and there is a deep wound down the side of my wrist. Both severed my main artery, nerves and tendons, damaging my dominant hand for life.

Above right: Some of the multiple stab wounds in the centre and left side of my chest, which hit the outside of my heart – his primary target.

Below: Taken outside the court when I gave my statement after Bobby's sentencing. I was completely broken.

© *Richard Vernalls / PA Images*

My first time being able to hold Leah – nearly one week on from the attack - both of us still so vulnerable and ill, but I am reassuring her that her mum is here now, and that everything is going to be alright.

Inset: The first photo I was given of Leah, on Sunday 6 March – Mother's Day. She was still in a coma, covered in monitors and being ventilated.

Above left: My ex-husband Ian and I completing 'The Wolf Run', just under six months after the attack – an achievement of which I was extremely proud.

Above right: All set for my 240-foot abseil in Birmingham, dressed in my Wonder Woman gear!

Below left: In June 2018, I started the Great Midlands Fun Run in Sutton Coldfield town centre. Trinity Hill, where the attack took place, is behind me. I ran 8.5 miles in sweltering heat in that flight suit!

Below right: Proudly holding my 'Inspiration Award' from Midlands Air Ambulance Charity, for fundraising after courageously overcoming a traumatic event.

The photos from the West Midlands Police Bravery Awards, being presented by Chief Constable Dave Thompson. These were the three men who helped save my life when the attack was in progress. Top to bottom: John Mitchell, Anthony Smith and Callum Gibson.

© West Midlands Police

Above left: In November 2018, I completed five marathons in five days, each non-stop, on a treadmill in the Queen Elizabeth Hospital Birmingham – raising money for both Midlands Air Ambulance Charity and the QE Hospital Birmingham Charity.

Above right: Dr Ravi Chauhan – the trauma consultant who saved my life on the helicopter that day – co-created the challenge with me and supported it to help raise money for these amazing causes.

Below: Proudly posing with critical care paramedic Steven Mitchell and pilot Richard Steele, in the helicopter (G-OMAA) which airlifted me to hospital on that fateful day.

In March 2019, I was given the 'Community Champion' award by the Aston Villa Foundation for my fundraising and work with anti-knife crime campaigns. It was given to me pitch-side at a home game. What a day!

Chapter 18

Happy Easter

EASTER WAS SOON AROUND THE CORNER, AN EVENT MY FAMILY HAS ALWAYS CELEBRATED TOGETHER. THIS YEAR IT WAS TO BE AT MY SISTER JANE'S HOUSE, AS PLANNED SINCE BEFORE the attack. Bobby and I had decided it would be ideal with a newborn to be up there so the older kids could have their Easter egg hunt, etc. with their cousins. But as we arrived at my sister's my heart sank, knowing this should have been so different.

Ian had popped up to see us all and when we were alone he asked me about practical matters, such as whether I had found my passport yet. It struck me that I hadn't and he urged me to get it cancelled straight away. After a couple of phone calls and a long-winded email to the Passport Agency, I managed to get it cancelled. To this day my passport has never been found. I don't know if Bobby took it for any reason, but it certainly vanished from my house, even though the kids' passports were still there. Maybe it was part of his plan, a scam? Who knows. One thing was for sure: I no longer trusted anything, and realising some of my ID was missing, and having a hint that finances weren't great for Bobby, I thought I'd better check out my credit rating – I needed to ensure he hadn't applied for any credit in my name. I signed up to one of the online credit checkers and had a report run. I breathed a sigh of relief when there was nothing untoward on it. I was advised to check again in a couple of months in case anything was being processed as I checked. It suddenly struck me how I really didn't know everything about my life any more. I was questioning everything, and it was an awful position to be in.

My life was then further called into question as the first concrete sign that Bobby had been lying to me suddenly came out when I contacted his cousin in Germany. She was shocked about the attack. The family had not given her much detail, so I filled her in. It was clear it had been played down to the wider family by his mother and siblings. Completely flabbergasted, she told me how much he loved me and had always talked about me. When she dropped in how his mother did not know about me being pregnant, I was shocked. He had told me the whole conversation he had with his mum about my pregnancy after my twelve-week scan and how she was disgusted and horrified. We had argued about her unreasonable reaction and the pressure she was putting on him about the pregnancy. It couldn't be true, she must be mistaken.

I sent her a message back telling her how Bobby had told me the conversation he had had with his mother in the September and her reaction to the news. A screenshot of a WhatsApp conversation between herself and Bobby in the October came back in which she asked him if he had told his mum about the growing baby bump and he replied, 'Not yet.' So, it was true, he hadn't told her. It was all a lie, 100 per cent fabricated. His cousin went on to say she was sure none of the family, aside from her, knew right up until after the attack. Tears flowed down my cheeks.

Why did he lie to me? Why hadn't he told his mum and sisters?

There was clearly a lot I didn't know. But this was only the beginning of the lies unravelling. I sat staring at my phone in disbelief.

After the madness of the Easter holidays, I realised I had still not registered Leah's birth, so I called the Registry Office, aware the deadline was drawing near. The woman on the phone was exceptionally surprised when she asked for Leah's date of birth. I was met with a stern voice questioning me as to why I'd left it so late to call to register her, and how most parents did it in the first couple of weeks. She went on to tell me the waiting list was long and I might easily miss the deadline. I waited patiently and quietly until she finished and then I spoke my apology.

'I'm sorry I haven't called before. I know I should have called earlier, this is my third child and I always have booked in straight away. However, I have had exceptional circumstances...' I began.

'That may be true,' she cut in, 'but you have to realise you could miss the deadline and then there will be repercussions.'

'As I said, I'm sorry. Listen, I will share with you as to why it has been so long for me to get in touch,' I started again.

'OK then,' she replied.

'I'm sure you heard about the heavily pregnant lady who was recently attacked in Sutton Coldfield town centre, stabbed repeatedly and nearly killed?' I began.

'Erm, yes.' The response not quite so forthright as before,

as it was clearly dawning on the woman who was on the end of the phone.

'That lady was me. I've been in hospital and then recovering whilst dealing with everything. That is why I'm late calling as it's been a hell of a lot to deal with,' I stated.

'I'm so sorry,' came the stunned reply, her tone completely altered from before. 'I'm truly sorry, it was an awful event. I heard about it on the news. Obviously we understand why you haven't called before, we can look for a date – add you to a waiting list or look at cancellations.'

'Thank you, I genuinely appreciate it,' I replied.

'No problem at all. So, will the father be coming along to the registration too?' she asked, obviously unaware of the whole story.

A short explanation later, more stunned silence down the phone and I had an appointment for the following week. It was decided my sister Mand would come with me. I knew it would be an emotional moment as I had made the decision, following advice, and a lot of careful thought, that Bobby would not be named on the birth certificate – protection of my baby was key.

Back home, the next milestone was waiting for me. With the kids still off school for the Easter holidays, we decided to venture, for the first time since that fateful Friday, into Sutton Coldfield town centre – a place I had avoided since the attack. It was a clear and dry day so we decided to walk. As we left the house I took a deep breath as I turned to walk in the same direction I had walked before. Terrible flashbacks and memories of the day came flooding back to me, but I had to press on. Emily walked alongside the pram with me and Isabel walked slightly behind with Ian, who was on annual leave and had offered to come along as moral support. As we approached the top of Rectory Road, which is opposite the end of Trinity Hill, just metres from where I was attacked, I could feel my heart racing and my stomach lurching. I was desperate to keep calm to show no signs to the girls that I was struggling. We walked to the zebra crossing, the very one I had crossed just before I walked down the hill. As I crossed, I felt Emily's hand grip mine on the pram. I glanced down at her and she smiled at me.

'It's OK, Mum. I'm with you, you'll be OK. I'm here, you're not on your own,' Emily reassured me. My young daughter, sounding so wise. My heart swelled with love, her care and protection of me was amazing. I always knew she was growing into a wonderful, loving young lady, but moments like this really proved it.

Tears prickled in my eyes. We didn't walk down Trinity Hill, but took the longer route around the front of the church. When we got onto the shopping parade, I felt sick but relieved: I had made all the way in to the town centre, the place I was aiming for on the day of the attack. That was my first time. I felt a small sense of victory inside telling me, *You did it, you got here! Yay! Well done you.*

Chapter 19

The Lies Begin
to Unravel

SO, EASTER HAD BROUGHT NOT JUST CHOCOLATE EGGS BUT
THE REALISATION THAT BOBBY HAD LIED TO ME. I TRUSTED
HIM COMPLETELY, *EVERYONE* TRUSTED HIM. BUT I WAS SOON
TO learn there were a lot of lies and deceit, to create a life
he wanted to live. A double, even triple, life in effect. To
make him out to be the perfect 'Bob' to everyone, except
it just wasn't true. The first lie had been exposed by his
cousin and it made me question, if he could do that so
easily about something so significant as his own developing
baby, what else wasn't true?

I didn't have to wait long for the next instalment of that
answer. Going a little stir-crazy trapped in the Sutton area,
I went with Mum and Leah into Birmingham. As I walked
around the Bullring, nervously looking over my shoulder
as my PTSD was flying high, I spotted the jeweller's where
Bobby had said my Rolex for my fortieth was purchased and
currently resided, ready to be engraved. His watch was also
in for repair there. I had to know so, with a pounding heart,
I walked in. I started off by asking about his watch and if

it was ready – it was. I said I would leave it there for now, then I asked if Mr Raja had a Rolex on order, which was being engraved. They scanned through all their records and there was no record of him purchasing a watch. Another lie. I nodded dumbly, knowing deep down all along that this would be the case, but my heart still twisting at yet another lie. As I walked out the shop, they asked what I would like to do about his watch, to which I replied, 'He won't be needing it for a while, he's currently in HMP Birmingham for my attempted murder. He's not due out any time soon, keep it for him.'

And with those words, I got the pram and walked out. I sounded much more together than I was and, as I walked back out into the main shopping mall, tears ran down my cheeks.

Why did he feel the need to lie so much? He didn't have to lie, it wasn't necessary. I didn't even ask for that watch, it's not as though I particularly wanted it and certainly didn't expect it.

Mum had been waiting for me outside the shop. She didn't need to ask the outcome when she saw my face – 'I'm so, so sorry, love.'

Whilst in Birmingham I went to see my plastic surgeon. Having met Bobby on a number of occasions, she was astounded. After examining my chest, we discussed the scarring. She concluded we could look at me having the implants back in after a year's recovery period, but I had to accept they wouldn't look the same as the scarring would cause some distortion. The surgery would be fairly involved as there was a lot of scar tissue to get through. I nodded, determined to have them back as part of my recovery. They made up a key psychological as well as physical part of me. And the last pair had helped save my life.

When I got home, I flung open Bobby's wardrobe and realised it was time I got rid of his things so I contacted Ruth and Louise from the police to ask their advice on what to do with them. They said if I packed them up, they would come and collect them and return them for me. They also told me I was allowed to attend the plea hearing; they offered to collect me and take me to the court. I accepted straight away and set about the task of packing everything up (I asked to be left alone in my room as I did it). Tears streamed down my face as I folded up his clothes, all so familiar but now a relic of a life I once had.

As I emptied drawers into boxes, I paused over cards we had sent each other. Most of them had already been taken by the police when they searched the house, but there were some left. Tears poured down my cheeks as I grabbed a sheet of paper and wrote a note for him to open when he was out of prison many, many years ahead. I explained the pain I was going through as I packed his stuff up, the disbelief that he had done this, the damage and destruction he had caused. After folding it up, I stuck it in an envelope in his stuff, hoping his mother wouldn't open it.

Just as I was putting the last of his things in the bags and boxes, I suddenly remembered a certain sex toy he had bought completely out the blue. I decided this should rightfully be his, so I lifted a couple of his jackets off the top of the case and laid the butt plug, complete with batteries, in amongst the clothes. The thought of his mother opening the case and rooting through his stuff to find that caused a wicked chuckle to myself. I then lugged all the cases and boxes downstairs ready for the police to collect the next day, which they did.

Mum was due to be away on holiday with my sister Jane

on the day when the plea hearing was set for, something I insisted she still did, as she needed the break. She fretted about being away for it (Mand and Dad would be there with me) and me being on my own whilst she was away so I contacted my friend Ava in Spain. She had already insisted that she was going to fly over to see me and immediately agreed to come that week and booked her flights.

Dad and I were soon discussing court arrangements and the topic of the car collection when I was in hospital came up whilst we were on the phone. He had talked to the owner of the car sat on our drive, who told him about the other car we had – the Mercedes SL that Bobby was driving the day of the attack.

'Well, I had a right game getting my car back as he had used it that day. I had to prove it was my car to get it returned. I told the police I had lent it to him on a long-term loan,' Dad relayed the owner's words.

'But the SL was Bobby's, not his. Bobby even told me how much he paid for it and how he was going to sell it now so he could buy a family car for us all,' I insisted, desperate for something else not to be a lie.

'No, darling, I'm sorry but it is true. No matter what Bobby said, the Mercedes SL was not his. None of the cars were his, apart from perhaps the knackered and battered Mercedes A Class he drove around in – he didn't have anything,' Dad reasoned in his calm, matter-of-fact way.

'No, that can't be true,' I said, raising my voice desperately. 'Bobby didn't have much, but that car was his.'

Even I started to wane at this point with the dawning realisation. I had bought a private number plate for Bobby on our first Christmas together. He hadn't put it on as the car wasn't his.

'Listen, darling, I know you still want to believe the best in him, God knows why, but you do. But you have to accept he's a liar. He lied to you about his family and the pregnancy, he lied to you on the day of the attack and he has lied to you about this. He didn't have anything, it was all a sham...' Dad broke off, sensing I could take no more.

I sat quietly at the end of the phone and cried silent tears. What else had he made me believe that wasn't true?

Other family members also started to question Bobby's background. My cousin checked out his business on a company website and the figures were poor. Also, Bobby was no longer a director and that had changed the Monday after the attack.

But he said the business was thriving, how he was getting such a good dividend from the company this year, plus how did they get him off from being director so quickly after the news of the attack broke?

We would have been facing maternity leave with little or almost no money.

Why didn't he say? We could have worked it out together.

But it was just a case of more lies.

Chapter 20

F***ing 13 April

AVA ARRIVED FROM SPAIN ON THE EVENING OF MONDAY, 11 APRIL. IT WAS THIRTY-SIX HOURS BEFORE I WOULD HAVE TO WALK INTO THAT COURTROOM AND SEE/HEAR BOBBY FOR the first time since the day of the attack. It was amazing to see her, she was full of her usual energy and life. On the day before the plea hearing, we spent a long time walking with the pram to keep my mind as clear as possible in an attempt to keep me relaxed. As we sat in a coffee house my phone bleeped a message from Bobby's German cousin: she had had an email from Bobby, telling her how much he still loved me and missed me. As I read the screenshot of the email for myself, I wept openly. The message tore through me as there was so much a part of me that wanted to hear that and believe what he had written. After all, I believed that right up to the afternoon of Friday, 4 March, but so much had happened since.

That night was fairly restless. Soon the morning of 13 April was upon us. My older girls had barely been gone ten minutes when my police family liaison officers, Ruth and Lou, pulled up outside. Taking a deep breath, I headed out to their car, hugging Ava and kissing Leah goodbye. Little did she know Mummy was off to see Daddy in court. The police drove me to the back entrance of the courthouse as there was already press interest in the plea hearing. We stood at the back gates of the court and I felt hollow as I was ushered through Security and then up to the witness protection room. As Mand and Dad arrived, in strode my barrister. A tall, relatively imposing-looking man, with a dark suit and grey formal court wig, but kind eyes and a lovely smile stood before me. He introduced himself and we ran through a few details.

I focused as best I could on what was going on around me, but I felt in a daze. Exactly one year to the day since I had been sat in the magistrates' court around the corner with Bobby supporting me as Jason's case for assault and harassment began. This time I was in court again, but with the very man who was meant to be my avid supporter being tried for my attempted murder and the attempted destruction of our baby – it was just unreal.

Much to my disappointment, the barrister warned there was a chance Bobby was going to defer the plea that day for some point in the future and he also said the plea would be coming in via videolink from the prison. I had hoped to see him in person and look him in the eye myself. Half an hour before Bobby was due in on the link, I was walked down to the courtroom. As I twisted down each level of the staircase, I kept my gaze down, not wishing to make eye contact with anyone. As I entered the court, the press were already there; some nudged each other as I walked in and I took my seat. Mand and Dad sat either side of me, the police officers flanking us. I looked around me: no sign of any of Bobby's family or his friends. I was expecting someone from his side to be there, but I guess they would have already known the plan.

The judge opened the session and drew our attention to the television screens situated on the walls of the courtroom. My eyes became transfixed one on the black screens. It soon flickered on and there was Bobby, clean-shaven, his hair cut, black top on. He looked calm and composed. Every bit of breath left my body: I couldn't believe he was there. Tears sprung from my eyes and I cried from the moment his image appeared until after he faded away.

The judge informed him who was in court, including me. The slightest of flickers crossed his face, but nothing of real note. He didn't speak much throughout the plea hearing, aside from confirming who he was and a few other minor details.

It was put out there straight away that a deferral had been requested for a psychiatric assessment. This was granted and the judge made a few points, all of which Bobby noted down on some sheets of paper in front of him, like he was taking notes on a video conference call for work. He seemed so much colder, so much more detached than I was expecting. I almost expected him to be in pieces, or at least seem a little bit emotionally affected by it all, but he was calm and in control. It was eerie. There I was, sat there in court in pieces, my world falling apart, yet he was the perpetrator in prison, having carried out one of the worst acts of violence a person could inflict on another. And his partner – eight months pregnant at the time with his baby. He stayed cool, calm and controlled throughout and both Dad and Mand were unsettled by what they saw – he was too controlled and seemingly unaffected by it all.

The plea hearing was deferred to 23 May – another five weeks to wait to hear what he was going to do. Before the session was completely wrapped up, the judge sitting in the courtroom placed a court order banning the naming of myself or the children, along with the banning of any images of or relating to us, which could identify us in any way. It was good to have the kids afforded that protection but, as far as I was concerned, it was a little late. My name and image had been out there from the beginning, I was no longer anonymous. If you typed in 'Sutton Coldfield Stabbing Pregnant Lady' my face would pop up on any internet search. It wasn't going to go away, I was locked in a digital log in time, never to be deleted. The story would be for ever with me in so many ways.

It was much later that I learnt the deferral had been driven by the fact that Bobby had swapped his counsel just before the day of the hearing. The psychiatric assessment wasn't really needed at this stage but it gave them more time. The new lawyer was a top-flight one from London, who marketed herself online as a defence lawyer for gangland crime, murders and contract killing. She must have cost a fortune. So much for holding his hands up and taking the rap as soon as he could, as Bobby later claimed he did. Instead, he did his best to make his sentence as light as possible.

The initial plea was soon over and the police officers whisked me upstairs to the witness protection room again, where we were joined by my barrister. I was informed that a letter had been written by Bobby's family, which they asked to be passed to me. The police and barrister had reviewed the letter and it would be passed over in the near future. I wasn't going to receive it that day, which I was exceptionally glad about, as the last thing I wanted to do was face their words.

The barrister addressed the issue of the photos of Leah that I wanted to send. He said he wouldn't stop me if I wanted to send any, but they needed to go through the police for them to review what was being sent to him. I was asked to keep detail to the minimum. Somewhat frustratingly, I soon realised my life was no longer my own – from now on, I couldn't make decisions on most things without needing to ask someone about it. Finally, the barrister told me that I was allowed to return on 23 May for the plea hearing before I asked again!

Ruth and Lou, the two policewomen, took me back to Ava and Leah, all my energy spent. I called my mum from the car to update her. She was disappointed for me that it wasn't further along, but in five weeks' time he would have to plead one way or the other and the case could crack on. It was just another small delay in a long, mountainous road ahead. Focusing on the end point wasn't much use, the enormity of getting there was too huge and bite-sized steps made it a little easier to face.

Once back, I spent the rest of the week with Ava distracting me as much as she could from the case and she took it in turns with me to get up for Leah's night feeds as I was just so exhausted. I still ached for Bobby and missed him with every part of me. The grieving process was only just beginning. It was hard and confusing as I knew that I should hate him. Ava listened to my ramblings and to a degree she understood why I felt like I did. She just hoped beyond hope that my life would eventually creep on and I would naturally let go of this perceived connection with him.

That Friday, Ava flew back. It had been amazing, having her stay – it was just the matter of trying to get on with life now that was the issue.

Chapter 21

How the Hell Do I Get Normality Back?

I READ A POIGNANT PIECE BY CATHERINE WOODIWISS ABOUT TRAUMA. IN IT, SHE STATES HOW TRAUMA PERMANENTLY CHANGES US. THERE IS NO SUCH THING AS SIMPLY 'GETTING over it' AND returning to the old you: you are changed for good, full stop. And it was true. My original 'Plan A' was gone and out the window. As Sheryl Sandberg, with the support of her psychologist Adam Grant, writes in *Option B*, you have to accept sometimes that Plan A is gone forever and you must make the most of Option B. Sometimes there is no choice. I just hoped that life at this point wasn't my permanent new normality as it was a living hell.

My new normality threw up physical aspects I never expected, such as shedding skin (my entire damaged left hand peeled off in nearly one sheet), the hairiness of scars (at one point I feared turning into Teen Wolf!) and the emerging stitches which had hidden themselves to only come popping out now and again as the scars were massaged (and ably removed by myself with a pair of tweezers!). As it heals, the body does some amazing and weird things. But, as much as

I could sound light-hearted about those aspects of my 'new normality', in truth, other parts were harder, such as having a newborn to deal with in addition to the rest of the trauma.

I was referred to a mother–baby counsellor at my local hospital. The purpose of this extra support was to discuss ways I could bond further with Leah and work on reducing the natural stress associated with the situation and having a newborn. An appointment was booked and, one lunchtime, I went off to see the woman, wheeling Leah along with me in her pram, fast asleep. The counsellor was very warm, slightly eccentric (in a good way) and quite a spiritual person. She introduced her role as a support to new parents who have had to deal with an unusual/abnormal situation, including those whose babies have passed away or are in Intensive Care for a long time. As she seemed well equipped to discuss emotionally tough stories, I began, but she was horrified. She had read about my story but it was clear that for her to hear the details first-hand really did move her. She could see how hurt I was emotionally by it all, in addition to the sheer physical trauma of the whole situation. By the time I had gone through the attack, the build-up and my feelings now, the session was as good as over. We booked in another session to discuss bonding, etc. further, as we hadn't had time to touch on this.

As I left the room, I felt drained, but reminded myself that this was to help Leah and I long-term. However, I was soon to learn this wasn't to be. As I walked into my next session, the counsellor told me right from the start how much I had affected her last time. She said how she went home and was really upset by my story, so much so that her husband noticed and hence she shut herself away in a room for the evening. She went on to tell me how she couldn't help me any further as it was too traumatic for her and she felt out of her depth dealing with me. It seemed that I was 'too tragic' a case for a qualified, experienced counsellor, who had dealt with baby death, etc. Bewildered, I left the room feeling terrible that I had affected someone like that.

Was there too much detail?

But I had just told her my story just as it was, the harsh reality of it all and where I was now. As Leah carried on sleeping, I pushed the pram back home with tears in my eyes.

My situation is so shit, even a counsellor can't help me.

I couldn't have felt much lonelier or isolated than I did at that point.

My emotional feelings and mood did not lift with my interactions that week either. Bobby's close friends from school days, guys he had known for thirty years, came to see me. The first time we had met since the attack, it was surreal talking to them without Bobby there. They had seen him for the first time the day before in HMP Birmingham. Apparently, he seemed relatively normal, mainly talking about football and what was happening in the outside world. Even the guys said it was surreal. Little had been said about the attack so I talked them through it all and they were visibly distressed by the details. Before heading off, they asked if there was anything they could help me with around the house. The only thing we could think of was the garden, which was huge and pretty unmanageable. It wasn't the best pick for Bobby and me as we both hated gardening. They arranged to come back with mowers, etc. and then off they went after I'd hugged them goodbye through my tears. Afterwards, I collapsed on the sofa and quietly wept to myself.

The darkness and grief built up each day with me. Another contact from his cousin in Germany. Another email to her from him, in which he wrote about how much he missed me and the kids. *I'm sure he does locked up in his cell,* I thought cynically. To add to the emotional turmoil, Emily crashed a little more, as she broke down at school and told her teacher how she had heard it all unfold on the police officer's radio – the police officer who had been looking after them after their nanny had been taken off to the QE. The police officer hadn't got her earpiece in and the radio played out. Emily heard words such as 'life-threatening injuries' and 'critical condition'. She pretended she hadn't heard and hadn't told anyone for weeks, but then it all came flooding out. My heart broke as I learnt more about the depth of my girls' trauma. I hated the life they had been thrown into – I had spent my whole life protecting them yet this blew everything out of the water, it seemed.

With the darkness fast descending on me, I was scared I could go under and not resurface again. The kids needed their mum so I could not afford for that to happen – I was a mum, always a mum. With that in mind, I switched to work mode, got a pad and pen and started writing down some basic goals/things to investigate.

Move away: UK or abroad?
Investigate and quantify the real possibility of moving abroad to live and work
Organise my fundraising for Midlands Air Ambulance Charity (MAAC)
Meet Ravi, the doctor from the Air Ambulance.

List done, I had a focus: I had some objectives/goals, even some actions to reach those goals. It was what I was used to and gave me something to work at and shape this new normality.

Chapter 22

When the Angels Are on Your Side

I ARRANGED TO MEET WITH DR RAVI, AS PLANNED. HE WAS AMAZED HOW FAR I'D COME IN SUCH A SHORT SPACE OF TIME AND APPLAUDED MY RESILIENCE, SOMETHING HE HAD noted from the moment they came to me in the land ambulance. I asked him more about that day to piece more of the puzzle together.

The landing of the helicopter had been a significant challenge being a busy town centre location, on a traffic junction, on a slope, with buildings, lampposts, cables, etc. all around, as well as an onlooking crowd, which the police had cleared back successfully. Richard, the pilot, used all his skill to execute a tricky, yet safe landing. Ravi told me how when they were circling to identify a landing spot, they received updates on how critical I was, so as part of his planning on how to best handle the situation he formed a three-point plan. Plan A was based on me being conscious, by some miracle, when they got to me. They would load me as fast as possible into the helicopter, no interventions, and airlift me to the QE as fast as possible. Plan B involved me being in cardiac arrest, as suspected, when they landed. They would then have c-sectioned me in the back of the land ambulance parked on the hill and got Leah out and off to hospital before attempting to resuscitate me.

Ravi then paused, so I asked about Plan C. He claimed not to remember, hence I replied with a smile, 'Well, Plan B wasn't looking too good for me, so I'm assuming Plan C involved me being past resuscitation?'

'I can't remember,' he replied, obviously concerned how I would take the news.

They fully expected me to be in cardiac arrest when they landed and I'm sure Plan B was whirling through their minds. My blood pressure was just above what was the minimum required to preserve life and I was still haemorrhaging internally and externally, thereby reducing my blood pressure further by the minute. Plus, being eight months pregnant and supporting a baby with my diminishing blood supply made it truly touch and go.

Although by some complete miracle I was conscious when they stepped into the back of the land ambulance, it was evident I wasn't going to hold on much longer and despite knowing my lung had collapsed, there was no time to fit a chest drain – they just needed to airlift me. Once loaded, they leapt in and started to lift. The day was very cold and the rotor blades showed signs of beginning to ice up. Cloud cover was also getting very low and it was questioned whether they would get into the QE, where visibility was starting to become compromised. But they knew the time to divert to another hospital would prove potentially fatal for both Leah and I, so Richard used all his skills and training to negotiate safely through to the QE. Ravi later told me that he reckoned Leah and I had less than five minutes left when we touched down, it was that close! He observed how calm I was in the helicopter and how that had probably helped me stay alive. As he summarised it in his own words, 'The angels were with you that day!'

And it was true: the angels were with me. When I reflect back, my life-saving passers-by – Johnny, Tony, Carmello, Callum and the police foot patrol were all in the right place at exactly the right time to jump in and save me. Then, whilst West Midlands Police and Ambulance services fought so hard to keep me alive on the ground, the Air Ambulance overcame weather and location adversity and got me to the QE as fast as possible, making the difference between life and death. It is all incredible and that's why it has always been so important to me to support the 100 per cent charity-funded Air Ambulance. Ravi and I went on to discuss some of the fundraising ideas I had before Mum, Leah and I left him to return to work.

I knew I wanted to look at my own charity work, potentially setting up a charitable foundation at some point in time, which could support victims of major trauma as current available therapy/support for PTSD is very hit-and-miss across the UK. But how to go about that? When I contemplated my best contact, one person jumped out at me: Katie Piper who, in 2009, set up The Katie Piper Foundation for victims of serious burns. Of course I was familiar with Katie's story and the horrific attack. I took the first steps of contacting her foundation to see if I could get in contact with her. Her charity manager, Ezinna, contacted me back and we had a long chat on the phone about the work they do and the possibility of me talking directly to Katie, which Katie agreed to. It was amazing how a little self-belief and reaching out to people could encourage that first step along a new road in life. A teleconference date was set in the diary and a few months later, over FaceTime, I got to see both Katie and Ezinna. They showed kindness, empathy and support for what I was going through. I discussed how I wanted to write this book and asked about getting involved in charity work. Katie gave me her invaluable insight and advice and I am grateful to both her and Ezinna for their support.

Now I had one focus, a plan to develop longer-term around charity work, but I still had the pressing issue of the immediate need to support a charity I felt personally committed and involved with: Midlands Air Ambulance Charity. As I built my stamina and fitness back very slowly and carefully in the gym, I noted a team from the gym were signed up to The Autumn Wolf Run. It would be a huge challenge for me – a 10K obstacle course one-handed, with a chest full of scarring and abdomen still sore – but a perfect goal to set myself and raise money too. In the early summer of 2016 I signed up to my gym's Wolf Run team and set up my JustGiving page. Everyone thought I was crazy, which was and probably is true, however I wasn't going to be told no. I set a target of £2,400, which correlated to Leah's birthweight of 2,400g, and then reached out to all my friends and family for support. And support they did! I reached target in a matter of weeks, so I doubled it to £4,800 to push the challenge even further – and to repay the fact that *two* lives were saved in my airlift, not one!

The gym also helped in my mental recovery, negating the need for pills as it became my antidepressant, my natural serotonin hit, my happy hormone, and it is something I still rely on to this day.

Even with physical tasks like the gym underway, I still needed help. One Saturday afternoon, Bobby's friends turned up and cracked on with the gardening. It was lovely for them to do it for me, but hearing their laughter and chatter made me miss Bobby even more. I could almost hear his voice amongst them, interjecting with his dry wit and quick humour. But the silence in the space that should have been his voice echoed in my ears. Tears prickled my eyes as I saw them quickly gather up their belongings as a full downpour set in. They loaded their cars, promised to be back and I thanked them profusely. As soon as they were gone though, I broke down in tears. I missed Bobby so much and I knew, at this point, I couldn't have them over again. Not because I disliked them in any way – quite the contrary, they had shown kindness and support – but because they inherently reminded me of Bobby and the pain was too much to bear.

That evening my best friend, Anita, suggested we went out. Up to this point, I hadn't gone out and I was nervous and apprehensive. Mum was still living with me and kindly said she would stay in with the children so we went to a couple of bars (she drove us there in case I freaked out and needed to get home quickly). In both bars, I found myself retreating from the crowds – I felt scared and found myself shrinking with my back against a wall to protect me. As I watched the commotion going on around me, the laughter and the drinking, I envied each and every one of those people. Their lives seemed so carefree and I felt locked in some parallel universe, looking into their world, crippled with fear. I would never be able to be like that again, to laugh and not worry about who stood behind me or who might approach me, I felt, so we soon returned home.

I was slightly disappointed by my fear, but knew I had taken another small step on the road to recovery.

Chapter 23

My Precious Girls

I HAVE NEVER FELT BEFORE THE PERSONAL LOSS AND GRIEF I EXPERIENCED AFTER LOSING THE BOBBY I THOUGHT I KNEW. ON 4 MARCH, HE CEASED TO EXIST, AS DID THE NATALIE who entered the top of Trinity Hill. Metaphorically, he killed us both off that afternoon. For weeks and months after, I said how I still loved Bobby, how much I missed him and I cried for him every day. After all, I had spent twenty-five years of my life thinking he was a good person with a kind heart. He had never threatened or hurt me in any way, I adored him. But it wasn't just me missing him, grieving him, Emily and Isabel were really suffering as well.

As I sat on her bed one evening, Isabel fell into my arms, sobbing.

'I miss Bobby. Why did he do it? Our family isn't safe!'

Her words came pouring out between gulping sobs. I had no answer, I just silently wept into her hair as I rocked her back and forth gently to soothe her. Eventually, I settled her and went in to see Emily: she was in bed with her duvet up around her nose, her eyes glistening.

'Mum, why did Bobby ask Isabel and I to help him with asking you to marry him before baby bump came? He asked us around your birthday to help him as he wanted to ask you properly before you had Leah.' Her eyes were wide and brimming with tears.

The air went out of me; I sat on her bedroom floor and hung my head down.

'I don't know,' I replied softly, desperately trying to sniff back the tears as I stared at the floor.

He actually asked the kids to help him propose just a few weeks before he tried to murder me. What?!

'But also, Mum,' Emily continued, 'he told Isabel and I how much he loved us. If he loved us, why did he try to take our mummy away?'

With those final words she broke down sobbing, burying her face in her pillow. I got up from the floor quickly and rushed over, pulling her away from the covers. As we both cried, I hugged her hard. I had no answers for these perfectly reasonable questions, the same questions I asked myself every single day. I couldn't understand it as a relatively intelligent forty-year-old woman, so how on earth two young children could ever grasp it, God only knows.

As I tried to push on, there was one ultimate demon I had not yet faced: Trinity Hill. One weekend, as the children and I walked into Sutton shopping centre, me pushing myself along mentally every step of the way, we reached the top of Trinity Hill. As I went to set off around the front of the church to avoid it, Emily pulled at my hand.

'I think we should go down there, Mum. We are with you, so you'll be safe. I think it's time we went down there.'

We had stopped and I turned to look at her face. She stared right back at me and I could see every part of her willing me to walk down there. I don't know her reasoning for wanting me to do it. Maybe she thought that it would help me with the next step in my recovery. Whatever her logic, I could sense a steely determination. She wanted to show me her ultimate support; she wanted me to trust her and Isabel to walk me down there as we pushed Leah in the pram. My stomach flipped and my heart raced.

I can't do it, I just can't do it... I'm too scared.

My head was saying no way! But my heart folded when I looked at Emily's face. I knew it would mean so much to her if I went down there with them, as it would show we could face it together as a family and I trusted her support. So I nodded and we turned the pram towards the top of the slope. My heart was beating so hard it was ready to burst through my chest. I felt physically sick, but knew I had to do it. My hands, sweating, gripped tightly around the pram handles as I walked down the hill nervously, Emily's arm hooked through mine one side and Isabel walking alongside me the other, resting her hand on the pram.

The flashbacks came thick and fast, like a tidal wave. As I reached the point I remembered hearing him run behind me, I found myself glancing over my shoulder again. It was like I was re-enacting a reconstruction of it all. Then I reached the point where he had caught up with me, grabbed me and plunged the knife in. A wave of bile surged up my throat. As I swallowed hard, desperate not to be sick, I stared ahead of me. The town centre was bustling with people going about their normal day as they must have been doing whilst I was being brutally attacked, unaware of the horror unfolding just a few hundred yards away. I then noticed the distance between the point where I was first stabbed and the gates I collapsed against. It seemed so short, looking at it now. I felt I had run a good distance, but the reality was I had probably stumbled not too far before collapsing. Not surprising really.

As I stared at the gates of the Baptist church I noticed a gentleman, clearly someone who worked there, standing in the doorway. I hadn't had a chance to discuss with them about me going in to say a proper thank-you for their generosity – they had a massive collection for me the Sunday after my attack. I had written a thank-you card, but not had the chance in person to thank the congregation, so I made my way over. Needless to say, he was very surprised when I introduced myself and he invited me and the children in straight away. He and another gentleman from the church talked about that day and how they had been locked in the church for six or seven hours as it was treated as a murder scene, Forensics crawling all over it. After seeing me slumped against the gates, they had spent their time enclosed in the church, praying for our survival. With tears in my eyes, I thanked them. It was very surreal, meeting people who had seen me in that horrific state. They told me I was so badly injured, as I lay on the pavement propped against the gate, they willed me to live.

I thanked them for their prayers and for the support from themselves and the congregation. I was overwhelmed by their generosity and thoughts. It was so important for me to come along to thank the congregation personally so a date and time were chosen. I would take my sister Jane with me and then, during the service, they would call me up to the front to say a few words. I knew it would be very emotional, but I would go prepared – it meant so much to me to thank them personally. As we left, one of the ministers insisted on walking us down to the bottom of the hill. He told me I was incredibly brave coming down again and facing it. I said I had my wonderful daughters to thank for that, to which both my older girls smiled, embarrassed and proud.

After saying a fond farewell, we made our way into the town centre and the nearest coffee shop. As we flopped onto some chairs around a table, both Emily and Isabel burst into tears. I grabbed both of them under each of my arms, pulled them to me and let them sob, kissing the tops of their heads. A few people turned, looking slightly bemused, but I didn't care – I let them cry it out, they needed it. Their release valves had been loosened by that walk and meeting the people from the Baptist church; they needed to let it out.

That day was not only another step forward, it bonded the girls and I even more in a way I could never have imagined before. Now, we have a special link for life that nothing could ever break. I'm fiercely proud of them and what we have shared together is a devastating experience, but one that has united us even further. From then on, I knew I had to hang onto that, even in the darkest days.

Chapter 24

A Proper Thank-You

I FELT LIKE A TIGHTROPE WALKER STEPPING PRECARIOUSLY ONTO A THIN LINE HIGH ABOVE THE SHOW RING. ALL EYES ON ME AND KNOWING THE ODDS ON ME STAYING UP THERE whilst balancing everything were slim. But I had defied the odds already and I was to keep defying them – I had no choice, three little people relied on me.

Having goals certainly helped me. I met with both the Midland Air Ambulance Charity fundraising director and the area and events fundraising manager, Jason and Jo, at a nearby hotel to discuss fundraising ideas further. At the meeting, Jason introduced me to the idea of doing a video of my story/rescue, to be used at fundraising events to showcase what they do. Being such an unusual case, it would really highlight the breadth of cases they attended. I loved it and said it was something we should discuss further. As I mulled over the video idea, fundraising started to pick up pace as Emily ran an event at her school with her school friends, which raised £500 – well over her initial £300 target! Jo from the charity came along, with

Dr Ravi and Steve, to collect the cheque and give a talk at the school. Emily was rightly proud, but nowhere near as proud as I was of her.

As the plea hearing rapidly approached, my nerves began to reach a new all-time high as I thought about his plea. I was sure he must plead guilty, but a small part of me worried if he didn't and we had to have a full trial. I also had further statements to give to the police, such as relaying my feelings and the effect this whole attack had on me in a formal Police Victim Impact Statement. Needless to say, it was a lengthy document.

When the two police officers, Ruth and Lou, came to finalise my statement they brought with them the long-anticipated letter from Bobby's family. I saved opening it until after they'd gone. Both the police and the Crown Prosecution Service (CPS) had read the letter and approved it to be passed on. I took myself out into the back garden to read it. With trembling hands, I tore open the envelope and pulled out the A4 sheet inside. It was a photocopied version, the original most likely still in the possession of the police. The letter had clearly been planned out meticulously (Bobby's youngest sister is a lawyer). They wrote about how they had wanted to contact me for some time but were not sure if I would want to hear from them. They were aware I wished to attend the court so they wanted the initial contact before we faced each other. They told me how they were thinking of me and my family, and how they could only imagine how things must be for me.

That I very much doubted.

They told me how they didn't want to cause any upset at all, but offered their support. They said they wished to meet us all, but understood if we didn't wish to meet them.

Strange for a family who wouldn't have spat on me if I was on fire before.

They told me we were in their thoughts every day and they were happy to hear from me at any time. They left a phone number for me to contact them on and signed the letter from his mum, sisters, brother and brother-in-laws. It struck me how Tom's Sikh wife, who hadn't been accepted either by Bobby's mother, had been left off the list.

I read the letter over and over a number of times. They had point-blank refused to accept me for the eighteen months of my relationship with Bobby, actively pushed for him to have nothing to do with me. Yet now I was accepted? Now they wanted to meet me and my family? I hadn't fitted in with what his mother wanted: I wasn't a Muslim, I was Catholic. I wasn't a Pakistani, but a mixed British-Portuguese woman. I wasn't chosen by her and she relentlessly pushed him to reject me. She manipulated him, telling him how he had shamed her, made her feel like she wanted to die, repeatedly forcing guilt upon him. My daughters, my family and myself had paid the ultimate price, our lives forever affected. I was scarred, both physically and mentally. And for what? His sisters had married white Englishmen, not Muslim by birth, yet were accepted by her.

As I read the letter again, it all felt as if it was too little, too late. The notable exclusion of Tom's wife showed that lessons hadn't been learnt. Bobby's mum's acceptance of me was not through a realisation that she had been wrong – she would have been accepting of Tom's wife now, had she seen the devastation she had already been a part of. It was a well-timed piece of literature for the CPS and police to see. Plus, she wanted to see her precious son's only child, Leah.

But I did acknowledge the letter with a text. I thanked them for the contact and said I needed time to process everything – I had to get through plea hearing first.

As each week passed, it felt more details about the attack or the days around it came out. Such as the day I met by chance the community support police officer who helped lift me into the helicopter on the day of the attack. He recounted, 'You looked so vulnerable. I remember looking at your face when the Air Ambulance doctor spoke to you. You opened your eyes really wide and stared at him, like a small child would stare at their parent or another adult they trust completely.'

I probably had. Dr Ravi was my lifeline to get me to a place of safety.

Then one of the school mums, Sheridan, who had her baby the same day as the attack, told me how her mum had passed me in her car as I walked up the final part of Rectory Road before crossing to Trinity Hill, literally moments before the attack. Had I not survived, she would have been the last person who knew me to see me alive.

As I tackled all this new information, I had my weekly routine engulfed with hospital appointments or challenges through the lack of feeling and use of my left hand. I was having to retrain myself to use my right hand now as a dominant hand. Frustration was key. The surgeon planned to operate further to try and improve the function, but he couldn't predict the outcome. He gave me one good piece of news, though. After convincing him that as I had an automatic car and therefore didn't need to change gear with my damaged left hand, plus my own little bit of begging, I was told I could now start to drive! As soon as I was home, I started my car. The low battery light flashed at me and I drove slowly and a little nervously, not having driven for months. But it didn't take long for the car to be running fine and for me to have the baby car seat transferred over and at last some freedom!

On the day before the plea hearing, I went to the Baptist church, as arranged, to thank the congregation for their amazing generosity. My eldest sister Jane came to my house early and as we started the descent down Trinity Hill, once more my heart started to race. My mouth went dry and vivid flashbacks seared through my head. Jane clasped my hand tightly and I took deep breaths, focusing on where we were heading. I slipped in through the door, grateful to be inside and caught my breath.

The church was packed and once the children had left for Sunday School, the minister reminded the congregation of what had happened to me and murmurs went round about how terrible it was. He then said that he was pleased to say I was actually there to say a few words to thank them for how they had reached out to me. A shockwave rippled across the congregation. Taking a deep breath, I got up from my seat at the back and walked down to the front as a sea of faces turned to look at me. It was the first time I had spoken publicly about the attack. After thanking the minister, I took my place at the lectern. I spoke slowly and carefully, my voice catching when I talked about my baby daughter and I being saved. Tears swam and members of the congregation too wiped the odd tear away. People stood and clapped as I returned to my seat.

After the service I was there for at least a further hour as people came up to me, to congratulate me, to tell me how touched they were with what I had said, and to offer hugs and best wishes. It was truly lifting to feel so included and to have so many people willing me on. However, I still had the next day to think about and prepare myself for...

Chapter 25

Guilty or Not?

CLEARLY, HE WAS GUILTY, BUT UNTIL I HEARD BOBBY ACTUALLY SAY IT HIMSELF, I COULDN'T BE SURE OF WHAT WAS GOING TO HAPPEN NEXT. I BARELY SLEPT THE NIGHT before the plea hearing.

He had five charges against him:

Two counts of attempted murder (myself and John
  Mitchell, who had been stabbed in the hand)
Assault occasioning actual bodily harm (Tony)
Attempted child destruction (Leah)
Possessing an offensive weapon in a public place

Already, his lawyer had issued a plea bargain about the one count of attempted murder relating to John Mitchell. They said he would not plead guilty to that, but would accept the lower charge of unlawful wounding. So it had already been agreed to downgrade this.

Ruth and Louise, the police officers assigned to me, picked up Mand and I from my house and we were taken in again through the back of the court building to avoid the media and met my friend Annabel and Dad up in the witness protection room. The proceeding hour was a blur. The barrister came to see me, various investigating officers popped their heads in and we all sat staring at each other on low-slung sofa chairs, white plastic cups of water clutched in our hands. I was told a couple of Bobby's friends were downstairs, waiting to go in, but none of the family were in attendance. When I was walked down to the courtroom, we were told he was coming in via videolink again.

I was disappointed as I wanted to see him in person.

The courtroom was packed when we took our seats. Bobby's two friends were turned away at the door as the media filled the remaining seats. His lawyer, a hard-faced, slim woman, walked into the court. Very official, and looking very much in control.

It wasn't long before the judge came in. We all stood and he addressed the room as we took our seats. Our attention was diverted to the screens mounted high on the courtroom wall and, very shortly, Bobby's image was again on a screen in front of me. Almost instantly, my eyes filled with tears, watching him. The judge addressed him and made him aware of who was in the courtroom, highlighting the fact I was present. Flanked either side of me were Dad and Mand. They squeezed my hands as the charges were read out. Bobby nodded to show he understood what was being read out to him.

On the charge of 'attempted murder of Natalie Queiroz', he uttered the immortal word: 'Guilty.'

My body collapsed from the inside. There was of course relief that he was pleading guilty, acknowledging what he had done, but also an overwhelming grief that a man I loved with all my heart was actually saying, 'Yes, I tried to kill her.' I sobbed loudly and muffled my mouth as best I could with the endless supply of tissues being handed to me from all angles.

They had to read out the second charge of attempted murder, which was the 'Not Guilty' plea, as we knew it would be. Bobby's defence lawyer then piped up, 'Mr Raja would like to make it clear that his only intention that day was to murder Natalie Queiroz.'

I knew this was the case, but hearing it said so coldly just broke me that bit further. As I stared at him on the screen, there was barely a flicker of anything, no shame or remorse came through.

He of course pleaded guilty to the unlawful wounding of John Mitchell instead, as well as attempted child destruction of Leah, assault causing actual bodily harm of Anthony (Tony) Smith and possession of a knife in a public place.

Throughout the whole proceedings I didn't stop crying. I could see the press watching me, taking notes, and the glances from people behind me, who I later learnt were Tony Smith and Callum Gibson, two of the men who came to my aid. Bobby, on the other hand, seemed fairly impassive. For him, it was a clear, methodical process, it seemed. No emotion was shown.

The judge concluded there was a lot to consider in this case – the evidence around the planning and the psychological reports on Bobby – so sentencing was set for 23 June. A few final words to which Bobby nodded graciously and the screen was cut. Calm, in control, polite and courteous, he had played it well, yet he had just admitted to being, in essence, a murderer. It was only by the grace of God that I was sat there and he wasn't on a full murder charge.

Bobby's lawyer dashed out to have a debrief over videolink in a separate room. Hollow, I asked the police to just get me out of there and take me back to the witness protection room. I never spoke to Callum or Tony – I didn't know for sure who they were. Later, I felt horribly guilty when I learnt exactly who they were, that I hadn't spoken to them. They must have thought me so rude, I was just completely broken.

The media were going crazy. It was a big story, but it was still my life… my horrible, surreal life. It was of course good news that Bobby had pleaded guilty, we weren't going to have to have a trial now. But I felt empty.

I turned to Ian Ingram, lead investigator.

'So, can I see the evidence now? Hear what you found in your investigation?'

Ian smiled as he knew I would ask, as I had been asking repeatedly about what they had found out, but they couldn't say until we had reached this conclusion. He nodded and we set a date for the day after tomorrow, the 25th. Mand agreed to come along to support me.

'What is the main reason he gave for why he did it?' I asked before we departed.

Ian sighed, clearly not wishing to cause me any more upset or personal grief,

'He said he felt under pressure, he did it because he was under pressure from everything and everybody. We will go through it all in a couple of days.'

Ruth and Lou drove Mand and me home. Drained, physically and emotionally, I never expected to feel so bad. The triumph I knew I should have felt never came, just more questions.

Why was he so devoid of emotion? Why did it all seem like a 'normal', mundane process to him?

I thought about how he must be, sat in his cell. What did he think about? How much did this affect him, aside from the obvious restrictions on his liberty?

Wednesday, 25 May. Mand came over and we headed for the police station. My stomach flipped, but I had to do it – I had to know what had been found out, no matter how awful it was going to be. My sister agreed to take notes for me as I had a list of pre-prepared questions I wanted to ask and seek answers to. I clung to them as we made our way from the car to meet Ruth, who led us from the car park and up to a conference room at the top of the police station. Mand and I were seated as Ruth went out to fetch Ian Ingram. My eyes scanned my notes, the questions I needed answering, to help me put some of this jigsaw puzzle together.

Ian came in with a warm empathetic smile, listened to some of my questions and then went through what they found.

Bobby's car had been parked in the car park by the TGI Fridays' restaurant in Sutton Coldfield, a relatively short walk away from Trinity Hill. When he arrived in Sutton, he went first to M&S food hall, dressed as normal, to buy a sandwich, etc.

He went and bought lunch?

I stared, incredulous, at Ian and Ruth.

'He bought his lunch before he tried to murder me? He actually went and looked for something to eat first?'

Both nodded.

'A receipt for his food was found in the car, timed at 14.48,' Ian confirmed.

'14.48? I called him at about 14.55 to say I was on my way!' I said, shaking my head in disbelief.

Bobby went from M&S to McDonald's, where he was caught on CCTV, but he didn't go in. He then returned to his car, most likely to get changed.

McDonald's? That's at the foot of Trinity Hill. Was he seeing if it was clear on there before he carried out what he was planning?

He was not picked up again on CCTV until he appeared on Trinity Hill. It is unknown where he was waiting for me.

'You have to know, when questioned in police custody, he answered, "No comment" to all the questions we asked him. The only time he spoke and gave any details was when he was assessed by the police psychologist to see if he was sane and fit to be questioned. This was on the Saturday morning after the attack. He was not questioned at all on the Friday night, he spent it in the cells at the station,' Ian continued.

He and Ruth then ran through the attack as I knew it had happened with Johnny, Tony, Carmello and Callum all coming to my rescue. Then the police foot patrol turned up and arrested him.

'There were photos taken during the attack by someone who lives on Trinity Hill,' Ian said, interrupting my thoughts.

'Photos? Photos of me and him, photos of the attack?'

'Yes, but I don't think you should see them. They have been submitted to the judge, but I doubt they will be made public. One photo of him has been selected to give to the press to show how he looked during the attack – you know, he was heavily disguised,' Ian warned.

'I want to see them,' came my inevitable reply.

Ian and Ruth did their best to dissuade me, but Mand said, 'She won't stop asking until she sees them.'

'We had guessed that, we just don't want to distress her

further,' came the reply. But as I explained, knowing the photos existed meant I needed to see them to add to the collage of information in my head. It was agreed they would show them to me before I left.

When it came to the motive and how long he had been planning it for, it transpired from his discussions with the psychologist, that Bobby had been feeling low for about three months. He was initially excited about becoming a dad – in his words, 'overjoyed and ecstatic at the time', but then the pressure started to set in. Living with me and the girls was not what he had expected. It was much harder than he expected (he had never really lived with anyone before, aside a short period with a girlfriend straight after university, which he never told his family about). His feelings for me had diminished and he felt trapped; he didn't know if he wanted to spend the rest of his life with me and was unsure too if he could provide for the baby and I. He told the psychologist that he had never talked to me about it and that I wouldn't have had a clue about any of these feelings – he hadn't said anything to anyone. As far as myself or anyone else was concerned, everything was good between us.

When asked how long he had been planning it for, the answer wasn't clear-cut. He said he had been thinking of harming me for some time, but had no specific plans. He admitted that he had planned it as he could 'see no other option'. He didn't know if he had any specific plans to kill the baby, but accepted that what he was planning to do to me would, in all likelihood, kill her as well. He didn't know how he was going to do it exactly as 'he had never done it before'. He finished up by saying he didn't know why he did it, 'Let alone to someone I care about, or to my own child'.

Bobby was deemed fit by the psychologist to be inter-viewed. It also came out in that initial assessment that he had got the clothes and the knife from his mother's house in the days prior to the attack. He talked about how she had disapproved of our relationship and how he had lied about the money being there to transfer to me.

In the police investigation, they discovered he had been carrying a rucksack under his top on his front to pad himself out and disguise himself. Inside was more clothing and a spare pair of shoes. In his back pocket he had a black bin bag, with a charity wrapper around it (sent out to collect clothing donations). He was prepared to take my life and then change, bag up his clothes and get away. In terms of what he was actually wearing, he had two pairs of gloves on – the inner pair were latex surgical gloves, whilst the outer pair, made of a rough material which I remembered brushing past my face, were gardening gloves. He had two pairs of trousers, the pair closest to him were the work trousers he had left the house in that day. A pair of scruffy jeans were worn over them. There were four layers on his top half too, including a dark hooded top – he had the hood up to hide his identity as much as possible. The planning element was clear, this wasn't a spontaneous act.

During the attack, the blade of the knife broke. In fact, the knife had hit me with such force the blade was completely bent when it snapped off. In the press photo released of him, depicting him coming at me for a third time (just before the police arrived), the knife in his hand shows clearly that the blade was broken off. He had already stabbed me twenty-four times at that point.

It was also confirmed from eye witnesses that Bobby

repeatedly punched me in the face when he came at me the second time, hence my eye being in the state it was in hospital – knocked out of alignment and bruised/swollen.

We discussed more details as I asked about Pakistan. The police had no details about whether Bobby had ever been arrested over there. They did confirm that the flights had been booked a long time before he actually went that December, not booked on the day as he said. He also always had the return flight booked for New Year's Eve, no record of any flight being booked for the 22nd, as he had said. Clearly, he knew well before he left that he was never going to be around for Christmas, yet he said nothing and let me plan everything as normal.

They confirmed that from further questioning his family, they didn't know I was pregnant. It was all a lie that he had told me they knew.

There wasn't much more they could add at this stage as he had not answered any of their questions directly. They checked once more if I really wanted to see the photos, which of course I said I did. Ian Ingram went off to print them out as I was left reeling from all the new information.

DI Ingram came back into the room, clutching sheets of paper to him. One by one, he showed me the images. Truly graphic, they clearly showed how vulnerable I was, propped against the brick pillar of the Baptist church gate, holding my bump protectively with my left arm whilst I put my right hand up in a 'stop' gesture to protect myself. My top was slashed open in lots of places across my chest and bump, my face and hair sprayed with blood. The photos were very hard-hitting. Mand struggled to look at them, but I pored over the details.

He was determined to kill me, come what may.

Two and a half hours on from arriving, Mand and I left the police station. We had to dash back home to collect Leah for her hospital appointments. Emotionally drained, a huge void sat within me. Mand looked at me and I knew she could see my heart physically tearing in two that bit further.

His personal feelings had diminished for me kept playing over in my head. But I loved him so much. I had spent ages looking for other people's confirmation and view of Bobby's feelings for me and everyone thought the same, that he loved me completely. It seems he didn't – I was devastated.

Mand and I collected Leah from Mum and dashed back over to Birmingham Women's Hospital. We went to see the physio first, but Leah was so distressed, she refused to do anything for them. We then went to see the consultant. She went through everything that had happened after Leah was born. I sat there crying as I listened again to how desperately ill my daughter had been, knowing I couldn't be there for her. The consultant then told me how Leah had suffered Moderate 'Hypoxic Ischaemic Encephalopathy'. Basically, she was significantly starved of oxygen, which affected her brain. The central grey matter of her brain was unaffected, so her motor (physical) movement should be unaffected. But the swelling was all over her white matter, the learning part of the brain. There were also eight small bleeds across her brain. This could affect her learning long-term, but there was no way of predicting how much or in what way until we got to her milestones and saw at each stage where she was. I cried some more. The consultant told me not to get upset as we could work on her cognition, her learning – the fact that her physical ability ought to be unaffected was fantastic.

I knew she was right, but I was exhausted. It had been a mind-blowing three days and I could barely take anything else on board.

My partner had pleaded guilty, he had fully intended to kill me. I just had to learn to one day accept it and try to move on.

At this stage I just didn't know how to.

Chapter 26

Killing Me Softly

AS THE GREAT LAUREN HILL AND THE FUGEES ONCE SANG ABOUT, BOBBY WAS KILLING ME SOFTLY WITH HIS WORDS. WHEN I HAD RETURNED HOME FROM THE HOSPITAL, HIS German cousin texted to tell me Bobby had emailed her again.

'He wrote that he loves you. I did not ask him, he tell me. He said he had everything he wanted with you. He loves you and your girls too.'

I threw my phone across the kitchen.

How could he say that after I heard that evidence for myself? What an absolute pile of steaming horse manure!

My head could barely take anything else. There was new information coming out all the time and we had no idea what the future held for Leah. But I had to keep going, I had to keep focused.

I managed to get a break away with the girls at my aunt and uncle's house in Wales, but even there I received messages from Bobby's cousin, telling me how he had written to her, telling her that he loved me now and always will. He wrote that it was clear that he loved me so much as he lived with me and chose to have a baby with me. He added a piece at the end about how (his words) '*my baby is twelve weeks old now*' and drew a smiley face. I was livid, my head couldn't take all these contradictions. I didn't know what games he was trying to play, but he was killing me inside slowly as I fought to hold things together.

Further messages came via his cousin when I got back home, saying how he wanted to see me, and how his mum sent her love to me and the girls. I was really at about my limit with it all. Trying to process everything Bobby had said when first questioned by the police psychologist, mixed with what he was saying now and learning about all his lies was taking its toll. I felt I was going backwards emotionally. Anna said, first, it was not surprising. The layers of trauma being so many, one of them alone would significantly affect someone, let alone having so many piled up. It would never be a straight road journey, there would be peaks and troughs along the way, where the troughs make you feel like you are slipping backwards. But I had to remember that I was not going backward, as every day I was improving a tiny bit overall – after all, every day was another day I had made it through. I just couldn't see that at the time.

Second, as she told me, it was the beginning of 'acceptance', one of the hardest stages in the grief cycle. Accepting this was my life was not coming easily to me: I had to focus on the future and remind myself of who I was. As a small token to keep me focused on me, Natalie the fighter with the slightly rebellious streak, came in the form of a P!nk key fob for my car keys. My car gave me freedom, and P!nk (who I adore and admire) reminded me of the strong person I was. I could feel a little spark of the original Natalie trying to ignite back in me.

However, even with steely resolve I had endless unwittingly insensitive things people were saying to me to deal with/ smile at. I made a list of some of my 'favourites':

'Oh, those scars are looking good now! You will hardly see them soon enough'
They were still bright red, raised and prominent, they did not look good. Please don't patronise me.

'Well, at least she is pale!' in reference to Leah.
Yes, that was really said to me. More than once. Really? You mean she doesn't look half-Pakistani? Ah, that's OK then! What?!

'You look thinner/better/like you've put on weight/ well' (delete as appropriate)
All could be said in a matter of days from different people. It astounds me how when someone goes through something traumatic, people feel they have the right to comment on their weight and appearance. You would not normally go up to someone and say, 'Oh, wow, you've put on weight! Great!' Yet this was a perfectly acceptable focus of conversation?

'At least he will be locked up for a long time'
Oh, that's OK then, I've just got to live with it and tell our child all about it. Oh, and face him coming out at some point and probably trying to see my daughter.

'Oh, you just need to get on with your life now and forget this'

He hasn't even been sentenced yet, for pity's sake!
Really? I sincerely hope your life is this straight-
forward, too.

And then my all-time favourite: *'Oh, we thought it might have happened because he thought it wasn't his baby'*
I was lost for words over this one, just sign me up to
Jeremy Kyle. I actually had my neighbour ask if Leah
was Bobby's, 'Because you know people do talk and
wonder why he did it.' I was left speechless.

Time was passing on rapidly and getting close to the big day
of sentencing. Whilst the country prepared to go to the polls
to vote on Brexit on 23 June 2016, I was preparing myself
for a day that would affect my future personally. Anna
created a report to submit to the courts about my mental
wellbeing and how the attack had affected me, whilst DI Ian
Ingram held a press conference about the upcoming event.

Six days before sentencing, I went in for my hand
operation at the QE. Done under a nerve block so I was
awake for the whole procedure, it wasn't as successful as
they hoped as they couldn't get the tendon in my little finger
to release properly and stay straight. I was plastered up to
my mid forearm and discharged the same day. It was the
first sign that my finger would probably never return to full
function and certainly would not be near the same as it was
pre-attack. This was in addition to the loss of nerve in the
other half of my hand. I had the plaster taken off just before
sentencing and my hand was put in another splint.

As I got myself finally together for court, I typed letters
to all the people who had come to my rescue. I hoped to see

them at court so I could give these letters to them personally. If they weren't there, the police agreed to take them and pass them on for me.

Thursday, 23 June arrived – sentencing day or Brexit voting day as most people would remember it. At 5am I was wide awake, unable to sleep, so I got up to get ready for court, before feeding and changing Leah. My friend Claire had kindly offered to look after her for the day to allow my mum to come along to court. Mum, who was still living with me, got herself ready and took Leah over to Claire's as I paced around further.

Mum, Dad, both my sisters and my friends Anita and Annabel were all coming along to support me. My ex-husband Ian had also taken leave for the day to attend. He wanted not only to support me but hear the evidence and see Bob sentenced for what he did. After all, it was his children who had been so badly affected by this, his children who had lived with this man, who unbeknownst to any of us was planning to try and murder me.

Anita travelled with me to the court. Police officers Ruth and Lou once again drove me as the rest of my family made their own way together. My stomach was somersaulting all the way. I felt physically sick as we pulled up around the back of the court house. The press were already there in force and I was rushed from the car to the back gate before any of them realised I had arrived. In the court building, I was taken once more to the witness protection room, where I met up with all my family.

'There's a lot of people who want to be in the courtroom, but we will make sure you all have seats. The press interest is huge and we believe there are quite a few members of his family here,' I was told. I just wanted to get down there and get a seat. Taking a huge ribcage-stretching deep breath, I followed the team of police down the stairs with my family following on behind. As we got to the courtroom, I was asked to wait for a moment outside. Even though we were early, Bobby's family had already taken up the front row of the public seating. They were asked to move to the back seats to clear the row for me and my family, which they duly did.

As I stepped through the double doors I could feel myself starting to crumble. His mother, auntie, sister and two brother-in-laws were all sat there. I refused to make eye contact with any of them as I didn't dare speak. My family took their seats and I positioned myself best to see the dock, where he would be sat. The dock was enclosed in perspex and less than ten metres in front of me. As I sat there, I could sense his family sat right behind me.

It was a relatively small courtroom and every seat was taken. Anita and Annabel were seated not in the public gallery but opposite us on seats usually reserved for court officials. The press filled the rest of the public seating as well as the rows of seating near the judge, usually taken up by the jury. I focused on my breathing and the grounding methods Anna and I had worked on in preparation for this day. Then, after some time, the door of the dock opened and in he walked with the prison security guard.

My heart leapt and a numb feeling passed across my body.

He's here! The man I loved so much and who has turned my life into this.

I stared hard at him, willing him to look over. Wearing a smart dark blue suit, he was clean-shaven and had obviously not long ago had his hair cut. He looked like 'normal' Bob.

He made no eye contact. As he walked in, his eyes were firmly fixed to the floor. He was seated so he was facing the judge directly across the opposite side of the courtroom to him, so he looked only straight ahead. I was on his diagonal left, but he didn't glance over at me at all. Not once. Not at all, throughout the whole day.

It must have taken some self-control to not even glance around.

After the judge was in and we were all seated, the prosecution opened proceedings by running through the events of the day and the days leading up to the attack – how Bobby had got the knife and clothes in the days before and had left them in the car. The events of the day, as captured on CCTV and his food receipt, etc. from M&S, were also gone through as a timeline. Photos of Bobby were shown during the attack. None of the photos with me on were shown though, just handed directly to the judge and referred to. Photos of my clothing, however, were shown: my shredded leather jacket and blue top, what was left of it, all appeared on the screens. When I saw them, I flinched – I hadn't seen the forensic photos before. They were mutilated, holes visible, shredded in parts and soaked in dark blood. It was like a scene from a horror movie. There was a referral to my breast implants and how they contributed to my survival – they prevented the knife going all the way through my heart. There was also a discussion about how my bra had protected my chest from the knife too – I wasn't aware I had put on a Kevlar bra before I left that day!

My victim impact statement was then read out in full. There were points where at last a reaction was evoked from Bobby. He wiped away the odd tear and shook his head, especially when the impact on the children, especially Leah, was outlined and the fact I had been suicidal since the attack. Other victim impact statements from Johnny, Tony and Callum were also touched upon and how it had affected their lives so significantly.

After the prosecution were finished, the defence opened her case. She discussed the psychiatric reports on Bobby and how he was affected. However, we had to stop for lunch before she could get any further. Bobby was taken out first, again not looking over at me at all. I watched his back retreating through the open door with the guard walking out with him. It just wasn't real. The seating then started to empty. Bob's mum walked straight over to me and took my arm. She kept saying sorry and how 'Babur really loves you'. Lost for words, I just shook my head. I had cried silently throughout the morning and my eyes stung with tears at her words. I didn't catch the rest of what she said, but Bobby's sister, Shazan, pulled her arm and said, 'Mum, leave it. Not today, not here.'

When I glanced up, the press were all watching. I stood there numb, fixed to the spot. Bobby's auntie then came past and drew me into a hug, apologising for it all. I stood there, stiff. His sister tugged her arm too and mouthed, 'I'm so sorry' at me. I just nodded slightly and through my tears quietly replied, 'I know.'

With his family out of the courtroom I was able to move from the seating area. As I walked to the double doors, I spotted Callum standing there. I went straight over and hugged him hard, whilst sobbing into his shoulder and repeatedly saying, 'Thank you, thank so much! You saved our lives.' After fumbling for the letter I had for him, I gave it to him. I then told my family who he was and Mum instantly grabbed him and hugged him, My sisters thanked him profusely, as did my dad. It was very emotional.

Aware that we were being watched by the national press, we made our way back upstairs. Unable to eat as I felt so sick, I sipped some water and, before I knew it, we were being called back in.

Taking our seats once more, I watched them bring my former partner back in. He kept his eyes down again as he took his seat, only looking up to face the judge directly.

The defence laid out her case. She read out texts Bobby had received from his mother, begging him to leave me. Telling him that he was bringing shame upon her and the whole family by being with me. Her life was not worth living if he continued the relationship with me. There were also texts from the sister sat in court behind me. I turned my head as the texts were read out, she looked down and his mother pulled her hijab around her face. They wouldn't look me in the eye now.

His mother was a massive focus of the blame for the pressure put on Bobby. It was outlined that he had been going back to her house most days and although she knew we were a couple, she couldn't fully accept that he was not with her any more.

I guess that makes sense as to why he came home so late and wasn't hungry most evenings – he was going to his mum's on the way back from work, probably eating with her. He was in effect leading a double life but the other woman was his mother?!

It was reported from the psychiatrist report, paid for by the defence, that the pressure from his mother sent him temporarily mad. 'Adjustment Disorder' was labelled as the condition he had suffered. A temporary disorder caused by the changes in Bobby's life and the pressure he felt. The fact his family did not know about the baby and that he had no money were other pressure factors listed. It was announced he had £11.36 in the bank when I was attacked, not the thousands of pounds he had promised me.

The defence lawyer left no stone unturned when she presented his case. She had even arranged for him to write a letter to the judge. In it he stated his remorse. He wrote about me and his thoughts about me – '*Natalie is a beautiful, confident, independent, intellectual woman, which is why I fell in love with her and why I am still in love with her*'. He told how his life was now destroyed on losing the love of his life and the baby he had always wanted.

I nearly choked, listening to it. Having known the contents of his conversation with the psychologist, it just didn't ring true: you don't murder someone you love.

He went on to refer to the fact that he hadn't talked to me about any of his fears and worries. Indeed, he hadn't talked to anyone about them and he had exploded. He didn't lay any of the blame on me, but other pressures from his family and finances.

He denounced Islam and declared himself an atheist.

It was like theatre. The joke of that last part was that during this very day, it was Ramadan and Bobby was actually fasting throughout the day – not drinking any water nor eating. A funny thing to do if you've just declared you aren't Muslim.

The defence lawyer stated that I was not a 'vulnerable' person just because I was eight months pregnant (the prosecution had declared me vulnerable as that could affect the length of his sentence). I kept quiet, just a small snort under my breath. I'd been briefed by DI Ian Ingram that I would not like what the defence said and I was to not react, but to let it pass over me. It was so very hard, but I did it.

The judge then took time to consider this statement and came back with his summing up. In summing up, he stated how Bobby knew from the start how his mother would react to us – especially because she had nothing to do with his youngest brother who had married a Sikh girl – yet he still chose to be with me. He said how I had a good career and two children already; that I didn't need any more kids at this point in my life, but clearly had one for him. A baby that was planned for, and wanted by both of us: a baby who he knew what the consequences would be with his family. But he kept going. The judge told him that he had his head buried in the sand and when he couldn't cope and chose his mother, instead of terminating the relationship with me, he chose to terminate Leah and myself instead.

He went on to say that Bobby was dangerous as given the same set/level of circumstances or pressures, he could easily do the same thing again.

It looked as though he was going to get a life sentence and it was brought up, but then the judge referred to his good character. The defence lawyer had accumulated a lot of character witnesses from people Bobby knew from various professions to testify what a good person he was – an 'exemplary' character – so it would start at thirty years. He then reduced the sentence because of Bobby's early (he deferred his first plea?!) guilty plea, reducing it by a third. Then the good character references and the fact he had only one record of dishonesty (involving a stolen car he was found driving, but claims he did not know it was stolen) but no other criminal record, took his sentence down to eighteen years.

Bobby was told he would have to serve a minimum of twelve years before being eligible for parole. He would have an extra four years on top of that, where he would be on 'licence' so his movements would be tracked.

The judge then referred to my family and praised us for our conduct throughout the case. We nodded, but my tears crippled me from doing or saying much more. I was absolutely broken in two, I had cried all day.

As soon as the judge left the room, I asked to be taken out straight away. DI Ian Ingram and I went quickly back up the stairs before the press could catch me. I was so angry with the sentence that I didn't dare speak until I was safely back in the witness protection room. As the door shut and the group turned to me and asked what I thought, I exploded: 'Twelve years? He could be out in *twelve years*?! Leah would only be *twelve years old* when her father comes out of prison – how is she supposed to be kept safe from him at such a vulnerable age?'

I absolutely let rip, I was so angry.

The prosecution barrister came straight in and I repeated all I had just shouted and asked him what he thought. He conceded that the sentence was lenient, but not unduly so: to get an appeal, it has to be deemed unduly lenient.

I couldn't speak any more, I was so angry. I paced the room as my dad spoke out, 'But it is by the grace of God that Natalie is still here. Complete luck and miracle. So how is it not sentenced the same as murder? After all, his actions and intent were to all purpose the same.'

'I know,' the barrister conceded once more. 'But she survived and, legally, it is viewed differently, although I do agree with your point.'

'Natalie,' Ian Ingram ventured, 'do you still want to give

your statement? The judge has lifted the ban on your name for today to allow you to make a statement. It does mean going out there now, though.'

He looked at me with concern.

'I don't know if I can,' I replied, exhausted. My eyes were swollen and I hadn't eaten all day. 'But will it be easier if I do?'

'They are less likely to turn up at your house if you make a statement now, as you will have given them what they want,' came the reply.

'OK, I'll do it, if it keeps them away from my home.' I nodded before glancing at my face in the mirror in the witness room. My make-up had run, I was pale and drawn. Luckily, I had taken a pair of sunglasses with me – they would disguise my eyes and act as a shield between me and the awaiting cameras.

It was agreed that Ian Ingram and Ruth would go out with me and Ruth would read the prepared statement from me. Drained, exhausted and full of apprehension, I followed her and Ian to the doors of the court. Lee, the police press officer, had got the press assembled and ready. As I walked out onto the steps a gathering of cameras and journalists with microphones stood waiting, cameras clicked and flashed. Cautiously, I stepped down the stairs to the awaiting crowd and stood between Ian and Ruth whilst she read out my statement:

'I am unable to find the words to describe how I feel about today and the events of the last sixteen weeks, other than I have been left devastated by the attack on 4 March.

'As far as myself, our families and all our friends

were concerned, Bobby and I had an exceptionally happy and loving relationship, living together and looking forward to the birth of our daughter, his first child. A child which he very much wanted right from the start of our relationship.

'The attack he committed on me was completely unprovoked and totally unexpected. Luckily, I was saved and my baby was born alive. My daughter and I continue to recover, which with this case thankfully concluded as it should be, we can now clearly focus on this.

'I want to take this opportunity to give my heartfelt thanks and pay tribute to the courageous people who came to the aid of myself and my unborn child, along with the West Midlands Police officers who were at the scene, the paramedics, the crew of the Midlands Air Ambulance and the staff at both the Queen Elizabeth Hospital and the Birmingham Women's Hospital, without all of whom my daughter and I would not have survived.

'My attention is now on our recovery and rebuilding my family's future. To this end, I ask you all to please respect our privacy in this continuing difficult and traumatic time.

'I have no further comment to make. Thank you.'

I found myself nearly breaking through parts of this speech and my face contorted as I did my best not to break down in front of the cameras. At the end, I walked silently back up the stairs with Ruth whilst Ian took more questions.

My day was done. The media were already breaking the story online and news channels were reporting his sentence.

Wearily, I made my way with Ruth and Louise back to their car at the rear entrance and drove home in relative silence, just picking up on parts of what was brought up, such as how dangerous my partner really was, how unpredictable and how his life was clearly being led under two different guises between me and his mother.

I spent some time with the family at home before the kids were collected from my different friends who had them. We watched the evening news at 6pm and I saw myself on the court steps standing by Ruth and Ian whilst my statement was read. It was all so very surreal. As I looked at the person standing on the screen I knew it was me, but I looked broken. Everyone saw the true impact of the attack on me that day: no pretence, no mask, raw emotion.

When the kids arrived back, we cracked open a bottle of Prosecco and some Shloer for them. We toasted the fact it was all over.

I showed the girls the photo that had been released of Bobby during the attack in case they saw it in the following days. They were surprisingly fine with it. Emily just said, 'But, Mum, how did you not guess it was him? Look at the nose!'

That did make me laugh – the one and only time that day.

Eventually, I got the kids to bed and collapsed on the sofa. I still couldn't face food. Exhausted, I talked to my family for a while longer, dissecting it all, until I fell into a deep sleep, Bob's words playing in my head.

Killing me softly with his words…

Chapter 27

You've Got Mail

NOW SENTENCING WAS DONE, I WAS FREE TO CONTACT BOBBY DIRECTLY ON THE PRISONER EMAIL SYSTEM VIA A SPECIALIST ONLINE SERVICE, MONITORED BY A PRISON GUARD. A SYSTEM which allows you to pay for a reply sheet to allow the prisoner to write back to you.

I penned my first email to him late that night.

Bobby,

This is one of the hardest things to do.

Thursday – sentencing day – was awful, but I wanted to make contact now I am free and able to.

You may have heard from others that I wanted to see you myself, on my own.

I believe you have to sort out the prison visit request, and I'm writing to ask if you could do this for an imminent date.

I have waited a long time to do this, so I hope you are in agreement and this can be arranged relatively quickly.

I'll leave this with you,
Natalie

Five days later, I received a reply.

Dear Nat,
I will do this, I just need your telephone (mobile)
number and I will get you on my list.
  It means nothing, but I am sorry.
  Yours
  Bobby

And that was it: short, to the point. It was the first time he had had a chance to write sorry to me. But it felt empty and hollow, an afterthought almost.

The local papers came out less than a week from sentencing. They had all covered it in detail. I stared at the papers on the rack; I looked at the haunting image of me standing on the court steps and I looked broken. I knew it was me but I realised how badly I had fared as I scrutinised my gaunt, pale face.

I wrote a reply to Bobby's email almost straight away, telling him how it continued to be one of the most stressful and horrific periods of my entire life. I sent him my temporary mobile number, as the police still had my phones. I told him I was writing as I was sat at the hospital with Leah having her neurological check-up. I wrote about how she looked just like him at times and I told him that I would send him photos of her as, '*No matter what, you are her daddy and I want you to at least see her. You should be holding her. And that breaks my heart.*'

I signed off with the line, '*As ridiculous and stupid as this probably makes me, I hope you are as safe as you can be in there. Nat.'*

Heartbroken, I missed him so much. It all channelled out through my email to him. I bought a card and printed off photos of Leah to send to him, then stood at the Post Office counter to send it recorded delivery, trying to sound normal as I could as I gave his full address for their system, watching their eyes flick up as I read out, 'Prisoner No. ******, HMP Birmingham, Winson Green Road...'

I had the Bobby from before 4 March in my head. The man on the hill was still a stranger to me.

Again, his reply came about a week later,

Dear Nat,

Thank you for the number. I will put you on, they may contact you to ask if you want to be added as a visitor.

It will take a few days, so could you please reply and let me know what days and times are best for you over the next couple of weeks.

I mentioned to Shazan that you had written to me so she may mention the process to you.

Yours
Bobby

When I reflect now on these emails, they seem bizarre. The conversation was as if we were long-lost lovers or best friends, not a conversation between a murderer and his attempted victim. Emotionally, I was clearly still in a very hard place and as for his mental mindset, God only knows!

After Bobby received the photos, I received another email from him,

Nat

How are you? How are the girls?

I got the photos. Thank you soo much. She is beautiful, a real credit to you. I am blessed that she has you to look after her.

I have tried to put you on as a visitor but had a reply saying that I cannot put you on.

I am not sure what to do next, I will speak to some people/officers to see what to do next. I really would like to see you, but it may take longer (how's your patience?). It may be worthwhile speaking to someone from your end.

Either way, I hope that you keep in touch.

Yours

Bobby

I smarted when I read the '*I am blessed that she has you to look after her*'. Tears of anger broke through. He seemed to be treating our contact like everything was all OK now. It was time to put pen to paper and write a longer letter than email allowance would allow to explain exactly how things really were. Meanwhile I pinged a reply back, saying I was warned that this might happen. I then told him, '*I'm destroyed, devastated and cannot believe this has happened. Physically and emotionally so hurt – that is the abbreviated version. I trusted and loved you so much. You were my world. I thought this was forever.*'

And then I went on and talked about how he had only taken me to that gorgeous hotel in Kensington just a few weeks before he did what he did. I then asked what I needed to ask, but knew I would never get a response to,

How was your action ever an option?

I signed off,

> *This should never have happened. You have destroyed everything. I'm heartbroken.*
> *Nat*

His reply came soon after,

> *Dear Nat,*
> *There are some things that I need to say to you, face to face, and other things that no matter what I say, you may never believe.*
> *I know my actions do not bear this out, but I really do truly love you. Every single day when I wake, you and the girls are the first thing on my mind. You and them are the last thing on my mind. I can't explain why it happened, which is the hardest thing, but I am truly sorry.*
> *I know that you doubt yourself, but please do not. It is not you, it was me. You truly are a wonderful, loving, intelligent, caring, beautiful and sexy woman. You truly are the woman I want to marry and though it will never happen now, you are the one that I want to be with for the rest of my life.*
> *I am sorry for the pain, emotional and physical, that I have caused to you and your daughters, your mum and dad, sisters, their husbands and their children. Words are never enough to take away that pain for you. I feel ashamed I have done this to you and them.*

I hope that I do see you, so that it may help you.
Until then,
  Love Bobby

On first reading, you may think how sweet his sentiment was. Then read it again, knowing what he did. 'How patronising!' could spring to mind.

I hope that I do see you, so that it may help you...

Really?

The fact he thought about us the second he awoke and the second he went to bed was not exactly surprising. After all, when he woke up, he would be locked up in his cell and would have thought about it on a daily basis

And finally, you cannot miss the corker,

I know that you doubt yourself, but please do not. It is not you, it was me.

Did he seriously just use that line in this instance?

I shouted at the screen, 'Of course I know it's not me. YOU tried to murder ME! I didn't think it was me at any point during this!'

I couldn't decide if there were subtle mind games going on or if he really thought it was acceptable to write half of that. The problem is no matter how angry his emails made me, I also collapsed emotionally every time I read them. I hurt so badly. I couldn't live with the fact so much in my life had been a lie, although it was clear a lot had been.

And there was more to come.

Whilst all this was happening, I was having increased

contact with the Midlands Air Ambulance team. Jo invited me to their annual fundraising ball and awards night and I could bring a 'plus one'. This was a no-brainer: my mum had been my absolute rock and support every day since the attack. The night was incredible as well as very emotional. They flew *G-OMAA*, the actual helicopter that airlifted me, into the grounds of the venue and if that wasn't emotional enough, the pilot was none other than Richard, the amazing pilot who so skilfully flew into Sutton Coldfield town centre that afternoon – I hadn't met him up to this point.

As I saw the helicopter coming into land, my heart started racing. The noise rang in my ears, taking me right back to Trinity Hill. I was desperately fighting off the flashbacks.

Not here, not now. Please…

Tears pricked in my eyes and the odd rogue one escaped down my cheek. I sat quietly by myself as I watched it come in. A round of applause erupted when it was down. I clapped and wiped away my tears. As everyone filed back into the main room, I remained seated in the stands, watching and waiting for the pilot to get out. Then I saw him disembark.

'Thank you,' I muttered quietly to myself.

Halfway through the dinner, Richard was brought over to me. I grabbed him, hugged him and started crying. Between stifled sobs, I thanked him again and again for what he did. He was exceptionally modest about it all, as had the two medics been. He told me how well I had done when I was in the helicopter in staying calm. He was also amazed at how well I looked. I did comment that, hopefully, I did look a lot better than when he saw me last!

The rest of the evening was filled with fundraising events. They played a video of a rescue they did of a young girl involved in an extremely serious road traffic collision. It left everyone in the room in awe of the work of Midlands Air Ambulance Charity. Seeing the difference the film made to the Air Ambulance's fundraising goal, I made the decision then that I definitely wanted my story to be used for one of these video case studies so, the day after the ball, I emailed the charity to give them the go-ahead.

It was an honour to have my mum with me that night. Afterwards, we got a cab home and collapsed into bed in the early hours, shattered but so happy to have been part of something so positive.

The following week saw me at long last get some of my property back: plastic evidence bags containing different parts of my belongings, all sealed with evidence numbers and reams of paper to sign to confirm receipt of them. One of the bags contained the many cards Bobby had written and given to me during our times together. Taking it, I retreated to my bedroom and shut the door firmly behind me. Tearing open the plastic, I emptied the cards straight out onto the duvet and surveyed the mass of them covering my bed, *our* bed. The cards that had once been left, one at a time, on my pillow, waiting for me to get home from work. I picked through a selection of them and pored over the details.

Dear Natalie,

Thank you for the best five months of my life. You are perfect and I wish I could explain how important you are and have been for me. You really have supported and helped me in ways that you may not understand. I love you. I want you. I need you. I have never opened myself out to anyone the way I have with you. I do so because I trust you implicitly. Not

*just not to leave me or tell anyone my secrets, but I
trust that you will be there for me, trust that you will
love me and I hope you know that I will be here for
you until the day I die.*

    Love always
    Bobby

His other cards talked repeatedly about how he loved me
more than anyone he had ever loved in his life. He told me
how he wanted me to be his wife, the mother of his children.
In one card, he promised to '*be your shield when you want
one. A sword when you need one. Your partner, companion,
lover and friend for life*'. The irony being that he was the
very person I needed protecting from, as it turned out.

In a few of the cards he talked about how I inspired him
to be a better man and how I showed him that he was worth
something. He told me how if a woman, a person like me,
was interested in him, then he could achieve anything. How
he woke each day thinking of me and making sure he was
worthy of me and would be a man, a boyfriend, I could be
proud of. I had always been proud of him and at the time I
used to tell him how daft he was to write those things. But
now, looking back over those cards, I wonder what opinion
he really did have of himself. He clearly knew he wasn't the
person he portrayed and maybe that charade just got all too
much for him.

One card, though, really made me sob,

*Dear Natalie,
In my heart, there is only room for one
I want that one to be you,
I need that one to be you,*

There is only one,
I sleep and it is you,
I wake and it is you,
I see no one else,
I want no one else,
I need no one else,
You
Now and Forever,
You
Love Bobby

I had believed it all, every single word. Right up to the point the knife cut through me.

How could these have been sent by the same man who tried to take my life? Who really was this man that I believed in and loved so much?

My next contact from the police was to inform me that my mobile phones were ready for collection from the police station. One of the investigating officers brought out a couple of brown paper bags, both with biohazard warnings on them. They were soaked in blood. On the day I had my personal mobile on me, the one I had spoken to Bobby on as I walked into Sutton, and it was in the inside pocket of my jacket. My work mobile was in my handbag. My personal phone had definitely come off worse: it was caked in dried blood. Once I was sat in the car, I fired them both up, having to replace their SIM cards and get a power line into them to get them working. As I scrolled through the messages from Bobby from that day and in the days building up to the attack, my stomach lurched. They were all so normal and loving, as they always were. The reality of reading them all on the phone made me weep. I then scrolled through my work phone and my stomach turned again. The last missed call I had was from my mum: 15.17 on 04.03.16. She had called me whilst I was being stabbed. To think she was trying to get hold of me as I was fighting, literally, for my life makes me feel physically ill.

I emailed Bobby to let him know that I had looked into the process for me to get into the prison and that it required me seeing a special Victim Support probation team. Unfortunately, the police family liaison officers could do no more than pass their number to me. I called and spoke to the probation department for Victim Support. When I made it clear that I wanted to arrange to see my former partner, I was told that it could be looked at further down the line if it was deemed appropriate.

Frustration doesn't even begin to describe how I felt at this point. It was clearly going to be a long process and I had so much inside of me waiting to burst out.

I had to get in and see him!

I told Bobby that I had sent him a letter, which I warned would not make for easy reading. I also reiterated messages from some of the cards he sent me and said how I was at a complete loss to understand any of this.

There was no reply, even a week later. Not knowing if the email even got through, I wrote another one. I asked him to let me know if he had received my letter. I reiterated a conversation I had had with his sister on text, who said the family were willing to support me. I had more pride than to ask his family for money. However, as he was Leah's father, I told him that he should be organising this. I said that I now knew he had pretty much no money, but he needed to sort something out. He had left me high and dry financially and, after what he did, I had very little sympathy for his financial matters. I touched upon his email and told him how I found it very hard to believe he was still in love with me, or if he ever was. I signed off by telling him how I was been a guest at the Midlands Air Ambulance ball and what an amazing night with incredible people it was – I wanted to show him I was doing some things to move my life on.

A reply quickly came from him, saying he had received my letter and that he had written one back to me. He said that if I didn't want to contact him again, he would understand but he hoped he would see me at least once. Another email followed shortly afterwards, where he talked about the letter he had sent me and how he was truly and absolutely sorry. He said he could not explain what he did and may never be able to.

He then wrote,

I know you may never believe me, but you were (are) my life. I have never loved anyone the way that I loved you. I still only think about you and the girls. I know that you are a fabulous mother. That is why I wanted a baby with you.

My heart broke that bit further and I wept. I read the rest through blurred vision. He said he was glad I was moving on with my life and that I went to the ball and how he couldn't thank '*those special people who kept you alive*' enough. He wrote that he hoped I would trust his family enough to spend a little time with them. That it wasn't their fault, but his.

Funny how he relied heavily on it being his mother's fault in court.

He reiterated how much he loved me and how his time with the girls and I was the best time in his life.

Again, strange, that's not when he said to the first psychologist he spoke to...

He signed off,

Love Bobby
Ps. I bet you were the most beautiful woman at the ball.
Pps. I claimed Portugal's victory for myself [football] as I have a quarter-Portuguese daughter!

That final line just about finished me off. I was angry, hurt, and I wept. He acted like everything was fine and normal, like Leah was his child in the usual sense and that he had a claim on her when, in fact, he relinquished all rights the moment he carried out that despicable act. His emails left me speechless at times – and I still had his handwritten letter to come in the post...

Chapter 28

The Letter &
Other Firsts

IT SEEMED TO TAKE AGES FOR HIS LETTER TO ARRIVE. HE HADN'T PROVIDED ENOUGH POSTAGE, SO I HAD TO GO DOWN TO THE MAIL CENTRE TO PAY THE EXTRA AND COLLECT IT.

I recognised his swirly handwriting on the front, our address emblazoned across the envelope by his own fair hand. I took it shakily and walked back to my car, gulping down breaths as I paced back. The second I was in the car, I locked the door and opened the letter – I knew I wouldn't be able to wait until I got home, I had to know what it said now. It was handwritten on five pages of lined A4, each one numbered in the corner.

His letter started off with a thank-you for having written to him and sharing how I felt. He told me if ever I wanted to write to him about anything, then please do – he was there for me if I needed it! He acknowledged he had destroyed my trust and that he wouldn't be able to get it back. He went on to preach that he didn't believe in God or any afterlife, that this was the only life we lead, and he felt there was no death-bed redemption. Therefore, the taking of someone's life is the worst thing any human being could do, something he struggled to reconcile with alongside his actions. Plus, in his words, he did it to the 'two most important people' in his life.

At this point I was loudly sobbing in my car; tears streamed down my face and I rested my head on the steering wheel. I read the letter as it perched on my knees below my head, as my tears ungracefully ran down the side of my nose and dripped onto the paper.

He went on to repeat how much he loved me and still loves me. Again, he told me how he wanted to marry me. Then he wrote the classic line, '*You are not perfect, but you are perfect for me.*' What? A man who tried to murder me and his unborn child tells ME I'M NOT PERFECT?

He told me how he had trusted me more than anyone else.

Which may have been true. I think he let me in too much and he feared the lack of control and the fact I was starting to see the real him.

He enlightened me that our trip to Lisbon was the best holiday of his life: '*It was as close to perfect as any man could ever have and it is one of a million happy memories I have that help sustain me in here, all of them revolve around you.*'

My chest crumpled. Then the sentence I was dreading, '*The real problem for me is trying to explain why I did what I did. The reason is because I can't explain it. I try every night to resolve what I feel for you and my basic beliefs about life with what I did.*' He went on to say he wondered how he could do that. He said he was sorry his lawyer had belittled Leah's injuries, but she was doing the best for her client! Then he rounded up by telling me, '*But know this: it is not your fault. You are in no way to blame. Neither are your children or your family or our baby. It is not even my family's fault, it is all mine. I am the only one to blame in all of this. It is my fault, my burden and my responsibility.'*

How noble of him!

A postscript probably gave me more new information than the rest of the letter. He claimed that the clothes he wore in the attack were from his mother's house – but fetched to do the gardening! He then claimed the knife wasn't from his mother's house, as stated in that first interview, but was already in the car! The first interview he had, he was still affected by a temporary mental health disorder and didn't know what he was saying – psychiatrists he has since seen have not been able to help him remember any of it. The only thing he does remember (conveniently, I might add) is that he didn't think about doing it until he looked at his bank balance when he was in Sutton. Then he doesn't know why, but that was the trigger for him carrying out the heinous act. An act he claims to remember nothing about, not even getting ready for it.

So, he expected me to believe that he thought about it after looking at a balance at an ATM? Then in what would have been less than half an hour, he planned to get changed to disguise himself, pack spare clothes and a pair of shoes into a rucksack (fortunately, in his car), luckily, find a large carving knife and a bin bag in a charity wrapper in his boot, as well as two pairs of gloves in the boot. Then, after prepping himself, go find me and follow me to murder me in broad daylight? Jeez, that was one hell of a quick plan! Not only did it not ring true, it totally contradicted what he said when first interviewed – where he stated he had been thinking about killing me for a couple of weeks!

He ended the letter reminding me it wasn't my fault and he left for work that day in the hope of a good day and wonderful life with me and our family.

His final line, '*Again, I'm sorry for the pain, hurt and betrayal.*'

Bobby HATED gardening. It was the end of February/start of March when he claimed to have gathered those clothes. Not many people, even the keen gardeners, venture out then in cold, icy conditions. Plus, he had plenty of spare clothes at home, so why would he need to get extra ones from his mum's? We had a packed weekend planned, so when was the gardening going to happen? It was so ridiculous, it was beyond a joke!

I didn't drive anywhere for a while; I just sat flicking through the pages again, checking I hadn't missed anything. Most of it had been said in emails before. I was hoping this letter would have shed new light on it all, but it was mainly sanctimonious, self-important nonsense. After I had composed myself, I turned on the engine and drove back home to see Mum with Leah.

A couple of days passed and, slowly, the contents of the letter sunk in further. I started searching for a greater understanding of what happened, which made me turn to social media. His mother was on Facebook, so I searched for her page. As I scrolled through photos, my heart stopped: there was a photo of Bobby in a suit, at what looked like a large family celebration. I scanned the date: 26 December 2015. Boxing Day? The day he'd been texting to telling me he was sat waiting at an airport, trying to get a standby seat to fly home. Yet he was fully suited and laughing at a family party. There was another photo taken that day, posted by his uncle, who I knew was an avid Facebook user. I clicked on his profile page and scrolled back to 26 December. There was a plethora of photos, all taken at a family wedding. A wedding where Bobby was part of the wedding group, carrying the bride in and taking his place on the main stage. His clothing matched the wedding party. Then came the photo that really turned my stomach, him dancing around in a group, carrying his cousin's baby, laughing and clearly enjoying himself.

I'd been a fool. What life was he living? What else didn't I know?

Despite the fact he made out he hadn't known about going to Pakistan until the day he flew (which was starting to unravel as a lie from the police investigation) and the calls I received, telling me he'd been arrested and was 'stuck' in Pakistan, desperately trying to get home for Christmas, it was clearly a lie: he had obviously gone for his cousin's wedding. It had certainly been planned for a long time (probably the summer before, when her parents visited the UK) and he must have known he was never going to be with me over the Christmas period.

Why didn't he tell me the truth? It was becoming increasingly obvious he had one life he showed to me, another to his family. A double life that he couldn't keep juggling and that was starting to unravel.

In his psychologist's interview he had reported feeling down for about three months. It would have coincided with his trip to Pakistan. This would make sense as the pressure of all the different stories was most likely starting to weigh him down. It still didn't make sense why I had to be the one murdered and disposed of in this web of lies, but one thing was clear: the Bobby I thought I knew was not 'real'. That night, I cried myself to sleep as yet another part of the life I had believed in came crashing down.

The following week, I had my final visit from Ruth and Lou, my police family liaison officers. I had said I would like my clothing returned to me and not destroyed, as offered by the police. They came to my house with numerous large brown bags, all sealed with cable ties and biohazard warning labels on them.

'They do let off a bit of an aroma,' I was told tactfully. 'They also do have a lot of dried blood on them still, just to prepare you and, also, be careful where you open them.'

Nodding, I put the bags to one side in the living room as I signed to say I had them back. My driving licence was still missing, but was believed to be with Bobby's belongings in another police station; they promised to chase this up. The signing over of the clothes done, we realised this was probably the last time they would visit me. It was an emotional realisation as they had been with me since the beginning, their support invaluable. They had become part of an extended family I now had, a family created out of dreadful circumstances. I couldn't imagine not seeing them again after all these months together. Whether it was usual or not, we hugged goodbye. I could feel the tears welling up as their departure meant another step on the journey and I was left alone with this awful reality as part of my new normality.

Ruth, Lou and DI Ian Ingram are all officers I have the greatest respect for: they showed humanity, empathy and kindness throughout the investigation and afterwards. They are a credit to West Midlands Police and I will always have a special place for them in my heart, as I know my mum and sisters will.

Later that day, I braved opening the bags onto the patio. As I cut them open, the stench of dried blood made me heave. I tipped the clothing out and, despite having seen photos in court, the reality made my blood run cold: my fitted blue top and leather jacket were shredded. Dark blood stains soaked the front of the top and the sleeves, the leather on the jacket was stiff with blood. My maternity jeans were soaked in it, as was the umbrella I'd been holding. It appears I must have fallen on the umbrella as there were pools of dried blood in the folds.

After laying out paper from a large plain roll, I put each item of clothing out, one at a time, and took photos. The gaping holes where the knife had torn through were a screaming reminder of the atrocity of the attack. My hand involuntarily reached up to my chest and my wrist as I traced in my mind the holes in the clothes onto my body. Tears filled my eyes as this stark reminder of the horror lay in front of me.

Mum stayed in the house whilst I picked over them – she didn't want to see, the photos in court had been enough for her. Once the photos were complete, I bundled the clothes back in their bags and sealed them back up, before dragging them back into the garage, ready for disposal.

Disposal of them came a few weeks later when I took the girls and Mum back to my aunt and uncle's house in Wales. I loaded the bags into Mum's car, hidden away from the children so they didn't ask what they were. Once they were tucked up in bed at my aunt's house, the light evening afforded the chance to take the bags out with my uncle. Together, we carried them across their farmland, to where my uncle always has enormous bonfires. My sister Mand, who was aware of what I had planned, had made a special trip up to Wales to be with me whilst I burnt them all.

I opened the bags and, once the fire was going, threw them on alongside the bags they'd been carried in. The flames soon engulfed them and as they licked high in the air, a silence descended as we watched them turn to ashes. Tears ran down my cheeks as I silently said goodbye to another part of my life, the horror they embodied. As the flames died down, my uncle made his way back up to the house, leaving Mand and I staring at the smouldering embers. She put her arm around me and said, 'They are gone! Well done for seeing through another step in your journey to recovery. Now, let's go in as it's getting cold!'

I smiled at her, we turned back to the house and walked up the drive together.

The summer was now well underway and due to the thank-you cards I had sent out to the people who had come to my aid, I had contact with Tony, the amazing man who jumped fearlessly onto Bobby's back to pull him down and try and wrestle the knife off him. We arranged to meet so I could thank him properly to his face. My heart was pounding as I negotiated the pram towards him. We hugged straight away and I repeated myself over and over again, saying thank-you. The words sounded so futile. Here I was, meeting the man so involved on that fateful day. The man who risked his own life to save mine and Leah's, enduring injuries in the process.

Tony told me how eerily calm Bobby was and when he grabbed his arm with the knife and pulled it back, Bobby's large dark eyes bored up into his. The memory of that hard stare had stuck, so sinister in his look and demeanour. It was clear the attack still had a massive impact on Tony and we shared our pain of the memory of it all.

Time rolled on and, in August, my damaged left hand deteriorated further and it was decided more surgery was needed to try and improve it. I was also fitted out by the scar-management specialist nurse with a compression bandage for my hand and wrist to aid scar healing. But most significantly for me at this time, I had my first visit from the victim liaison officers of the Probation Unit, Catherine and Bernadette. Catherine was my designated point of contact, assigned to be in touch with me throughout Bobby's sentence. Bernadette was the mediation coordinator who managed victim contact with the perpetrator of the crime.

They sat in my lounge as Mum made us all a cup of tea and went through Bobby's sentence with me to make sure I understood fully the different aspects, the jail term set, the minimum time period laid out before he would be eligible for parole (something that still turns my stomach to this day) and the extended licence he will be under when eventually released. By then I knew his sentence in detail, but listening to it in black-and-white terms hit me hard.

We discussed my request to see him and they warned that the process can take a very long time. I told them I had had contact with him via email and letter, and that he had said he wanted to see me as much as I wanted to see him, undoubtedly for very different reasons. I pressed hard about how soon I could see him, but they insisted the process could be longer than I was wanting it to be. It was of course a fairly unusual case: the basis of Bobby's and my relationship up to the point of the attack, the fact I'd been pregnant by him and was now the sole parent and that I was almost murdered in such a violent and horrific way yet wanted to face my attacker so relatively soon after the attack meant there were many aspects to consider. They told me they would have to contact the prison to try to arrange to see him. This in itself raised its own issues: HMP Birmingham is predominantly a remand and holding prison, so it wasn't a prison they visited very often and therefore didn't have the right contacts in place. It was to be a very long and frustrating process. After they left, I felt lost and downhearted. I had hoped the visit could be sorted quickly and without issue, but this battle was going to draw on all my resources.

Less than two weeks later, another step in my journey was taken. I had a phone conversation with Bobby's sister, Shona (the one I had met in Sutton all those months before, when she told me she was pregnant). My heart raced as I dialled her number, passed on to me by his other sister. The call was certainly enlightening: Shona had been told by her sister how I'd been in the hospital the same day she was discharged, how I'd seen her but not called out to her. She told me how sad she found it that the situation was such that I hadn't felt able to do so. Of course she understood why, as she knew that as far as I was concerned, the family were aware I was pregnant but continued to blank me. But they knew nothing about my pregnancy until after the attack. I asked her about the day I'd seen her leave the hospital – there was a question I had mulling in my head for some time.

'When you left that day I saw you at Good Hope,' I asked, 'who picked you up from the hospital?'

'Bobby,' she replied. 'He was waiting outside the main door in his car for me. He drove me home and settled me in the house before he left.'

My heart sank: another lie, another part of his double life. Bobby had told me he was stuck at work. He had me go to hospital with my mum as he couldn't be there with me straight away, despite my fears about labour starting and the baby being at risk of being premature. He must have seen me walk into the hospital with Mum. His car must have been parked up there, waiting for Shona – after all, she left just a few minutes after I arrived.

'He was there at the hospital, waiting for you?' I stammered down the phone.

'Yes,' came her solemn reply as she realised exactly what this meant. 'I don't know what to say to you, Natalie. He drove me home and he was his usual chatty, relaxed self. He talked about how I could rely on him to be there when I go into labour, how he would be on standby for me, how he would take me into hospital if needed or look after my kids. He chatted so normally and spent time with me at home, yet all the while you were in hospital with his first child, not knowing if you were in labour or if the baby was OK. I have no words for him, I'm just so sorry.'

'You weren't to know,' I told her. 'But he did – and yet he chose to lie to me again.'

She went on to tell me how he had been at hers the evening before the attack, babysitting and cooking her dinner. He'd been happy and relaxed, yet hours away from committing the worst crime possible. This was the very evening he texted to say he had a late drop-off with a car for work, but would be home soon.

His lies were never-ending, it seemed.

She went on to tell me how Bobby always told lies when he got himself in a bad situation to cover up mistakes or wrong decisions. They were always elaborate in nature too. Which led me to ask her about Pakistan and what she knew about his trip there over Christmas. She confirmed what I had already found out: that he had gone over for a family wedding, a wedding he had known about since the summer before and one he agreed to be a key part of. She had thought it strange that he was going to be away for Christmas, our first Christmas, knowing how important it would be to me, as it is for her husband's family. She soon learnt that I had no idea about the wedding, that I had found out through Facebook photos. I asked if he had actually been to court whilst over there or even been arrested.

'No, none of that happened. I'm afraid that was all more of his elaborate lies.'

My heart sank. I knew this would have been the case, but again I was being forced to face up to it.

She told me how she would like us to have a relationship and hoped we could meet. I said I would think about it, there was so much to take on board. She mentioned how she had seen her brother a couple of times in prison and how he just couldn't explain why he did it. Before finishing the conversation, I asked her the one thing I'd been dreading, but needed to know.

'Did he have anyone else? Was he married to someone else in Pakistan?'

To my relief the answer was no. He had always turned down any arranged marriages their mother had tried to set up. She knew of no one else.

We closed the conversation with an agreement I would think about meeting up face to face. The call left me drained and upset, so many lies to face up to. The truth of my life with Bobby was far different to the one I had believed all the time I was with him. I spent that weekend composing a very long email to him, calling out all his lies. If I couldn't face him yet to tell him, I would damn well write it down and make him realise I was finding out the truth for myself.

As we were well into summer, I realised that I hadn't actually booked a holiday for the kids and I. We were just about getting by in my head, but time away was so important for them to have that normality and another step in showing I wasn't defeated. Mum and I booked a family room for the girls and I and a single room for her in the Premier Inn in Swansea. As we tucked down on the first night there, I realised it was my first time with the kids alone overnight. Mum still lived with us at this point. It showed me I was far more in control of things than I thought.

The time down there was lovely, we even managed the beach and the sea, although Leah was distinctly unimpressed! On the way back from Swansea I stopped at my lovely friend Harrie's and her husband Graham's, just outside Cardiff. As I sat and chatted late into the night with Harrie, I realised how lucky I was to have such amazing friends.

Once home, I decided I was ready to make the next step. Mum and I chatted when we got back and I suggested she started to stay some nights back at hers. She needed the time back in her own house, she had lived with me every single day since I had come out of hospital. At some point I had to face the real world and she needed to recoup some of her own life. Early September, six months on from the attack, Mum started to move back to hers. I was scared but excited that I had made another stride forward in my independence.

Chapter 29

A Barrage of Emails

ALL THIS TIME THE EMAIL CONTACT BETWEEN BOBBY AND I HAD BEEN CONTINUOUS. AS EACH LIE SURFACED, I NOTED THEM DOWN MENTALLY AND ACCUMULATED THEM TO SEND and face him with the facts as I had now discovered them.

My emails went from trying to prove to him how strong I was to emotionally crumbling, telling him how much I wished he was still home and that none of this had happened. I frequently told him how I still didn't understand it and I knew that I probably never would. I was in a dark place and struggling to come to terms with it all.

As we went through August, I had hit a period when I had sent a couple of emails with no reply. Then, unexpectedly, on a family trip to Twycross zoo, my email inbox suddenly went crazy with messages from him.

I stared at my phone as notification after notification popped up, four in a row. As much as I wanted to leave them and not read them until I got home, as I was out with my family, I just couldn't. Eventually, I excused myself from the group and wandered off distractedly, phone in hand, pushing the pram with my elbow. I logged onto the system and downloaded all his messages: it was one long email, written over four separate email reply sheets, each numbered so I could follow them as one long document and it hit me like a train.

First, he apologised for the delay in his reply, saying it was down to 'the system'. He discussed the fact that Leah was the most precious thing, after me, to him. He went on to say that he counted the weeks since her birth and that although he has not met her, he loves her like he has never loved anything, aside from me. She was his world and he was thankful to me for all I have done and do for her every day. How I balked at those words when he was prepared to murder his child before she was even born!

He claimed that he did not remember anything he told the police psychologist and said that he could not remember much at all about those first few days. He told me life wasn't easy with the girls and I, but he insisted he wanted it. He then referred to the things said in court, especially in reference to the downplaying of the long-term effects on Leah, and told me how they were said as they were the best for him.

'*I know that may seem wrong to you, but it was my defence's job to do what they could for me. I know it sounds harsh, but it was the rest of my life on the line. I know that you don't want to hear that, but it does matter so what was said was felt to be the best way to do what was best for me.*'

I almost choked on reading that paragraph. It had been mine and Leah's lives actually on the line!

Of all the self-centred, self-absorbed things to write!

He continued to put it to me that whatever truth I wished to believe was up to me. He believed that he loved me and

my children and his child and always will. He continued
to talk about the lies I had raised and still maintained he
was arrested in Pakistan (something I have since been told
categorically by his family was not true). He finished with
telling me that I was '*incredible – kind, loving, generous,
intelligent, a great mum, fit and very beautiful*'. He said he
was lucky to have me in my life and grateful that I was the
mother to his child and he was so, so sorry for all he had
done to hurt me, signing off, '*Love, Bobby*'.

I bit back the tears. The wave of nausea, a feeling now
so familiar, washed over me once more. It wasn't the place
to break down, though – I was out with my children and
family, so I had to put my mask back on, take a deep breath
and step back into the family craziness. I spent the rest of
the day functioning as normally as I could for the children's
sake until we eventually got home and I put the kids to bed
and then sat and re-read the pages again. I broke down in
tears and cried to myself for the rest of the evening before
collapsing into an exhausted sleep on my bed.

My reply to this four-page epic waited. Too emotional to
reply straight away, I made the decision to take the emotions
out of it as much as I could when I did eventually write back.
There was no point going round in circles so I focused on
what was now important and, cold as it sounds, that was
sorting out the finances. After all, I had three children to
raise, one of them biologically his. He had left me in one of
the worst situations possible and I still had to live my life, pay
the bills and keep my children secure. I was just about getting
by and had no idea if and when I could return to work even
with the amazing support I had received from my company,
led by Sara, an amazing occupational health nurse. It was a
situation that couldn't be left undecided forever.

He had said so many times about supporting me, but I'd seen nothing material in that direction. It was time to discuss what support he actually was going to provide financially. I closed my email to him by saying, '*I'm continually hurt by you, even when you are in prison. Do the right thing by me financially at least now, don't put me through any more. I have our child to bring up. Show you have some shred of morals, show me the man I believed you were at least this way.*'

It was a couple of weeks before I heard back. He told me that his mother was trying to sell some land in Pakistan in which he had a share and when that was sold, his share would go to Leah and me. I knew this was something that might never happen and was certainly not going to happen for years as it was an ongoing issue. No other support was offered.

Whilst waiting for this email about finances, I had Bobby's first birthday away from us to face. His forty-second birthday – the rest of his forties were destined to be spent in prison, not facing release until he was at least fifty-three. In my highly emotional state I found myself (crazily, now I look back) sending him a card from Leah, alongside a book I knew he would enjoy. I even sent a card from me, adding inside that I did not know why I was sending it, my head and heart were hurt and confused. I included further photos of Leah in the card. It was the last time I was to send any photos of Leah to him. However, when I sent them, I was at that point still so determined he saw the beautiful person he had not only been part of creating but also tried to destroy. I wanted him to face what he had lost. But now I can see it was useless and in vain. Luckily, Leah has changed so much now from those photos that you wouldn't connect them to the wonderful little girl she is now.

It was time to take that next step. I had shown him what she looked like, I could do no more – now I just had to cut off my emotions as much as I could.

Something I knew would be far easier said than done.

Chapter 30

Pushing the
Boundaries

THE DAY OF THE WOLF RUN ARRIVED – A TEN-KILOMETRE OBSTACLE COURSE THROUGH FORESTS, STREAMS AND ACROSS FARMLAND, INCLUDING A 50M OPEN-WATER SWIM ACROSS A lake. Even for the physically fit it was a challenge, but I was attempting this just under six months from the attack. My body had been slowly recovering, the stab wounds in my chest and abdomen gradually healing, but still angry and sore (and undoubtedly meshing a network of scar tissue underneath). My hand was still useless, something that would always pose a problem on an obstacle course. But I had been patched up as best as possible and the Wolf Run was one of my key goals for the year.

My fundraising had already reaped over £6,200 in sponsorship for Midlands Air Ambulance Charity, smashing my initial target of £2,400! Ian, my ex-husband, had filled an empty place that had turned up in our team. I was really grateful for his support and stepping in – I knew I would need someone close by me on the course, especially for the obstacles, which might involve a degree of rather ungracious shoving from behind. He had seen me give birth to our two children so we had no secrets or shame!

My sister Mand also came with me, Emily and Isabel (Leah had been left at home with Mum). Anita met us there too. Ian and I registered, had our numbers written on our foreheads in black felt tip and headed off for a warm-up. Before we knew it, we were off! Mand, Anita and the girls stood near the start line and cheered their support. The course was already quite muddy and soon I was covered in thick mud. Cold, heavy rain set in and the mud grew wetter and more slippery, but we pushed on. The obstacles were tough at times and I did find myself dropping off a tall climbing wall when my hand just couldn't hold me almost at the top.

The fifty-metre open-water swim was horrific. I would class myself as a fairly strong swimmer, but as I waded into the icy water, weighed down by thick mud stuck to my trainers and clothes, I started to panic slightly. The water was full of swimmers, most of whom were struggling. The hardest swim I have ever done, it brought home to me how much muscle strength I had lost, especially across my chest and arms, which had obviously borne the brunt of the stabbing.

In the final kilometre, I felt my legs turn to jelly. Ian jogged alongside me to check I was OK. But I just nodded – I had to focus on the end. There was one last high metal climbing wall and my heart sank. I was so tired, but I had to finish. One last unceremonious shove from Ian and I pulled myself up the rope with my one good hand. As we jumped in the mud-filled lake at the end, my gym teammates, Ian and I raised our hands and cheered.

I'd done it! Less than twenty-six weeks before I had been in an induced coma, unable to walk further than the end of my bed, needing a wheelchair to get any distance and as good as stabbed to death, as well giving birth. Yet I had completed my challenge. The feeling of achieving that goal was incredible. I have continued to always set myself goals – nothing unrealistic, but stretching and focusing on things I know I want to achieve to jump onto my next stepping stone of recovery.

Feeling positive after the Wolf Run, I met up with Shona, Bobby's sister, for the first time. I left Leah at home with Mum as I prepared myself for an emotionally charged meeting. Shona came striding in after I arrived, pushing a pram with her little boy, only a few weeks younger than Leah. Tears prickled in both of our eyes as we sensed the gravitas of this meeting to both of us. As I peered in the pram to look at her sleeping boy, I was shocked: he was Leah's double. The similarity was so striking, it took my breath away.

Shona and I talked for four hours. It soon became apparent to her that I knew a lot about Bobby, and at times it seemed, more than the family knew. We discussed Bob's previous relationships – it was clear the family weren't aware of half of what he did in his private life. They had no idea he was heavily involved with a German cousin in his teens or that he was engaged in a two-year relationship with another close, younger relative. Shona practically choked on her cup of tea when I let out those revelations!

As we talked further, the web of lies Bobby had weaved started to become transparent. It came out that he had even gone so far as telling them that he was going on a golfing holiday with the lads to Lisbon (a free trip apparently as one of the lads had supposedly dropped out and no wives, etc.). This lie, like all the others, was elaborate in detail and he was actually going on our family holiday to Portugal. Shona had called him out on that lie on their group messaging, asking him why he was lying when it was obvious he was going away with the girls and I, but he never replied.

Throughout our conversation, it became clear that Bobby had lied many times in his life to get out of bad situations and a lot of those lies became quite tall tales. He once borrowed Shona's car, promising her repeatedly that he was insured on it, only to be involved in a crash, write it off and then give his younger brother's name at the scene of the accident as he wasn't insured. His family had bailed him out.

From speaking to Shona, it was obvious Bobby had been brought up differently to his siblings, hailed as someone special. His mother favoured him from a young age and his father bestowed more money and attention on him than the younger children. Truly the golden child who could do no wrong, he had been bailed out repeatedly through his life. If he did make mistakes, they were soon covered up and dealt with – he never had to get himself out of a tough situation.

From his late teens, he began escorting his mother to family functions – weddings, etc. – as their father took no interest in such events. The relationship soon evolved into more husband/wife as Bobby was always at his mother's side in place of his father. They had an extremely 'involved' relationship, *too* involved many might argue. He was 'hers' and no woman was ever going to fit in her plan or be good enough/right. It seemed everyone was bewitched by this amazing, kind man, myself included. Bobby the 'untouchable', Bobby who could do no wrong. Except the truth was, of course, he *could* do wrong.

He never had any responsibility, never really grew up.

His whole life was spent lying to get out of bad situations to maintain his 'perfect Bobby' image. Whoever he was with, he created that perfect persona to them, even if it wasn't based entirely on fact. But I believe I had been his step too far: I started to see the real him and I questioned things that didn't seem to add up. Then there was my pregnancy, the lie he couldn't cover up and, in my belief, the lie he had to get rid of.

Before Shona and I parted ways, we discussed finances. I said I had just addressed the very subject with Bobby via email, but was still waiting for a reply. She told me she would look into it, but wasn't too hopeful.

The meeting had been better than I expected.

The very next day, I had Catherine and Bernadette from the probation team visit me. They had seen Bobby in HMP Birmingham and came to update me and plan the next steps. I hoped this would mean getting some dates sorted for me to go in, but that hope was soon dashed. Their meeting with him had been brief. They couldn't tell me much about what he had said, aside from the fact he focused a lot on Leah and wanting to see her. This turned my stomach. I also felt hurt: where was the remorse? The probation team felt overall that he still wasn't ready to see me; he needed more time to reflect, especially as he claimed not to remember much. He seemed very controlled and collected about it all, almost detached.

Frustrated and angry, I argued that I just wanted to eyeball him. But they wouldn't budge and said, with time, I would get so much more out of a meeting with him. Little did I know at that stage they were doing me a huge favour and clearly doing the right thing. There were so many steps to take to reach the ultimate goal of facing him. I was adamant

I was not going to let this go – I would fight to the end to face him and they could see my grit determination.

In the following week, I made the huge step of going to Spain with Leah to visit my close friend Ava, who lived out there with her husband Rich and two children. My older two were at school and Ian had them every evening. I hadn't seen Ava since the April and I couldn't wait to see her. As I strode through Customs, with a sense of pride I had got that far without freaking out (my fear of being out alone was uncontrollable most of the time), I was met by a beaming Ava on the other side of the security gate. We hugged hard and both of us shed a tear to see one another again.

I stayed in an upstairs room in their villa, alone with Leah. I was completely safe, Ava and her husband were only downstairs. But it was my first time of being alone with Leah this way and that in itself felt strange, yet I knew I was taking another small step to recovery.

It was an amazing five days away. Ava's mum and dad also live out there in the same village. She, Rich, their children and her parents couldn't have made me feel more welcome and, for the first time, I experienced small glimpses of relaxing. When it came to leave, a sense of dread enveloped me: I could be in a bubble in Spain but, as with all bubbles, this one had to burst. Ava and her mum drove Leah and me back to the airport. We all cried as we said goodbye and I looked a forlorn figure as I pushed the pram to the security gate, sealing my return 'home'. But as I walked into the departure lounge, I reflected on the wonderful fact I had developed an extended family out there with Ava and her family. Out of all the horror, it was another positive rising like a phoenix from the flames.

Back on UK soil, all my usual anxieties were once again

heightened. I still found myself petrified every time I went outside the door on my own, even walking to the shops required mental preparation. I had transformed from someone so confident before the attack, who would travel anywhere alone, to someone who couldn't pop to the shops for a loaf of bread without panicking. I knew I had to do something to try and at least partly combat my fear. Self-defence seemed a natural route to go. Emily's martial arts instructor Dan and his amazing black-belt wife Jenny offered to spend time with me each week on one-to-one classes and refused any form of payment. They were absolutely fantastic! They took me through different self-defence mechanisms, should I ever be grabbed or find myself in a threatened position again; they were brilliant with their time and patience. But my fear of being out alone continued and I was so frustrated by it.

Frustration described how I felt about most things in the imploded world I was trapped in. I didn't feel in control of many things – unable to do so much for one reason or another, my outward persona hiding what was going on in my head, making it so hard for people to understand. I wanted to feel more 'normal' but I knew that normality looked so different to before. When I first met with my work colleagues, it was of course lovely to see them again but I felt like an outsider. To all intents and purposes, their world was the same as when I last saw them, but mine was unrecognisable. I couldn't express to them how I had changed, and they understandably saw the old Nat they wanted to see, but I knew she was gone forever.

Chapter 31

When Spoken Words Just Don't Seem Enough

I SOON FOUND I WAS STRUGGLING WITH GETTING ACROSS TO THOSE CLOSEST TO ME WHAT WAS GOING ON IN MY HEAD WHEN MY EXTERNAL APPEARANCE DIDN'T TELL THE WHOLE story. My psychologist Anna suggested an open letter to pass on to those key people around me.

Open Letter To All Those Who See the 'Normal' Face of Me

You all mean so well with your comments on how good I look, how the scars have shrunk and how well I'm doing. There is no malice, just a desire to share positive comments to help boost me. But all you see is my mask. The mask I put on in the morning and keep on all day, to be shed only in the privacy of my time with my psychologist Anna, when I'm on my own or with very few nearest to me.

It is joked how I asked for my fake tan and make-up bag whilst still in hospital. The sad truth is this was not vanity or 'Nat being Nat', but the sheer fact that I looked in the mirror and couldn't face the person staring back at me. The woman in the mirror was so pale and heavily scarred with bright red scars, bruised and emotionally vacant. It wasn't me, it was a damaged shell that once contained life, love and hope. Desperate to get the cover up of that shell at least, I smeared fake tan over my body in a desperate bid to mask some of the scars and applied make-up to my face to look more like 'Nat'. Comments were even passed after I started wearing make-up that I looked more like me, so the mask worked.

I could see people didn't know what to say to me and I felt like I had to make things easier for them by at least looking more normal. So the mask remains: the fake tan still gets slapped on and make-up covers the pain and destruction as best it can. Whilst I look more like me, and I smile occasionally, even make the odd joke, what's really going on, what is it that people do not see?

They don't see the moment I wake up in 'our' bed and look across to see it untouched, no Bobby. Or the heartache as that instant reminder of life hits. They don't see me getting back into a big, empty cold bed at night and lying there wide awake, unable to switch off and feeling so alone, missing the man I thought I was with.

They don't see the fight inside to be a normal new mummy to my three children. The smile I put on my face as I hastily wipe silent tears away, the shield I put up as best I can to protect them from this horrific situation.

They don't see the physical pain in my chest I feel when Leah's eyes pull an expression just like her dad's, or the fear I feel every time I think of the future and what effect all this will have on my precious baby. They don't see what is going on in my head from the moment I wake to the moment I eventually go back to sleep, reliving every moment of that fateful day – the morning cuddle in bed, the kiss goodbye, conversations on the phone. The moment I heard him following me, the moment he grabbed me, seeing the knife being pulled out and plunged repeatedly into my chest. The aftermath of the attack, the fight to live. The real fear I was going to die. I think about it all day, every day, as well as the heartbreakingly good memories of my life with Bobby and our plans for the future.

How I wish every day that my life was normal. I see everyone else's life moving on and mine trapped in a living nightmare.

People don't see my brain processing lie after lie that Bobby told; the fact he may well be a psychopath, working it out and fearing the future. They don't see how scared I feel every time I walk somewhere on my own or with the pram, the racing heart and the gripping fear another man might just grab me. They don't see me checking over my shoulder every few minutes to make sure someone isn't there, or my pace quicken whenever I'm faced with another person on their own. Or the tight grip on the pram handle, my stomach churning until I reach my destination.

They don't know the intense sick feeling I have

every time I'm in Sutton town centre, when I see
Trinity Hill or go into M&S – when I glance up at
the security camera that caught Bobby purchasing his
lunch just half an hour before the attack. How I trace
his steps every time, how it crushes down on me, or
how every Friday I look at the clock and relieve those
steps as 3pm approaches.

They don't see the mistrust I have of strangers
asking how I am, not knowing if they have an angle
or are preying on my vulnerability. I'm seeing the
world through such dark, mistrustful eyes. They don't
see the internal flinch every time I spot a heavily
pregnant woman. The overwhelming sadness I feel
and how I want to share my story with them, not
that I would, as I feel they are the closest person who
could begin to recognise the fear you might feel, being
that vulnerable and being attacked. How I feel robbed
of my pregnancy; how he stole that memory, cut it
short and destroyed any good thoughts of it. How he
took my dream of becoming a midwife away.

They don't see my pain when I see mixed-race
couples together. Seeing an Asian man with a white
woman leaves me wondering why it couldn't work
out for me. Asian men pushing prams and holding
their babies... I have to bite back the tears, the
overwhelming upset engulfs me.

They don't see me constantly stretching out my
deformed little finger, curled up with scar tissue and
oh, so painful. Or the number of things I have to
do differently or not at all with my left hand as it's
too weak, or the stabbing pain is too great, like a
sharp iron bar is pressing down in it. They don't see

my frustration when at times I can't do the simplest tasks, such as switching the TV channel over with the remote as my hand just won't work properly.

They don't see the sharp twinges I feel in my chest when I run. The reminder the scars are still there. The internal flinch when I see my naked body in the mirror, still so deformed.

They don't see the loneliness I feel every day. No one knows what it's like to have been through what I went through. People who've had bad car accidents or a partner cheat, or even had a serious illness usually find someone who has been through something the same or similar and can empathise and understand what it's like to have been there. But not me – no one knows what it's like to have the set of circumstances I had, I feel so alone.

Although I survived on that hill, Bobby in essence killed the real Natalie. That Natalie died on that hill and I'm left struggling to function. At times I wish that Bobby had been successful and that I wasn't here having to deal with this. Having to listen to people tell me I'm doing so well, how the scars are fading or aren't that bad (really?). How it was a good job it was me who was attacked as I'm strong and could survive it when others couldn't. The real Natalie is destroyed and I feel like I'm in the midst of a stormy ocean, trying to keep my head above the water, but failing and sinking as I tire of treading water. But when you ask me, 'How are you?' I will say, 'Fine, it's tough, but I'm getting there.' And you nod and agree. Because if I told you the truth, or took off this mask, you couldn't look at me, you couldn't deal with it. You would feel uncomfortable. It's easier to say I'm fine and we can all pass over it and another day is done.

If you want to know how I really am, this letter tells you: I'm still destroyed, I'm still petrified and I hurt beyond belief. But the mask goes on and I pretend I'm fine, getting through another day.

The letter was met with tears from my mum, sisters and closest friends. They already knew it deep down, but the stark reality in black and white truly conveyed what I just couldn't say.

Writing letters to express my inner feelings had become a regular channel for me. Following Anna's suggestion, I wrote numerous letters to Bobby. Letters that would never see the light of day, locked in the back of my notebook. They allowed me to 'talk' freely to him, to tell him exactly what was going on in my heart and mind. Some were filled with pure anger at what he did, others filled with pure grief for what we had lost and how much my heart missed him. They mirrored the confusion in my head.

Whilst I battled with the darkness, I still had practical matters to attend to, finances being key. Bobby's sister Shona and I had kept in touch and we arranged to meet to discuss the next step in sorting out money owed from Bobby's business. I decided I would take Leah with me, a massive decision. As Shona arrived, pushing her son Leo in the pram with her, she gasped when she saw us. Tears clouded her eyes as she was about to meet her niece for the first time, the baby none of the family believed they would see. She poked her head in the pram and saw Leah, eyes closed and perfectly at peace.

'Crikey, she does look like Leo!' she exclaimed, as shocked as I had been by the stark similarity.

Once Leah was awake, I scooped her up and told her about her auntie sat across from me. I asked Shona if she would like to hold her and she nodded eagerly in response. Shona's emotions were clear. I knew it wasn't her fault that her brother did what he did, yet I also knew this would almost certainly be one of the few times she might see her niece – I didn't know how much interaction with the family I could cope with long-term. Also, I had to protect Leah from Bobby and being heavily involved with his family was not going to make that easy once he was released.

So many punished over one action.

We spent time chatting over coffee and deciding a plan of action about recouping the money owed from Bobby's business partners. All the while Leah and Leo sat happily on our laps, listening to this seemingly normal conversation play out. A couple of women who were sat nearby cooed over the pair, asking if they were twins. Clearly, the similarity wasn't just noticed by us mums. We smiled and replied they were in fact cousins. And for a moment we paused and glanced at each other, the reality of that simple statement sinking in. I felt my heart and stomach twist.

Why did you destroy this, Bob?

A plan formed, we parted company knowing the next time we met, we would hopefully be taking a step towards regaining money we were of the understanding was rightfully owed to Bobby.

As was becoming the norm in my life, the emotional roller coaster didn't stop there. Just four days after meeting Shona with Leah, I stepped nervously into a lounge bar near the town centre to meet a very special man for brunch.

Having written to John Mitchell – Johnny, the first man who came to my rescue – he had at long last contacted me. Understandably, he needed time to come to terms with it all before making contact. As I pushed the pram through the door into the warm bar area, I soon spotted him. He got to his feet as I negotiated the pram around the tables towards him. No words were needed, we fell into each other's arms and hugged. Tears poured down my cheeks as I repeatedly mumbled thank-you into his now-damp shoulder.

For four hours we sat and chatted. We talked about everything, the attack being a key part of it. He told me how he had been walking home with his headphones in when he spotted Bobby jumping on me. To start with, he thought we were friends just messing about. Then he saw the knife and the look of sheer terror on my face – he had never seen anyone look so terrified. After processing it all for a moment, he rushed towards us, unsure of what action to take. He lunged at Bobby to wrestle him off me just before Tony jumped on Bobby from behind. Both of them were so brave. When they all realised I had escaped somehow, he recalled Bobby's calm and eerie persona when he broke free of his grip, how he rolled calmly away and stood up, dusting himself down, ready to come at me again with the knife. Johnny felt helpless and the attack had left him significantly affected. So much damage caused.

Then I filled him in on Bobby and our relationship. I showed him a few photos, although he struggled to look at his face, haunted by the memory of Bobby's dark eyes boring into him, unsure if he would try and take his life too during that attack.

In those four hours, Johnny and I bonded. A deep connection would always remain between us, no matter where life took us. We had shared an event barely anyone else would truly understand. When we left the lounge bar, we walked back to the town centre. When I asked Johnny if he was walking back home up the hill, he said he was. I gulped and checked my watch: Friday, 3pm. I felt helpless, like a small child lost in a huge scary crowd. As I sucked in a sharp breath, Johnny glanced at me.

'Ah, come here, Missus,' he said and hugged me again.

We pulled apart and I watched Johnny walk off towards Trinity Hill, as he would have at that time on that Friday afternoon, eight months before.

* * *

Shona stuck to her word and arranged a meeting with Bobby's former business partners. We met late one morning in a hotel in Birmingham. My friend Vish came along with me as my support and witness to the discussions. I was exceptionally apprehensive about the meeting so I prepared as best I could. As Shona, Vish and I sat there waiting, my heart lurched as they walked in. I had to remain composed, I needed to understand what was happening with Bobby's business and if there really was any money owed to him.

After the initial pleasantries and discussion about their shock at what had happened, the men relayed how calm and jovial Bobby had been that very morning. How he had talked about how excited he was about the baby. They said they thought we were happy – they had struggled with why he did it. Then they said something that shocked me: they told how they had asked Bobby to leave the business the previous October. They had found he had been taking money, accumulating to a few thousand pounds, out of the business without discussing it, so it was agreed he would quit his director position and they agreed a pay-off equating to the time when he began to discuss the 'dividend' he was going to give me. But it wasn't a dividend, he was losing his business and never told me. I then remembered how he once flared up at me when we discussing this 'dividend' and I said I was stressed about money.

He turned on me and said, 'You think *you're* stressed about money. I potentially am going to lose everything I have worked for the last few years.'

I remember stopping in my tracks and asking him what he meant, but he brushed it off and retracted what he said. But he was telling me the truth. He had blurted out something he wanted to keep secret from me: he would have no money, no income and no business. Instead of talking and us working something out, he chose to keep it from me.

The partners said they were still happy to pay the money and it could go to me if they had Bobby's written agreement on this. Shona later sorted that out and it was forwarded to them. She also wrote up all the notes from the meeting and whilst we signed them, to solidify an agreement on the points discussed, neither of his former business partners did.

No money has ever been paid.

Chapter 32

'Your Scars are
Your Stripes'

I know that you show a brave face, but let me tell you that I know that you have the strength inside you to get through this. I know that the scars I have inflicted are your stripes. And that you will get through this as the she-wolf that you are.

I love you
Bobby

Yes, you read that correctly. Bobby really did email, telling me he knows I have the strength to get through this situation and that the scars he inflicted with a carving knife whilst trying to murder me are my stripes, my badge of honour. This was after he had told me that he missed me more than he could explain. According to him, I most definitely didn't deserve this and he kindly reminded me again that '*You are not perfect, but you are perfect for me.*' Well, I'm so glad I have such supportive life-coaching comments from the man who tried his best to end my life and that of my baby!

The emails were the result of a couple of interactions we

had after I had met with his business partners. I emailed him with an update from the meeting and then sent a second email, thanking him for sending through the consent regarding payment to me so quickly. The first email reply told me how he ached to see me and how he had cried on our anniversary. I too had suffered and noted the anniversary in my own way. On 18 October, I had driven to the prison for the first time and parked opposite it. As I leant against my car, staring up at the vast brick walls and barbed wire, a surreal feeling engulfed me to know he was somewhere behind that wall.

So close, but in reality, a world away.

The second email I sent poured out my grief: how hard I was finding it without him, how I missed him and wished it was different. I was grieving the loss of him so badly. It was the second email that prompted the reply above. He probably did me a huge favour as my despair and engulfing grief soon turned to pure anger. Disabled left hand or not, the keyboard was soon on fire as I typed out a reply.

I started by asking why he felt the need to keep telling me I'm not perfect. None of us are and I've never professed to be. Plus, after what he had done, it was actually quite insulting for him to say this to me. Then I addressed the part about my scars,

To describe the horrific scars/disfigurement you've inflicted on me as my 'stripes' is pretty sick. You think they are my badge of honour, my proof of survival? Something to be proud of? You've permanently damaged me, left me with twenty-four disfiguring stab wounds. Please, at least show a bit of respect.

I went on to ask why, if he loved me so much, did he do it? I believed that he feared being revealed as the failed man who had lied about everything and it was all unravelling, so he tried to dispose of Leah and me in a desperate bid to stop that happening.

I talked about how it could have been, how I would have supported him through everything. I described my conversation with the child specialists, who advised I told Leah about what happened from a young age – '*You've devastated so much.*'

My hurt was raw and it fell from the page like water streaming from a tap over it. Tears spilled down my cheeks onto the keyboard as I hit 'send', the disbelief I felt unbound.

It took time to get a response. When it came, he talked about the fact he hadn't got a date for when I was due to come in, but it looked unlikely to be this side of Christmas. He then turned to the matter of the last email,

> *I do think you should be proud of what you have been through, as you have come through it and I know that it is not over for you. I know that it is a process and that you may never be where you were before and I am sorry that I am the cause of that. So, be proud of the scars and take strength in all the good things that people say to you. Because this is how you are seen by everyone. You are strong, you are beautiful. You are the best person I know. And I know it means nothing, but I am proud of you.*

As I pored over each word, his familiar scrawl across the page, I was angry, hurt and confused: he was so detached from what he had done. If you read the emails you wouldn't believe he had launched such a violent attack on me. It was all so wholly wrong. He was mentally unstable still, of this I was sure.

But the emotional battering from Bob's emails could not stop daily life and whilst still in October, Mum, Leah and I made a trip up to RAF Cosford. Midlands Air Ambulance Charity had asked to capture a photo of myself with Steve Mitchell, the paramedic, and Richard Steele, the pilot with the helicopter, G-OMAA, which had airlifted me, for an article about my fundraising. As I walked across the air field to the distinctive red and yellow helicopter, my stomach flipped and tears filled my eyes. They opened up the aircraft and pulled out the stretcher I had been loaded on and it all came flooding back: the monitors, the tight space. My heart raced as I was transported back to 4 March.

When I eventually sat back in my car, I took a deep breath as I started the engine up. Mum glanced across to me.

'Are you OK?' she said.

I just nodded. I couldn't break, but I was becoming exhausted with the emotional pain. It felt as if I was in some endurance race and the finish line still nowhere in sight. Mentally tired, but having to keep going – there was no other choice.

Before I knew it, my regular follow-up hospital appointments came round. First, with the gynaecology team at the Women's Hospital to check my recovery. After being told I would have difficulties having another baby, I said not to worry as I didn't want any more children as I have three and 'let's be honest, the last pregnancy didn't work out well for me!' I asked for a sterilisation and after a short discussion was consented and booked in for January 2017. A key decision about my life – taken by me, completely by me, for me.

Whilst I waited for that surgery, I was back at the QE for more hand surgery. This was to be a tricky operation as the blood supply was starting to become compromised and I risked amputation of my little finger. The surgery was done under nerve block again and the finger fused. It was the end of the line for what they could do, but they had done their very best. I now had to adapt with a functionally useless dominant hand for life.

On the day I had been in surgery, the victim liaison officers Catherine and Bernadette had been in HMP Birmingham, visiting Bobby. It wasn't long before they were back at my house to update me. My disappointment was visible as my face dropped when they told me I still couldn't see him yet. He was still very detached from what he had done and said little about the actual attack. His 'protected' life in prison seemed to add to his denial of the atrocity of the situation.

I knew from his sister he was on the vulnerable person wing, protected from the mainstream of prisoners. He had a phone in his cell, which allowed him to call his mother and sisters on a bi-daily basis and was now a mentor, helping other prisoners learn English and Maths! His family visited every weekend.

Bernadette and Catherine concluded, as previously, if I saw him now, I would not get out of the visit what I wanted or needed. At this I exploded. Even if Bobby didn't say anything, I had to face him – I wanted to put it all to bed before the chimes rang out on 31 December 2016. But I could see that slipping away. My frustration came spilling out as I told them in no uncertain terms that I wanted to talk about this with someone higher up the authority line. It was affecting my mental health and, for closure, I had to see him.

They listened and nodded as I sobbed and ranted. I look

back at this moment with a degree of shame. They were doing their very best for me, but I was so upset and frustrated, I couldn't see that – I just wanted some control back in my life. I knew I was going to have to accept the fact I wasn't going to see him this year, but I would keep fighting.

The bad news kept coming too. I was officially informed that Leah's Criminal Injury compensation claim would not be considered. The Criminal Injury Compensation Authority (CICA) did not recognise my daughter as a person in her own right. The fact that she had been in the womb at the point of the attack in their eyes meant she could not be the direct victim of that crime. I was incensed! I was over thirty-six weeks pregnant at the time of the attack, she was a viable person. He had put the knife into my stomach with the express intention of trying to kill her, something he had pleaded guilty to in court and been convicted for. It was a matter of principle: any compensation paid out to her would automatically be placed in a trust fund for when she was eighteen. Leah had experienced the worst possible start in life and would have to live with what her father did for the rest of her life. She at least deserved to be recognised as the victim of that attack as much as me.

And so I instructed a Criminal Injuries lawyer and he launched a case for me. This was a battle: justice for Leah and for other unborn children directly affected by a criminal act whilst in the womb.

Chapter 33

'We Wish You a Merry Christmas'

WINTER WAS NOW SETTING IN AND THE WORST YEAR OF MY
LIFE DRAWING TO A CLOSE. I HAD BEGUN THE YEAR BELIEVING
A NEW LIFE WAS STARTING FOR ME, BUT CERTAINLY NOT THE
one that transpired. My marriage plans and 'complete'
family picture had been brutally snatched away but I had
another beautiful addition to my brood and still so much
to be thankful for.

With this positive mindset I fulfilled another of my
original goals: a tattoo to celebrate my survival. I had
always wanted one so I went off to the studio to sit with
an incredible artist who I found online, Marius. After
some discussion we agreed on a guardian angel with three
butterflies encircling it to represent the guardian angel
who I felt watched down on me that day, the butterflies
representing my children. The butterfly representing Leah
was to be positioned next to the stab wound which just
missed her. It was well into the following year before I got it
done, but it was something I did for me and, with that, I felt
empowered. I was finding some glimmers of that original

spirit of Natalie. The Natalie who had been destroyed, but was now determined to rise stronger, brighter and with more purpose than ever before.

With the surge of empowerment from this appointment, I went on to talk at a charity ball held by some of the mums I knew locally. One of them had tragically lost her beautiful baby boy to a rare genetic condition and in his memory held an annual ball to raise funds for the Birmingham Children's Hospital. That year, they decided to split the proceeds with the Midlands Air Ambulance Charity because of what had happened to me.

Humbled by this, I invited my two protectors, Johnny and Tony, with whom I was still in contact. Tony unfortunately could not come, but Johnny was available. It was amazing to be there with my friends and to have Johnny there with his partner was the icing on the cake. At the start of the evening, I stood up and said a few words. I hadn't planned very much, so it was mainly off the cuff. The response was heartwarming – Johnny received a standing ovation when I referred to the fact that he was actually there that evening. Throughout the night people came up to talk, offering words of support, encouragement or to relay their memory of that day. At times I felt overwhelmed, but then my friend Harrie took me outside for some space. It was a wonderful night, and I had taken another step: I had been public about my attack and talked to people who remembered what happened.

Whilst on this trajectory of positive momentum I attended a speaker workshop with the inspiring Richard McCann, son of the first victim of Peter Sutcliffe, the renowned 'Yorkshire Ripper'. Richard had lost his mother at a very young age and his life met many challenges since.

He has built himself up into an international motivational speaker, who runs workshops on developing speaker skills and empowerment and has written three books. He invited me to be a guest at one of his his workshops.

On 9 December, I drove myself up there. I had no idea who I was going to meet that day, how I would feel sharing my story in front of complete strangers and interacting all day in a foreign environment on my own without panicking. After a short pep talk to myself in the car, I pushed open the door with my shoulder and stepped out into the bracing cold wind and crossed the car park to the hotel lobby. My eyes searched around and, after a short moment, I recognised Richard from photos I had seen of him. He gave me a warm welcome and introduced me to a couple of people who had arrived already.

I sat nervously on the edge of a huge sofa and rubbed my hands together whilst looking down and waiting for the others in the workshop to arrive. We all had different stories to tell and many different reasons for being there. I met some amazing people that day and one of the girls, Sarah, I still have contact with to this day. Standing up and speaking about my experience made me realise that it was still so raw, but I could do it and I could really add impact to people's lives by sharing. I felt an energy run through me as I took to the floor. That day, Richard's workshop cemented in my mind the path I wanted to travel: taking my story and experience, sharing it and hopefully inspiring others to fight through adversity themselves.

With the workshop firmly under my belt and supporting my plans and vision of my future, I suddenly realised how Christmas was nearly upon us. Determined to make this the best I possibly could, I decorated the house until parts could have passed as Santa's grotto. The kids loved it! Key occasions can trigger tough emotions, though. Once more, Isabel hit a brick wall with it all. It was clear the hurt and confusion in her head was not only significant still, but not dissimilar to my own. I guess I shouldn't have been surprised at the enormity of it all to her when I myself couldn't process it and I had thirty-plus years of life experience on top of her! Both she and Emily were getting support through professional support services. The initial damage was done to them. As a mother, every instinct makes you want to be able to take the pain away from your children and I couldn't completely and never would be able to. At least I could get them every piece of support they needed and that is what I ploughed on with.

About a week before Christmas news of the riots in HMP Birmingham broke. My stomach turned.

Riots? How bad?

As my fingers fumbled at my phone to Google what was happening, my instinct, foolishly, was to worry about him. There were reports that segregation had been breached. I slept horrifically that night, cursing myself for even caring. The riots resolved and eventually a message came from Bobby via his family to say he was safe and completely unaffected. I was angry with myself for the stress I put myself through with the news – I guess I still loved the man I thought I knew and it would take a lot of time to change.

On the day of the riots, I ironically received communication from Catherine from Probation. She had received an email a couple of days before from HMP Birmingham and things seemed to be moving on a step, except now the riots had struck. A sure spanner in the works on gaining any access to the prison.

Before I knew it, Christmas Eve had arrived and the children were bouncing around, like pop from a shaken bottle ready to explode. The agreement had been a Christmas film for us all to watch together in our PJs, with Mum around in the late afternoon/early evening to settle them down. About halfway through the film, the doorbell rang. I prised myself from between my two very snuggly older daughters and peeped out the window, the curtains still wide open despite the night having drawn in: it was Ian. Still cautious about anyone just turning up at the house, relief passed through me. As I opened the door, I was greeted by a confused-looking Ian, his hands full with two large gift bags.

'Er, I thought all your presents were already here?' I questioned him.

'These aren't from me, they were left outside your porch. Did someone ring the bell?' he replied, sounding slightly confused.

No, I didn't remember hearing the doorbell nor seeing anyone on the drive. I took the bags from him and as he sauntered into the front room to see the kids, I carried them through to the kitchen. As I pulled out the cards, my worst fears were confirmed: it was Bobby's family, his mother to be precise. I opened a card to Leah from her and tears filled my eyes:

My dearest sweet Leah,
I am your dado (grandmother) though I have only
seen you in photos & I can tell that you are the most
beautiful & I love you very much. You are always in
my thoughts, my heart & in my dmas (prayers). May
Allah give you the happiest life full of joy, health, may

*you be the star & shine forever. I know one day Allah
willing I will meet you and will hug you so hard &
will never let you go.*

With love & kisses Dado xxxxxxxx

*What?! A happy life full of joy and health, after her precious
son – whom she supported – nearly murdered her?! I also
think she will find it is Natalie willing, not Allah, as to
whether she meets her.*

I was angry and upset. She had written cards to us all.
Then there was an additional card to Leah.

Surely not?

I tore open the envelope. It was a handmade card,
beautifully drawn holly with red berries on the front, with
the words 'Merry Christmas'. I opened it up and retched: it
was from Bobby.

*Dear Leah
I hope that you have a fabulous Christmas.
I love you more than I could ever say, I miss you and
I am very sorry.
Love Abu* [father]

That finished me, the tears flowed freely down my cheeks. I
ran into the utility room and sobbed into a towel to muffle
any sound. Ian came through, wondering why I hadn't
rejoined them, to find my tear-stained face and puffy eyes. I
chucked the cards at him and, as his eyes scanned them, he
shook his head in disbelief.

I looked through the presents but didn't open them.
His mother must have been to the house whilst we were
watching the film. She must have walked up my drive and

dropped them by the door. It was Christmas Eve. Bobby said she never recognised Christmas. I couldn't believe she had actually come to the house – she wouldn't come near when we lived here together.

I took the bags, along with the cards, upstairs and shoved them into one of my wardrobes – I was not going to look at them anymore, I had spent too much time away from the kids. I needed to get our Christmas Eve back on track, that family had ruined enough already.

The rest of Christmas was family focused. The house was full of family and it was magnificent. Jane, Andy, Louise and Ben joined us in the celebrations with Mum and Ian. The kids had a wonderful time with their cousins. Leah was slightly bemused by it all, but kept up her usual smiley face. I couldn't help but reflect on what had been happening that same time the previous year when Bobby had been 'stuck' in Pakistan. Except he hadn't – he had chosen to be there for a family wedding. He had chosen to lie to me and let me down without warning. I had shed so many tears that Christmas and to think he was spending this one in a prison cell, it was all too surreal.

Between Christmas and New Year, Leah had her routine follow-up with the paediatric neurologist to assess her development. The specialist felt her range of sounds was limited. She was still choking easily on food, probably related to the lack of muscle development in her mouth. I had always known the attack and subsequent oxygen starvation might cause such delays but with the reality starting to show, it was hard not to feel slightly overwhelmed again. She was such a happy baby and looked so perfect, it was difficult to comprehend that she might have any difficulties, but it was a medical fact that we just didn't know at this stage.

As the next few days passed, New Year's Eve soon arrived. A real landmark point in time as it marked the final day of 2016, a year I would never forget. Annabel was holding a house party and it had long been organised that I would go completely child-free. Before I headed off, I walked with another good friend of mine to Trinity Hill. I had written a note on a card and attached it to some flowers to lay on Nicola Dixon's memorial to mark her anniversary. As I lay them down, I spoke quietly to Nicola, thanking her, as I believed she had been watching over me that day. Maybe she was my guardian angel. Already there was a host of flowers there, probably because this year marked twenty years since her brutal murder. As my friend nodded towards the hill, my eyes widened with fear and I shook my head.

He smiled and said, 'Go on, walk it today as you leave the year – I'm with you.'

I thought about it and then shakily took his hand and we walked down. I felt physically ill and the screaming and shouts from that day in March rang through my ears. But with a reassuring hand, my friend walked me to the bottom.

I did it!

That evening we headed to Annabel's. The party was in full swing when we arrived and I felt slightly overwhelmed by the attention I received. I didn't drink too much as I was aware my emotions were fully heightened. As the clock struck midnight, the roar of the party went up and people leapt around shouting, 'Happy New Year!'

Tears streamed down my cheeks. It was as if I was in a parallel universe, watching them celebrate from outside some glass box containing them all and their merriment. The emotion of letting go of 2016 hit me like a train. For a few moments I stepped away from the main party and allowed myself to cry. My friend followed me and drew me into a hug as I sobbed quietly on his shoulder.

'Happy New Year, Nat,' he whispered. 'You keep fighting and show everyone what you can do in this year ahead. You've already come so far.'

I nodded, had one last hug, then pulled away. After I had wiped my eyes we joined the chaotic group, arms linked, for 'Auld Lang Syne' and as the remnants of 2016 washed away in time, 2017 started with a vengeance.

Chapter 34

New Year, New Goals

THE YEAR 2017 STARTED OFF SPECTACULARLY, ALTHOUGH NOT IN A WAY ANYONE WOULD HAVE PLANNED OR HOPED FOR. I WOKE ON 1 JANUARY, VIOLENTLY ILL WITH A STOMACH bug. Not quite the successful start to the year I planned, but a great excuse to stay in bed all day! As I lay staring at the pillow and ceiling alternately, I planned some goals/rules to live by (note: I am not using the word 'resolutions'!).

To get more sleep
To eat well
To continue to exercise and get stronger and fitter
To enjoy happy moments and create special memories
    with my children
To enjoy life now
To do what I have to do to get the life I want.

A couple of days into New Year and I was off to the Birmingham Women's Hospital for my sterilisation. I hadn't asked anyone to come with me as I didn't want to put them out and in some ways I needed to do this part of the journey on my own. It became a decision I soon regretted as I sat alone in the waiting room whilst everyone had someone else with them as support. Annabel by chance sent me a text and, after a short discussion, she arrived when I was out having the procedure. She took me home and as I lay resting that evening with a hot water bottle, I reflected how in such a short time period, I had undergone a life-changing event: no more children for me. But I didn't need any more, my three are amazing! I had taken back another bit of control of my future.

The next day I was back on my feet as normal and carried on building towards my goals and future. I had a phone call booked with Katie Piper and her charity manager, Ezinna. They were still so supportive and Katie gave advice on how she went about writing, publishing and getting into motivational speaking. As I came off the call, I reflected how surreal my life was. Here I was, discussing my future with the amazing Katie Piper! Never could I have foreseen I would be doing that, twelve months before.

A week later, my upbeat mood hit a slight slump and late one evening, I found myself composing an email to Bobby. No matter how much I wanted to forget him, my head and heart battled daily. I wrote about how I truly believed him to be mentally ill, how he put on a false persona to the outside world, how he had spent his life pretending to be someone he wasn't, that he had no real substance. I talked about how detached he seemed from what he had done and although in some ways I felt that I couldn't be bothered to fight to see him any more as my life was moving on, I still wanted him to look me in the eye. I mentioned the fact I had received no financial support and pointed out that I was doing all this on my own and he could at least have the balls/decency to sort out money as best he could from there. It was nearly midnight as I typed the final line. I hovered the mouse over the 'save' button, but tiredness overtook me and before I knew it, I had clicked the adjacent 'send' button.

A surge of adrenaline went through me and I sat bolt upright. I had always read through emails I sent him carefully before pressing 'send', yet the most important one I had ever written had been sent to flit off through the ether without a second glance. When I searched through my sent list, there it was: gone.

Maybe it was good thing. It would be in the hands of a prison officer before I knew it. I didn't know if they would pass it on to him after they had checked it as it may have been classed as far too contentious.

With Bobby and the prison at the forefront of my mind, I called Catherine at the probation victim support team. The probation team linked to the prison hadn't even been in to see Bobby yet to talk to him about my visit and make their assessment as to whether it would be allowed. This was definitely going to be a long process, but I had made a pact with myself that I would fight this every step of the way. Chasing, following up, asking what else could be done, I would get in to see him: one day, one way.

As January wore on, I had further meetings with the Midlands Air Ambulance Charity team to discuss my next fundraising challenges. Within one meeting, I found myself agreeing to – and subsequently signing up to – a 240ft abseil off one of the tallest buildings in Birmingham and agreeing to undertake the longest zip-line in Europe, based in Snowdon! Another JustGiving needed to be set up for donations. Recently, I had received an email from JustGiving about my fundraising efforts the year before, informing me that I was in the top one per cent of all their fundraisers for 2016. Later, I learnt I was actually the No. 1 individual fundraiser on JustGiving for Midlands Air Ambulance Charity in 2016. I was elated to have taken that place, although not as happy as I had been about the money raised for the charity in the first place.

In addition to these fundraising challenges, we discussed the video still to be made to explain my attack, airlift and recovery. A video that would be used at their fundraising events to really drive home how important the charity is and the difference it makes. For Leah and me, it was the difference between life and death. However, the video required my anonymity being lifted. At the first plea hearing of Bobby's case, the judge had imposed a reporting restriction on both myself and the children's names and images to help protect the children from the media. My photo and name had been everywhere in the press by that point, the internet full of images of myself with my name alongside the story of what happened so, for me, it was all too late. Applying for my anonymity to be lifted (but not the children's) would allow me to publicly raise funds for the Midlands Air Ambulance through using my story as an example of their work so I carefully constructed an email to the courts, laying out a reasoned argument. I was warned it might not be an easy process, but it was something I was determined to challenge. Just after the anniversary, the ban was lifted!

The good news kept rolling in after this as I met with my breast surgeon and got the green light to have my surgery. For almost a year I had lived with a deformed chest, saggy scarred skin, with hardly any breast tissue to fill it. I was a step closer to getting myself back to how I wanted to be, the old Natalie...feminine. An incredibly caring lady, Colette, from my health insurance fought to get me support with the cost and, amazingly, the company showed their true integrity and agreed to cover the cost. Surgery was booked for the day after my abseil – what a weekend it was going to be!

Chapter 35

First Birthdays and First Anniversaries

BEFORE I KNEW IT, FEBRUARY SET IN AND THE FIRST ANNIVERSARY WAS APPROACHING RAPIDLY. FIRST, THERE WAS THE HURDLE OF MY BIRTHDAY. I REFLECTED HOW ONLY twelve months earlier, Bobby and I had been away in London for my fortieth – I was so happy, life seemed so perfect with the man I adored and our baby on the way. My heart ached at the memory. A wave of grief came crashing over me and as I met with Anna, my psychologist, and sobbed at the loss, she suggested I should write another letter to Bobby. With terrible shaky handwriting, I scribbled out a short note to him; it was barely legible but he was never going to receive it. In it, I talked about all the details I missed, each envisaged clearly in my mind. Tears streamed down my face as I laid bare each memory. I wrote how I literally grieved inside and how I had believed he was my soulmate. I described the small hole which would always be left in my heart, but told him I had to say goodbye to him now.

On the day before my birthday, a card arrived in the post addressed to Leah Karamat. It was from Bobby's mother.

I was appalled. For a start she knew that was not Leah's surname and I had to question if it really was a coincidence it arrived the day before my birthday. She talked about how Leah was a part of her and she thought about her every day. I chucked the card to one side – I had an overload of that family in my head for the time being.

My birthday came and went. The children did an amazing job of treating me, starting with breakfast in bed made by their own fair hands. It was, however, a tough day from the moment I opened my eyes, yet together we got through it. It wasn't long after my birthday when Isabel started to crash emotionally. Akin to my feelings with the anniversary approaching and the memories that my birthday had brought being our final happy family moments all together brought tremendous grief and confusion. Isabel feared for my safety and even at school she was breaking down in tears. The school called me in to talk and I went on to gain even further support for her. I realised how deep the damage Bobby had done and it hurt immensely.

As I pushed on to hold things together and just less than a week away from Leah's first birthday and the first anniversary of the attack, another card from Bobby's mother dropped through the door, addressed once more to Leah Karamat and sounding even more desperate than the last. She had to step back so I called Bobby's sister Shona to make it clear how I felt. She advised me she was aware of a card coming from Bobby to Leah for her birthday. I had asked the probation team to tell the prison that nothing should come from Bobby to Leah, but the system somewhere clearly wasn't listening to the victim. I told Shona that the card must be stopped and nothing should come from any of them. She said she would do her best but she wasn't sure where it was. I was well aware it would be a mixed day as I marked the anniversary of a terrifying life-changing event as well as celebrating the life and first birthday of my precious daughter.

I didn't need any more pressure.

I carefully planned out how the anniversary would be marked and Leah's birthday celebrated – I wanted to make sure my grief did not overtake the key fact it was Leah's day and made it clear that I did not want to spend it in Sutton Coldfield. After school collection on the day before, the children and I went straight up to Derby to stay at my sister Jane's. I had planned a party, family and close friends gathering to celebrate Leah's birthday.

Morning broke and, as usual, Leah had me up at the crack of dawn. Her sleeping pattern wasn't going to miss a 5am wake-up call, especially on her big day.

'Happy Birthday, baby!'

I beamed at her little face staring at me through the bars of her cot, dummy poking out her mouth and little bits of hair sticking in all directions. *She's beautiful and perfect*, I mused. She raised her arms up towards me to let me know she wanted me to pick her up, so I hauled myself off the bed and scooped her into a tight hug, breathing in the top of her head. Tears prickled in my eyes: 365 days since I had stirred in my sleep and snuggled into her father, happy and content, with no idea about how the day was going to unfold. Just hours later, I was to be fighting for my life. How our baby was to be delivered and how Bobby was about to start a long period of his life incarcerated. How much could change in just one day, that day becoming an indelible mark on my life.

It should all have been so different. He should have

been here for his daughter's first birthday, one of her first major milestones.

The emotional pain tore through me, taking my breath away. I felt myself crumble and flopped onto the bed, still cradling Leah. Silent tears fell on the top of her head as she nuzzled tighter into my chest. My job was clear: he had bowed out of his duty, his responsibility, but I was mum to this amazing little person as well as two other amazing not so little people, and that role was the most important job I would ever have. I had to nurture and protect all three of them. From the moment they were born I had always sworn to do so and done exactly that, and I had fought to stay alive to continue doing just that throughout their lives.

As we neared 6.30am my head started to play out the time plan of what had happened the year before. Like a play, it all acted out in my mind. Except this time I was a bystander. I mentally screamed at myself: I could see myself completely unsuspecting, the completely trusting prey of the manipulative predator. My head searched each scene from my memory bank to see if I had missed any detail. Was there something I just hadn't picked up on? But no, everything seemed 'normal'. It was terrifying to recall. Life was so spookily normal yet he was coldly and callously building up to murdering me and our baby.

My musings were shattered by the door being flung open and my other two daughters came pounding into the room and jumped on the bed.

'Happy Birthday, Leah!' they chanted, enveloping her in cuddles.

After much nagging to get out of bed, the girls dragged me downstairs and into the kitchen, where a pile of presents awaited the birthday belle. Leah was mainly a spectator of her present opening as her sisters tore through the cards and gifts. Mum called to sing 'Happy Birthday' down the phone, a tradition of her's (she was coming up later that morning). I asked her to pop into my house on the way up, just to check if anything had arrived from Bobby or his family – I didn't want to return home on the Sunday to find anything waiting for me.

The rest of the day was spent getting ready for the party. Mum arrived late morning. I looked anxiously out of the window as she arrived and held my breath as I waited to see if anything had come from the family. She shook her head slightly, knowing what I was waiting for, and relief flushed through me – at least they seemed to have listened. In the afternoon the house filled with guests. I became fixated on the clock, giving myself the same mental time-check prompts of where I was that day, twelve months before. As we neared 3.10pm, my mobile bleeped: it was Johnny, texting to say he was around the corner. I couldn't believe the timing. As he walked in, I collapsed into a huge hug with him and tears spilled from my eyes once more.

Poor Johnny was then faced with the barrage of my family. Not only had he arrived at the exact time point of my attack when I had first 'met' him, twelve months before, but my family, who had been desperate to meet him and were feeling highly emotional, soon swamped him. It must have been quite overwhelming.

After Leah and I blew out her birthday candles following a rapturous round of 'Happy Birthday' and 'Hip, hip hoorays', I proposed a toast to Johnny in recognition of the fact he was one of the key reasons we could all be here on this special day. We exchanged glances, knowing how important this moment was, and a slight look of 'Thanks for embarrassing me' came from Johnny.

Everyone stayed on until fairly late in the evening. Johnny and I hugged goodbye as night started to set in. I settled the kids into their beds and once everyone was gone, I was truly wrung out: not only had I lived the day of the party but re-lived the day from a year ago. I had cried, tried to laugh, but overall celebrated a very special miracle child who had survived against all odds.

I also gave myself a small mental toast to mark the fact that I too had survived and was still here standing, one year on.

Chapter 36

Moving On Up

A SMALL VOID OPENED UP AFTER THE ANNIVERSARY. THE FIRST YEAR HAD PASSED AND A LONELINESS SET IN AS THE REALISATION IT WAS NOW ONLY ME TAKING NOTE OF the milestones as they came around again. Of course, there were first milestones still to meet, but these meant more to me than anyone else. After all, 23 June 2016 was far better known as the day the UK went to the polls and voted to leave the EU than the day Babur Karamat Raja was sentenced!

I could not stay in the past, though. New shoots from seeds I had already planted were starting to grow and I had to nurture them. Other positive branches stretched out from the carnage too as it was announced the members of the public who jumped in to wrestle Bobby from me were to receive national awards from the Royal Humane Society, as well as Police Bravery Awards. The police officers involved on the day and in the investigation would also be receiving police recognition awards. I was asked to help give out the awards with the Chief Constable, which of course I agreed to. The award date was set for May 2017.

Alongside those awards, I had the honour of being invited to the Pride of Birmingham awards ceremony. The Midlands Air Ambulance Charity crew were to be given the Emergency Service of the Year award. Such a deserved honour! I filmed an interview for them to use on the night at one of the Air Ambulance airbases. I took all three children with me so they could see one of the helicopters close up, something they had never done before. It was a fun but long and emotional day.

By the time we got to the awards, life had struck another blow with the devastating unexpected loss of my uncle in Wales, a man who I regarded as a second dad. The awards ceremony fell in the days before the funeral. I knew he would have wanted me to still be there despite the utter heartbreak I felt over his loss. The ceremony was filled with incredible people who have done incredible acts helping others. Mixed in between was a plethora of celebrities, most of whom I had to explain to my mum who they were! Katie Piper hosted the evening and it gave me the opportunity at last to meet her face to face, along with her lovely charity manager, Ezinna. I proudly went onstage with the crew when their award was given out and reflected afterwards how lucky I was to have been part of it all.

Good truly can come out of anything.

Channelling the positive opportunities also followed with the Midlands Air Ambulance case study video. After many months of planning, the time soon came for me to film my section of it. We chose a local hotel as a venue to film the interviews with myself and Mum whilst Leah kept Jo (from the charity) amused in the hotel's lounge area.

I saw the completed film about a month and a half later. The charity invited me to their offices to watch it. It started with scenes from Trinity Hill itself. I took a sharp intake of breath – I was not aware they had filmed there. It was logical, I guess, but seeing the very place I was attacked captured on film was very hard indeed. There was a reconstruction of what happened and my stomach turned: they had filmed Cassie, the officer who kept me alive on the pavement. Seeing her face again made me crumple inside. A box of tissues was slid across the table to me, I gratefully leant forward and took one.

The film included a recording of one of the actual 999 calls made and the communication from Control to the Air Ambulance instructing them of the job. It was so difficult to listen to, knowing it was me they were talking about. The film was full of emotion, with all those involved discussing their memories and views of the day. A real roller coaster, it then lifted into what I had been doing since with my recovery and fundraising. It was fantastically put together and exceptionally impactful. I don't think any of us in the room had a dry eye by the end! We all took a moment to compose and I just nodded that it was brilliant. My key hope, as it always had been with the film, was that it would make a positive difference to fundraising as people clearly see why the service is so key. The film can be found online.

A few days after the film, I wrote to Bobby again. It had been quite a few weeks since I had written the controversial email to him. I hadn't received a reply and was pretty sure it probably hadn't been passed to him. The focus of my latest email was my visit to the prison to face him. I still didn't have agreement from the prison nor a date, so I wanted to ask him directly if he still wanted to see me in case that was where the delay was. I told him how I still wanted to face him so I could at last put the man I loved and adored with the evil attacker on the hill that day – I think the film had really made me think about how calculated his act was and how incredulous I was about it all.

Then, after a long tedious wait (including more hospital appointments to discuss removing the metal from my fused little finger), I at last got the news I'd been waiting for: the prison were now in agreement I could see Bobby, we just had to get a date agreed. It was incredible, I was just a step away! I'd repeatedly imagined walking into the prison and now it was almost a reality.

Chapter 37

A Royal Visit

My Life – The Reality

I look at my life and what do I see?
A life tainted with fear and uncertainty
A life where I cannot just stroll without care
A life where I constantly worry who's there.
A life that blew up that Friday afternoon
A life that had hope with a new family soon.
My old life did end in a terrible way
Where a trusted partner did really betray
The woman who loved him – going to be his wife
The woman who was prepared to accept all the strife.
The strife from his mother who just couldn't approve
As my beliefs didn't match and she just couldn't move
From her deep, set-in culture and all she could see
Was her son only marrying the 'right family'.
I'm left with the legacy of the crime that he did,
My own prison sentence with my littlest kid.
A beautiful girl who one day will learn

Of the horror committed and how her father did turn
Into a monster that none of us knew
Not even his best friends nor family too.
But I won't let it define us
I'll push through the pain,
We will find joy and be happy again.
His act didn't finish us that fateful day
It will all work out and we'll all be OK,
Our lives will get better.
I've discovered new strength
A strength that will push me to a whole new length,
A strength I will build up with every day
I'll see better things, I'll see a new way
To live my life the best that I can
To smile and mean it and forget that man.
He broke my heart, I won't deny
But his act won't define me, no matter what he did try
So I look to the future – I've a long way to climb
But I'll get there eventually, I'll get there in time.
I'll endure all the comments so thoughtlessly made,
The ones to my face or on internet tirade,
'You certainly do pick 'em', have joked quite a few
Well, funny, I didn't know he'd murder – I just never
*   knew!*
People analyse my life and pass comment all the time
From my weight to my appearance or decisions that
*   were mine.*
I'll never be perfect, I'll still make mistakes
But I'll live life to the max and make the world shake.
So, be prepared for the Queiroz who isn't down yet
I just need my reboot and every challenge will be met!

Another expression of how I felt, in poetry form this time. Turbulent feelings swirled and crashed around inside of me. I had so many positive things to look forward to and be grateful for, but the hurt, betrayal and grief of everything I had experienced emotionally crippled me. Therapy was still weekly and critical to my sanity.

But positivity kept fighting the battle hard. Johnny had been selected, based on his act of bravery in tackling Bobby, to attend one of HM The Queen's Garden Parties. I felt extremely honoured when he asked me to go along with him. He said he had talked to his partner about it and they both agreed it was most appropriate that I went with him. A relatively strict dress code was enclosed in the invitation, so a new dress and hat were in order!

And the good news kept coming. At last I had the call I had been waiting for: victim liaison officer Catherine phoned with a confirmed date to visit HMP Birmingham to face Bobby. After all this time, this was it. My heart raced. There was joy that I had at last hit my ultimate goal of getting to face him and unease at the reality that in a matter of weeks I would walk through the entrance and into the Victorian stone buildings of HMP Birmingham. Friday, 9 June 2017 was the date set – 463 days since we had last been in close contact, sixty-six weeks since he plunged the knife into me. I would be sat opposite him in a meeting room, making him look me in the eye. There was so much to prepare if I was to ensure every minute of that meeting counted.

Catherine and her colleague Bernadette arranged to meet me at my house to discuss the visit with one of the prison officers – Gemma – who would be there on the day too. I started to put together an agenda of things I wanted to cover and questions I had, such as whether I could take photos of my clothes, my injuries and pictures of Leah. They came to see me on 9 May, one month before the big visit. We discussed everything, from the minutiae of the day, such as where I would meet Catherine and Bernadette, what would happen when I entered the prison, where would I be taken (it was to take place in an offender rehab meeting room, much deeper in the prison than the standard visitor area) to how he was and what I wanted to talk to him about. They took away my questions to get clarification, especially about the photos. All three were hugely supportive. It was such an unusual case and circumstances: a victim of an attempted murder wanting to see the offender. But I had to see him – I had to make him look me in the eye and talk to me about it. There was so much to go through and some form of closure was what I hoped for. By the time they had all left my house, I felt exhausted, every part of me wrung out. But I was nearly there, almost at that point so important to reach, so I had to keep going.

Luckily, I had a few milestones to pass through, which kept the time moving to 9 June. On Saturday, 13 May, I donned my Wonder Woman T-shirt and special Wonder Woman pants over my leggings, pulled on my Wonder Woman trainer socks and trainers and set off to Birmingham for my 240ft abseil off the top of one of the high-rise hotels. I did it with a fantastic group of people and as we mounted the final stairs, the reality hit as I looked over the edge at all my friends and family below, who had come to support me: it was a long way down! As I waited to be harnessed up, I strolled around the top of the building, looking across the concrete sea surrounding me. I soon worked out which direction roughly HMP Birmingham was, and as I nervously took myself over the edge of the building and steadied myself on the rope, I lifted the middle finger of my free hand in the direction of the prison and muttered, 'F**k you, Karamat!' Not particularly ladylike, I know, but it made me feel a whole heap better – he hadn't broken me and he wasn't going to break me.

The kids came leaping towards me as soon as my feet touched the ground and I couldn't have asked for a warmer welcome than the one I received from my children, family and friends. That evening, however, the calmness I had displayed at the top of a 240ft drop soon started to dissipate. The operation to reinsert my implants was scheduled for first thing in the morning and the thought of more surgery, especially in my chest, which had been so badly damaged in the attack, made me nervous. There was no guarantee how the operation would turn out, but I had to do it: it was about my self-perception.

As I lay in the anaesthetic room the next morning, my heart pounded. Anxiety raced through my veins but, before I knew it, I was out cold and then being stirred by a friendly nurse. I could barely move – there was a drain coming out of each side of me and the pain was already intense. When I spoke to the surgeon later, she told me that it had gone better than expected, but there had been a lot of scar tissue to cut through. The drains would be in for a full week and antibiotics were key. My chest 'reconstruction' wasn't perfect, but I knew it couldn't be – I was never going to look how I was before, but that was just part of the acceptance of the new me.

Thankfully, the drains were removed just before I was due to go to London with Johnny for the Garden Party at Buckingham Palace. As we sat on the train, I pulled out a couple of mini bottles of Prosecco and, complete with straws to add to the classiness of it all, we toasted our trip and settled in for the journey. When we arrived at Buckingham Palace, security was top-level as it would always have been but, additionally, the atrocious attack at the Manchester Arena had happened the night before at the Ariana Grande concert – countless innocent people killed or seriously injured by the diabolical action of one person.

Johnny and I soon found ourselves queuing with hundreds of others to get into Buckingham Palace. As we stood clutching our invitations, it reminded me of the scene from *Charlie and the Chocolate Factory* as the lucky winners of the sacred Golden Tickets stood anxiously waiting outside the wondrous factory with all its secrets held within. As we walked through the courtyard, we both looked at each other with a mix of nerves and excitement: we were about to step into Buckingham Palace! After passing briefly through a small part of the palace, we stepped out into the huge gardens behind. Tents were laid out, where we were provided with a selection of small savouries, cakes and cups of tea – all highly civilized, as one would expect.

When it came to the Queen and Prince Philip stepping out, the crowd gathered around the base of the steps leading down from the palace. I was taken by how the Queen is so relatively small in stature but her presence creates a huge aura around her. She was followed by Prince Charles and Camilla and a few other royals and dignitaries.

After the royals had disappeared to the royal tent to take tea, Johnny and I walked around the vast gardens. It was like a protected paradise, surreal that you were standing in the centre of London. We made our way home late afternoon, both exhausted but exhilarated by such an amazing experience.

Once home, the repercussions of the terror attacks were felt everywhere as the terror alert was at its highest level. As a consequence, the Police Bravery Awards were postponed to allow all officers to be available for extra duty. A stark reality of the world we live in nowadays, where adaptability to the rapidly changing environment was key.

Before I knew it, I was into June and just a week away from entering the prison. I had final hand surgery booked exactly one week before 'prison day' to have the metal removed from my fused little finger. My chest still hurt, but I pushed on with this important operation. As I walked out of the QE, I accepted that from this point on that I had essentially lost proper function of my dominant left hand forever, but compared to what I might have been left with, I was grateful.

Before I knew it, the countdown was finally up: Friday, 9 June was upon us.

HMP Birmingham, here I come.

Chapter 38

Final Goodbye

I HAD NEVER BEEN IN A PRISON BEFORE, LET ALONE UNDER HORRIFIC CIRCUMSTANCES. THE MORE PREPARED I COULD BE, I FELT, THE BETTER. MY FINAL AGENDA FOR THE MEETING consisted of four sections:

Factual – mainly what actually happened during and just after the attack and discussion of the main lies I had learnt about. Then the crucial question I had to ask – why?

Emotional – the damage he did emotionally, during and after the attack, including the damage to my kids and family.

Leah – thoughts on her? Expectations, family expectations? Why did he try to murder her? The brain injury she's been left with because of the attack and future contact (or lack of it).

Financial – limited funds I had to date. Any compensation from him to me? His business partners and their lack of fulfilment of promises made.

Questions on details filled each section. I had been granted permission by the prison that I could take in photos of my injuries, my clothes and photos of Leah that I might wish to show him. They were all collected together in a bright pink document folder. I felt prepared, business-like – my shield for when I was in there.

In the days before the visit an email arrived from Bobby, telling me he would answer all my questions honestly (*now that would be a first!*) and that he couldn't get hold of his former business partners, but would keep trying. He finished by saying that he would like at some stage to see Leah, but would never fight me to see her if it was against my wishes – he just hoped that he could have some contact with her at some time. He signed off, '*See you next week, Bobby*'. The email had clearly taken a few days to come back to me after he had written it.

Friday, 9 June arrived and I got myself ready. I made sure I looked strong and confident. 'You've got this,' I told my reflection. As I stepped out the front door, the very door I had departed from so innocently that day, I took a deep breath.

'You ready for this?' my friend Vish asked as I walked towards his waiting car. I nodded as I focused on my breathing. My feet nervously tapped away in the passenger footwell as Vish drove. We pulled up early and I stepped out of the car to get some air and stare at the vast prison towering in front of me: huge stone walls, barbed wire and a large modern blue entrance. My stomach lurched. Victim liaison officers Catherine and Bernadette soon came into sight and Vish and I said our goodbyes. As I clutched onto him, he whispered, 'You can do this.' I let him go and followed Catherine and Bernadette towards the steps to the entrance. As I made my way slowly up, I felt the building encapsulating me.

After initial ID checks, passing metal detectors and being patted down, we entered an 'airlock'-type double doorway. Prison officer Gemma and her colleague were waiting for us on the other side. She smiled and asked how I was doing.

'Nervous,' I replied.

She explained that we would be walking around the grounds of the prison, alongside the recreation area adjacent to the cell block buildings. I followed behind her as she strode confidently towards the door to the inner walled courtyard. The air was stale. The sun was shining, but the oppression of the surrounding high buildings bore down upon us. We were immediately stopped by a huge wire-covered steel fence with a sliding doorway. I tilted my head back to see just how high it was. We had to wait for a prisoner to be taken back inside. My hands nervously wrangled around each other as I did my best to hold a cool, calm composure. Once clear, the gate slid across and we were allowed in. The cell blocks loomed alongside me – tall, dark, grubby-looking Victorian stone buildings. The walk around was further than I expected. We eventually reached a heavy metal door.

'Well, this is it, Natalie. We'll take you straight upstairs once we are in so you can see the room, and then when you're ready, we'll take you downstairs to have a cup of tea whilst we go and fetch him.'

I nodded, my mouth too dry for a proper reply.

Once inside, bare stone and concrete faced me. We entered the meeting room at the top of the stone stairs. Two high-back chairs faced each other over a small low coffee table, then two plastic chairs were positioned either side each of the higher chairs. I was told I could arrange the seating how I wanted with the caveat that I had to be closest to the door, should they need to get me out quickly, and the two prison guards had to flank him in order to restrain him, if needed. I nodded and slightly adjusted the chairs. There was one small high-up window with obscured glass, slightly ajar, covered in bars. I adjusted my chair so I was facing it, with the thought it would be behind him, so I could flick my gaze to it, should I need to 're-centre' whilst talking to him.

I was told to let them know when I was ready. It would take twenty minutes to half an hour to fetch him, so I said I was ready now. We all made our way back down the stone stairs to the room we would be waiting in. One of Gemma's colleagues offered to make us all a cup of tea as we waited.

'That would be lovely,' I smiled.

That would be lovely?! I'm not at my granny's waiting for Countdown *to come on!*

I mentally shook myself and sat down at the chair furthest into the room in the corner alongside a desk. After laying my folder out on the desk, I flicked through it. Catherine and Bernadette watched me intently, checking I was really OK. The slight tremor in my hand was giving away how nervous I felt.

'Are you all prepared, love?' Bernadette asked kindly. 'You can have as long as you like before you see him, even when they bring him in.'

'I'm OK, I'll drive myself mad if I read this folder again,' I replied with a trace of a forced smile. I picked up the mug of tea in front of me and sipped it whilst my ears strained to hear them walk back in with him. Then I heard the outer door being unlocked and bang against the wall as it swung open. My heart stopped beating for a moment before racing off faster than a rabbit out of a trap in a greyhound race. Heavy footsteps came in and keys jangled loudly. *He was actually in the same building as me!* Heavy footsteps went up the stairs and disappeared into the meeting room. A few minutes later, Gemma reappeared at the door.

'He's here and we're ready when you are. Take your time and come up when you are ready,' she told me, searching my face to check I was still OK.

Catherine and Bernadette nodded as I scraped my palms down my jean-clad thighs.

'I think I just need the toilet before I go up,' I told them. I was led to the ladies' with a heavy steel door – a quick visit and a check in the mirror.

You've got this.

Maintaining my composure as best I could, I walked back into the office, picked up my folder and stood next to a waiting Catherine and Bernadette. Bernadette started up the stairs with me close behind and Catherine behind me. Adrenaline surged like a power wave through me. As I reached the top of the stairs, we stopped for a second so I could take a breath, then turned into the room.

There he was, sat in the chair facing me as I walked in. His elbows were resting on the arms of the chair, hands brought together centre-front of him, fingers touching. His eyes bored into mine and we maintained eye contact the whole time.

'Bloody hell!' I muttered as I sat down.

We were sat just metres apart, facing each other. My eyes misted with tears as I gazed at him silently and incredulously, slightly shaking my head at him.

Barbara opened the meeting, stating how I had worked hard to make this happen and therefore it was mine to steer. Bobby was told to wait for me to speak before he said anything, to which he nodded. His eyes didn't leave mine for more than a second. Barbara then handed over to me.

'Well, this has been a long time coming,' I said directly to him and he nodded slightly. I told him I had an agenda in the folder with four different sections I wanted to go through. He nodded with a slight smile, recognising the business-like Natalie he knew and lived with. I then added, 'Bob, you can speak back to me.'

I started with the factual section. Bobby maintained that he did not remember the attack to which I snorted in disbelief. I asked about where he had left the car, which way he had walked and when he first saw me and started following me. Despite feigning lack of memory, when pushed and asked a few times, he suddenly starting answering.

'I saw you go down Trinity Hill,' he told me.

I shuddered.

'I remember your leather jacket. I saw the back of your leather jacket and I knew it was you,' he recalled slowly.

'So, you remember connecting me to my jacket. You can remember consciously thinking that it was me, yet you could still go ahead and do what you did?' I questioned back.

But he had no response, he half-shrugged at me.

I wanted to fill in all the details so I talked him through the attack, step by step. He didn't seem overly affected by it all. Then I got to the part where he punched me in the face when I was on the ground.

'What do you mean, I punched you in the face? I didn't, did I?' he asked, clearly shocked.

'Yes, Bobby, you punched me,' I replied calmly. 'I thought you had stabbed me in the face but you put the knife just once to my face, leaving me with a tiny scar by my nose.'

He leant slightly forward to see the scar he had left. I looked at him enquiringly as to why he was so interested.

'But you hadn't stabbed me in the face, you had punched me. Eye-witness reports confirmed this and my right eye dropped into the corner, with bruising around my cheekbone,' I calmly went on.

He looked at me, visibly shocked. The detail apparently hit him hard. Both prison guards reported at the end of the day, all he kept repeating was, 'I can't believe I punched her.'

They were as confused as me that he could seemingly handle the fact he stabbed me twenty-four times and nearly killed both Leah and I, but he couldn't believe he had punched me?!

I went on to show him all the photos of my injuries and my clothing. He pored over them, as if reading a fascinating textbook. Absorbed in the images, he also kept looking at me to see where the scars were.

Undeterred, I continued with my agenda. I proposed why I thought he did it and he denied putting much planning into the attack at all. I pointed out that this went against what he told the police psychologist. He said he didn't remember that interview and it was all rubbish as he 'wasn't himself'. I pointed out that probably meant he actually was telling the truth more than any other time. I told him exactly what I thought about his gardening clothes' excuse and scoffed at the fact he hated gardening, especially in winter. He feebly tried to maintain the excuse, but it was clear even he couldn't convince himself of this made-up reality he had created.

I told him how I believed he did it as his lies were spiralling out of control, how I was the ultimate lie he couldn't cover up. That there was no one to bail him out this time, as his family had done for him, time and time again. He strove ahead into a life he could not keep up, and ultimately, chose to retreat back to his mother. As Leah and I no longer fitted into his plans, he had to get rid of us. He denied this, vehemently stating that he loved me still with all his heart, that I had given him everything he wanted in life – I was his everything in life.

I broke across him, 'But you tried to kill me and you tried to kill Leah. That isn't love, that's a monstrous act!'

He argued that he did still love me so I asked him the pivotal question, which deep down, I knew he couldn't answer: 'So, WHY? Why try and kill me? Why try and kill your own child?' I looked at him hard.

His head bowed slightly as he slowly shook it. 'I don't know, I can't answer that. I sit in my cell every night and it scares me that I have that inside of me, that I am capable of killing someone, that I tried to do it...' he began.

'So, you should be scared of that, Bob,' I cut across him again, 'because that isn't normal. That is mentally ill at best, evil at worst. There is something seriously wrong with you.'

'I don't know why I did what I did, I felt pressured, I wanted the baby so much but as the pregnancy went on, I got scared. I couldn't go through with it. And Mum, she was so angry about us, she didn't want us together,' he carried on, putting himself across as the victim of circumstance.

'You pushed for a baby! I was scared when I got pregnant, but you reassured me. I believed in you, I believed in us, I thought our life was together forever...' Tears prickled in my eyes.

'I know, it's what I wanted. I didn't know you were that scared,' he replied.

'Yes, you did,' I said evenly as tears fell down my cheeks.

'You said we were forever and then nearly made me pay the ultimate price for developing our family.'

He rubbed his head.

'So why, Bob, why murder? I understand that you were under pressure – your lack of money, your family not knowing about the pregnancy, your mother's disapproval. And people get to a point where they must take action. Firstly, why didn't you talk to me? You have always said that you could tell me anything, but clearly not this so you were at breaking point. Now at that point, some people may run away. You could have left me, you could have jumped on a plane to Pakistan – I wouldn't have found you. You could even have killed yourself. But to take that decision and leap over that line and choose to do what you did, that is incomprehensible.'

I sounded calmer and more in control than the spurt of emotion before.

He looked at me levelly, clearly floored. 'I didn't know what I was doing, it all just happened,' he replied eventually.

'No, it didn't,' I said forcibly back. 'It didn't just happen, Bob – you had it planned. You had the knife, the disguise with the clothes and the rucksack under your top with more spare clothes. You wore two pairs of gloves, took a bin bag with you. That wasn't a last-minute thought process when you supposedly lost your mind. I spoke to you as I walked down to Sutton, you told me you were stuck in traffic, you said that you loved me – that was twenty minutes before the attack. You were calm and clear all through that conversation. Do you remember that call?' I questioned him further.

'No, I don't,' he replied.

'Lies, Bob, it's all lies, like everything you have said for years, not just to me but to friends and family alike! You're not the person anyone thinks you are.'

I was disgusted by him, his lack of ability to even try and come up with a decent excuse. He wasn't even hiding behind the excuse of his mother and her pressure as much as he was in court, where he and his lawyer had blamed her for everything. That was clearly a tack he wasn't taking today.

He argued his lack of memory further and I told him outright that I didn't believe him. He then grew angry and agitated, saying he had thought what was the point of me coming today when he knew I wouldn't believe him. I was in disbelief – he dared to get annoyed and angry at me for not believing him! After all he'd done.

Clear that I wasn't going to get anywhere with this line of questioning about the why and the wherefore, I went through all the different things I had found out to be a lie, including the day I saw his sister Shona in hospital a week before he did what he did. How he had picked her up just outside the hospital as I sat inside that very building, believing he was stuck at work. I told him I wished I had called out to her and he had been exposed then. He shook his head. Like that lie and many others, he was unable to deny what he had done now he was presented with it all. I informed him that I had put straight a huge number of his lies to his family and they had set me straight on a few things too. At this he looked trapped, knowing I had really dug deep. He was shocked when I told him how I had informed his sister of the relationships he had had with his relatives – I had no loyalty to him now, which he conceded.

When I reflect how he was whilst we discussed such shocking, horrific factual evidence, I clearly recall how he seemed so detached from it all. It was cold and unnerving. He was sat there listening to me talking about an event he had nothing to do with, it seemed. My eyes constantly scoured every part of him, trying to work out what was going on in his head. He referred to me a few times as 'Sweetie' as he would have when we were at home. He looked like the man I lived with, the man who had left home that fateful morning – he was even wearing the clothes from home that I had packed up and returned to his mother. It was then I realised he was actually wearing the red polo shirt that I had bought him and the cardigan he wore at home. And those jeans looked familiar…

'You're wearing the top I bought you, nice touch!' I said, allowing sarcasm to slip in. This observation was met with a scowl and he retorted that he loved the top and the other I had bought him, so he had specifically asked for them.

'So…' I continued, 'does that mean your mother has unpacked your clothes that I had returned to her house?'

'Er, yes… I asked for those things,' he replied, looking slightly confused.

I giggled and his frown deepened.

'Why do you ask?' he questioned me suspiciously.

'No reason,' I giggled again. It was so strange but his unease and the hilarity to me of the news I was about to break to him broke all my tension of being in this concrete box room in the middle of a prison.

'C'mon, what's so funny?' he asked, slightly annoyed that I seemed relaxed and obviously amused by something.

'Well, you know that butt plug you bought, I packed it with the clothes you are now wearing, which means your mother will definitely have found it. Don't worry, I left the batteries in for her!'

I was really laughing at this point. I could almost hear the stifled smirks and mirth from the four people sat in the room with us. However, he found it less amusing and rubbed his shaking head. This just gave me even more joy. Catherine and Bernadette both told me afterwards with a wry smile across their faces that they both stared at their feet when I said that – that they couldn't look at him!

After that brief light-hearted break, the emotion surged as we went on to discuss the emotional impact on me, the kids and my wider family. I described the destruction he had caused me from that day, from the moment I had stirred from my coma and the reality of it all hit me like a train as I fought not to sink irrevocably in Critical Care. His emotions seemed less than authentic. It was as if he knew he should feel bad but his true remorse didn't stand out. For a man who had apparently temporarily lost his mind and carried out an act so heinous and out of character, he was amazingly composed. I would have expected him to be broken, crying, horrified by the details of all that he had done and the lasting repercussions. But he wasn't – he sat there without shedding a tear. Tears streamed down my face and I hastily wiped them away with tissues, not wishing to fully display my agony. But he was detached from it all. This wasn't, in my opinion, a man incredulous at the atrocity of his actions, a man who had temporarily lost his mind and was now full of regret. This man was trying to give me calculated responses, but the true feeling of remorse never shone through. Instead, he seemed cold and detached at times. Afterwards, I reflected how twice whilst I was there his eyes even flashed with anger, especially when the subject of his mother was being discussed. Both times he reacted like this, I held his stare as fear lapped over me.

When I had finished telling him about the everlasting

emotional damage he had inflicted, he leant forward and started an almost evangelical rant about how I must never think I was to blame for the attack, it was nothing that I or my girls had done. That it was all down to him and I wasn't to go blaming myself. I felt myself slump slightly in my chair and then something stirred in me and I sat bolt upright.

'I don't think it was me, I never have done. All I did was love you, care for you, give you what you wanted, and was one hundred per cent loyal to you. Anyway, regardless of that, nobody could do anything that is so bad to even begin to justify your actions. So, don't patronise me. I know YOU are to blame for this, completely YOU!'

Two hours had soon passed and I had exhausted the first two sections of my agenda – I needed a break. Leah was our next topic, but I needed some time out. I turned my head to Bernadette and nodded to her to indicate I was ready for a break. She quickly wound up that section and said we would take some time out. Bobby sat there motionless, instructed clearly that he was not to stand whilst I was in the room or he would be taken down. As I rose from my chair, I could feel his gaze assessing every part of me – the way I looked, the way I carried myself. I could feel his eyes on me until I turned the corner out of sight. Wearily, I made my way back down the stairs behind Bernadette. Once in our 'waiting room' – their office – I took a deep sigh. She and Catherine patted me on the back and both offered praise and support for having held it together so well so far. A cup of tea was soon asked for and I slumped in a chair and rubbed my temples with my fingers.

'That was tough, so tough,' I told them. They nodded, visibly feeling the steps with me along the way. We chatted about how the morning session had gone. Biscuits were offered, but I refused – I didn't feel like eating anything still. Bobby too was not eating or drinking, but that wasn't down to nerves but Ramadan. Despite denouncing Allah and anything Islamic in court, he was fasting once more.

I flicked through my folder to see what I had forgotten. In those first two parts I had covered practically everything and there were just a couple of sections which I highlighted to ask when we went back in.

I mentally prepared myself for that afternoon session. We were going to discuss Leah and that would be tough. I had no idea what would come out of that discussion. If he was going to show any emotion that day, something he had done very little of up to that point, then this would be it. I indicated that I was ready to go back. Bernadette went to check they were ready for us and so we ascended the stairs once more.

His face was still serious, eyes boring into me and every move I made. I kicked off the discussion with the couple of questions I had for him. I then paused and said, 'Oh, one thing... I have terrible flashbacks from that day. Do you have flashbacks?'

'Yes, I do,' he replied, clearly transporting himself to those moments.

'They're awful, aren't they? Tell me about yours, though,' I continued, a touch of empathy in my voice.

'I remember your jacket so clearly, I remember the knife in my hand. I remember the struggle on the pavement, I remember being kicked or something. I remember the police pinning me down and holding me against a door...' He spoke slowly, as if it took time to come out of his memory.

'So, you basically remember all the attack from start to finish. When you say you don't remember, that is clearly untrue as you've just recalled parts from all the way through it,' I evenly concluded.

He held his head down and slightly shook it, but no reply came back to me. He'd been rumbled, he clearly remembered the whole attack. It was easier though for him to say he didn't. I left that fact there, pausing momentarily and then, with a deep breath, I moved on.

'So, Leah… The part you have probably been waiting to discuss. Tell me, what are your thoughts, hopes/expectations when it comes to her? Bearing in mind everything we have discussed today about what you actually have done, including trying to murder her?' I looked him directly in the eye.

His hands had been covering his mouth and he moved them aside. I waited.

'Well, it's all up to you,' he replied. 'Whatever you decide, it's your decision.'

'Well, I'm sure you don't need to be Einstein to guess how I feel about you having contact with her,' I said.

He shook his head slightly.

'She's an amazing little girl – funny, loving, always smiling. Her sisters adore her, as do I. She's incredible,' I went on. He showed no signs of response.

My eyes bored into him. 'You tried to murder her – YOU! How did she ever deserve that?' I leant forwards.

But he just sat there, quietly shaking his head, no real words coming out. He went on to thank me for what I did for Leah – for bringing her up so well.

'You don't thank me, I don't need your thanks. I'm her mum, it's my job to love, care for and protect her, to bring her up. It's what you do as a parent – you protect your children.' I spoke clearly and forcibly at him. He slightly hung his head at that last comment. I was so angry with him, but I wasn't about to let it out now: I was in control and he wasn't going to have the outburst he might have wanted or expected.

'I have brought photos of her here, they are in this envelope.' I waved the envelope on my lap. 'They are not for you to keep, but for you to see what she looks like now so you can face the beautiful little soul you tried to destroy. Do you want to see them?' I asked, squaring his eye defiantly.

'Yes, I'll see them, if that's OK,' he replied.

I handed them directly to him. His hand stretched across the table and our hands almost touched as the photos passed from me to him. I watched intently as he went from photo to photo, barely pausing on any of them, turning them over far faster than the ones of my injuries or blood-stained clothes. Once he had gone through them all, he quickly passed them back again. I was shocked – I never expected him to go through them so fast and hand them back so promptly. I took them off him and slumped back slightly in my chair, trying to work out what was going on in his head. There wasn't a sign of emotion on his face. I thought the photos might have broken him slightly, but he seemed immune to them.

'What did you think when you looked at those photos?' I asked.

'That I'm a fucking idiot,' he replied.

'I could think of far stronger words to describe you' – I had in fact already used a much stronger word, a word I had warned Catherine and (especially) Bernadette that I was going to use without doubt. I had called him the C-word many times to myself, but vowed I would use it to his face. Bernadette hated the word, but did allow me to say it under the circumstances. So, I said it.

We went on to discuss some rules around Leah, such as no contact from him from there on in, and no contact once he was out of prison. When she was eighteen, she could make her own decision as to whether she wanted to meet him, but nothing till that point. I told him he could write letters if he so desired, but he had to keep them until she was eighteen and then she could decide what she wanted to know or hear from him directly. He agreed. I told him I didn't trust his mother around Leah, something he surprisingly nodded and agreed with!

Once we had discussed Leah, we went on to discuss the financial situation, or lack of finances, to be more accurate. There was no joy from his business partners, but he said he would keep chasing this. He discussed money from sale of his land in Pakistan, although we both knew the legal problems attached to this were huge and with him in prison, clearly very little was going to be done. He kept promising me he would do what he could to support me, but I had heard this before. We discussed compensation and he asked outright what I wanted. I knew it didn't matter what I said as there was no money he could give me, unless his mother released equity from her recently renovated, expensive house she now lived in alone.

'So, go on, what do you want?' he asked, cockily.

'£100,000,' I came straight back with, looking levelly at him.

'£100K?' he asked, surprised at the amount I had said.

I nodded.

'Yes, £100K. You asked what I wanted. Well, I want £100K off you and, to be fair, that's nothing after what you did.'

He floundered, clearly not expecting me to say anything. When it came to money, pride was paramount to me, he knew.

'I don't think I can get that sort of money, but I'll speak to Mum,' he said, clearly working out the next step.

We discussed other financial matters and before I knew it, the time had passed and I had covered everything I wanted to cover. I'd been with him another two hours at this point and I was getting weary, so I signalled to Bernadette that I was done. She asked him if there was anything more he wanted to ask. He shook his head. Bernadette then summarised all the notes she had made: our key agreement pieces. We both listened and nodded our agreement that all the main points were listed. She told us how she would have a debrief with us both separately, the agreement document with all the key points would then go to both of us to be signed. It was then time for us to say goodbye.

I stared at him across the coffee table.

'So, this is it, I guess... goodbye,' I said awkwardly. My time with him was finished and now I knew I had to say goodbye for good. Not just to the Bobby sat in front of me, the murderer, but the man I had loved so deeply and lived with. A man who had left me forever on 4 March 2016. My heart was breaking as I knew I had to stand up and leave this room and leave him behind for good. Slowly, I got myself to my feet and he looked me straight in the eye and said, 'I'm sorry, goodbye.'

'You need help, Bobby, serious help. Something isn't right in your head,' I told him as kindly as I could.

I turned to the doorway and followed Bernadette out and down the stairs. We returned to the office again. I felt agitated – I couldn't put my finger on it. Gemma came down the stairs to ask if everything was OK.

'I don't know,' I said. 'You are all going to think I'm mad after everything I discussed up there with him, but I felt like

I wanted to give him a hug goodbye. Even I know it sounds mental!' I paced around the floor.

'It doesn't sound mad,' Bernadette cut across me. 'It is clear how much you loved him and clear that at one point your relationship had a lot of respect and love in it. A hug is a natural parting from someone you once cared about, it is saying a goodbye to that person you remember from back then.'

Catherine and Gemma agreed. I was shocked – I thought they'd all think I was crazy.

'How would you feel about me saying goodbye again to him?' I asked Gemma.

'Natalie, you need to get everything out whilst you are here. You want to leave here feeling you have done absolutely everything. Don't leave with any regrets about things not said or done. No one is in your shoes, no one can judge. If you want to say goodbye again, I can speak to him and see if he agrees. I'm sure he will. I am happy you are safe to go back in there with him.'

I nodded that I wanted to say goodbye again.

'My family won't be happy and my friends will think I'm crazy,' I said.

'You may be surprised,' Gemma replied.

'I want it made clear this is me saying goodbye to the old Bobby I once knew. There is no hope or glimmer of me changing my mind about him. He shouldn't read anything into this, I am just saying goodbye properly. How I feel I should say goodbye,' I said firmly.

Gemma nodded and she and Bernadette headed out the room once she had triple-checked I was sure about it. Within a few minutes, she returned with a nod of her head. Bernadette had relayed my reasons for wanting to say goodbye and impressed upon him it wasn't to be read into any other way than goodbye.

I followed Gemma back up the stairs. He was sitting in another part of the room when I entered, under the window. I walked across the room and stood directly in front of him.

'I've come to say goodbye properly,' I told him as he remained seated in front of me. 'You are allowed to stand up now.'

He stood up in front of me, now eye-to-eye for the first time. My heart raced once more. The last time I was this close to him, he was stabbing me.

'Come here,' I said and held out my arms.

We hugged. He gripped onto me tightly and whispered in my ear, 'You look amazing! I am so, so sorry, I never meant to harm you.'

I pulled away from him slightly – 'But you did.'

He started to stroke my hair, I tensed and forced my way out of his grip. He wouldn't let me go to start with, but I pulled away, hard. Then I looked him in the eye.

'This is irrevocable, you know that. No going back, this is a final goodbye.'

He nodded and pulled me back into a hug. I felt cold toward him but hugged him one last time and then that was it, I released him. I knew I had said my goodbye: I had said goodbye to the man I once loved, but now it was time to leave. This man I was holding was no longer 'my Bobby', the man I remembered.

This man was a coward – a cold-blooded and evil man.

'Get that sorted, work out what is happening in there,' I said, tapping his temple. 'It's not right and you know that.'

He stayed quiet and I wasn't convinced he really did know he wasn't quite right in the head.

'Well, you've got a cell to get back to and I've got three kids to get back home to,' I told him and cuffed his arm in a relaxed manner.

He told me how I had to leave the room first and I nodded and said, 'Of course. Bye, Bobby.' With that, I turned and made my way to the door and down the stairs.

I was glad I did it. We called my sister when I returned to the room and told her we were ready to leave. As we called her, I heard them take Bobby back to his cell and when they returned, we walked back across the prison grounds. All the noises melted away around me as my head buzzed with all that had happened. As we got back to the front office, Gemma and her colleague said goodbye. Both hugged me hard and wished me all the very best of luck with life ahead. They said how impressed they had been with how I held it together – we had all been on a journey in that room that day.

At 3.45pm, about the time I was being taken away from the scene of the stabbing as the Air Ambulance landed on that Friday, exactly sixty-six weeks before, I stepped out the main door of HMP Birmingham. The relatively fresh air hit me as I stood on the steps outside and a sense of freedom flooded through me.

I was free from the prison he was caught up inside but, more importantly, I had freed myself a little more from him. As I walked down the steps towards my sister's waiting car, I walked away from him for the last time. My body heaved a sigh. This was *my* ending, my choice on how it was to be ended, not his. This was that chapter closed.

The end.

Epilogue

I FELT DRAINED FOR DAYS AFTER THE PRISON VISIT, BUT LIFE
DOESN'T GIVE YOU MUCH CHANCE TO RECOVER WHEN YOU
HAVE THREE SMALL PEOPLE TO LOOK AFTER. I HAD TO FOCUS
on the future. There were still pieces of my puzzle to find and
fit into place, but I also had a new life to forge. I collated
some more pieces when I met with David, the man who had
witnessed the attack first-hand. He was recovering from an
operation that fateful day and couldn't run to my aid, but he
called 999 and took photos of the end of the attack to be used
as evidence. The photos were the ones I had seen at the police
station with my sister Mand just after the plea hearing.

We met in Sutton on 29 June 2017 and he handed over
a flash disk with the images on. The photos were more
harrowing than I had remembered, but they helped piece
together the attack, especially as they were time stamped.
They also made me face once more the stark truth it was
Bobby with the knife committing the atrocity on that hill.

My 'new life' brought two more award ceremonies that
year, the first being the Midlands Air Ambulance Charity Ball

and Recognition Awards evening at the end of June, where the film of my attack, rescue and recovery was launched. To my great surprise, I won the Inspiration Award for having fought adversity to go on and raise money in a dedicated way for the charity – I was so humbled. I have continued to do more and will do so further into the future, with the Midlands Air Ambulance Charity, my love and passion, giving talks alongside my video as well as completing more crazy challenges to raise money for them.

The second ceremony came a few months later, 5 September, in the form of the postponed Police Bravery Awards, where I had the pleasure of standing with the Chief Constable, handing out the awards to all those involved in my rescue and subsequent investigation. It was a very emotional evening, but fabulous too as I got to publicly thank them all together.

The publicity surrounding the Police Awards meant I was hounded for interviews again and at last I overcame my fear of speaking through the media and had my first interview with a local digital TV channel before going on to ITV's *This Morning* with Holly Willoughby and Phillip Schofield (both of whom I adore). I also supported a piece on local BBC News about stabbings and the startling rise in numbers.

Life of course still had – and has – its challenges. I discovered a small hard lump in my right breast in July 2017, which luckily turned out not to be cancer but a piece of silicone left over from the shredded implants. It has been left in, so we are now friends for life! Then, one morning later that month, I woke to discover my house had been broken into whilst my three girls and I slept upstairs to get the car keys and steal my car. It made me feel so vulnerable. The car was recovered, using its tracker, only a few miles away in a pub car park. I only had it back about six weeks when an elderly gentleman drove into the back of me whilst I was stationary at a red traffic light! Fortunately, I have learnt to put so much into perspective. I have realised, 'I can get through this, *anything* can be got through. Focus on the outcome and ask for help when needed'. So simple really! I have also found reflecting on funny moments in terrible situations can help.

My therapy has been a constant, regular event. It has been a lifeline to get me through this, along with my amazing mother, who has literally been there every day, supporting me and my children. At the start of 2018, I got into my PTSD therapy, which has been extremely tough, and I have felt physically worse during the initial stages as I remembered parts of the attack which I had blocked out. Graphic details, such as the force he stabbed me in my bump, his intention clear and calculated to terminate Leah as well as me. I have also recalled how I would not look at his face during the attack, especially the second part, where at times he was right in front of me – my brain protecting me from the harsh truth that I just couldn't deal with then. The brain is a complex thing and I will always be scarred significantly, both mentally and physically, by this attack. For me the road to acceptance has still not ended and it has been a complex journey so far.

Like so many victims of trauma, I have learnt I have carried guilt and negative thoughts about myself, such as *How did I not foresee what he would do?* Or *How did I let someone like that in not only my life but that of my children?* Through therapy, I realised I viewed myself as weak, hence why I have been so scared out on my own, feeling I would be targeted as some vulnerable prey for anyone to attack.

Building my self-belief again has been hard and is still a work in progress, but I do now realise my worth a bit more each day.

In so many ways the attack has perversely enriched my life. I have met some incredible people with astounding stories, whom I would otherwise never have met. Although I would give up all those experiences to have back what I thought I had. But the reality is that life didn't ever exist. Bobby wasn't, and isn't, the man myself and so many thought he was as that person would not have even thought of doing what he did.

So, I embrace my new life, a life where I have also grown closer to so many of my family and friends, formed stronger bonds than could ever before be imagined. Mum, Jane and Mand have always been my support and stability, but that relationship has now lifted to a whole new level. My children have and still continue to amaze me every day. Emily and Isabel truly are outstanding young ladies. They are exceptionally protective of Leah and I, they show endless love and care, and to have got this far in an overall positive manner from an experience no child should ever be subject to is just incredible. Pride does not come close to describing what I feel for them. Leah has fought every single odd and astounds everyone she meets. I have three amazing children who show me every day exactly why I survived and am still here living: to be with them.

On Friday, 4 March 2016, Babur Karamat Raja committed one of the most heinous acts a man could commit. He nearly destroyed my life and in turn the lives of those around me. But I have pushed my way back, like a new shoot pushing through the ground, drawing strength and sustenance from not only what is within me but from all those around me too. I hope this story helps others see that you really can get through the worst and totally unforeseen tragic life events. The trauma, the aftermath, the memories will hurt and the road will be extremely tough, but now and again you will look back and realise just how far you have come. It will surprise you as it does me. One day you will stop and acknowledge that, yes, the pain is still there and may always be, but you know what?

I'm still standing.

Acknowledgements

SO MANY PEOPLE TO THANK.

MY MUM – MY ROLE MODEL, STRONG, INDEPENDENT AND FIERCELY PROTECTIVE OF HER FAMILY – HAS TAUGHT ME never to give in, no matter how tough things get. She is my rock, and always there for me. Her support is out of this world. I couldn't have made it this far without her – my gratitude is immeasurable.

My three incredible daughters. All outstanding. Their resilience and love inspires me to fight on and make the best of life every single day.

My two older sisters, Jane and Mand, my brother-in-law Andy, my niece Louise and nephew Ben, with their unending love and support.

Ian, Emily and Isabel's father, who has also shown absolutely amazing support.

Noele (Aunt) and my dearly missed 'Unc' – always there to encourage with softly spoken words and a safe Welsh haven!

My friends who have dragged me through some really

hard times, been on hand to listen, made me laugh with their much-appreciated humour and helped me refocus when needed!

One of my most crucial supporters – my psychologist Anna – words cannot describe my gratitude. She has helped me develop my sense of self-worth and facilitated so much of my continuing growth since the attack to be where I am today.

Regarding this book: after toiling for many months at my computer, whilst also fundraising for Midlands Air Ambulance Charity (MAAC), I was introduced by the lovely Sofia Voutianitis (MAAC) to Willie Thorne – snooker ace and true gentleman. My eternal thanks to Willie for reaching out and connecting me to the wonderful Rosie Virgo, then Managing Director of John Blake Publishing, for advice and guidance.

Thank you to Rosie Virgo for taking the time to listen to my story, read a selection of chapters and inviting me to meet to discuss my book further. Then, along with John Blake, for having the belief in my book to want to publish it.

At that first incredible meeting, I was introduced to another key figure in this publication – James Hodgkinson, my fabulous editor, who has shown endless patience and listened to my points of view on all aspects of the book. James has been a trusted partner, guiding me as I finished writing and editing this book to produce a final piece of which I'm very proud.

Thank you to all the team at John Blake Publishing, bringing my book to life – with special thanks to Katie Greenaway, working her PR magic.

Thank you to you the reader for taking the time to read my story – that means everything to me. Hope this inspires you to know you can come back from any setback, achieve and to never give up.

I couldn't possibly fit in every last name that I want to, but to those who aren't named here but have been with me on this journey – and you know who you are – thank you, too!

Finally, a massive 'thank-you' to Johnny, Tony, Carmello and Callum, West Midlands Police Force, West Midlands Ambulance Service, Midlands Air Ambulance Charity and the staff at both the Queen Elizabeth Hospital Birmingham and Birmingham Women's Hospital, without all of whom Leah and I would not have survived Friday 4 March 2016. Words will never be enough.

MIDLANDS AIR AMBULANCE

Midlands Air Ambulance Charity is responsible for funding and operating three air ambulances serving six counties in the Midlands. The three aircraft each carries a crew comprising a pilot, two critical care paramedics (CCP) or a CCP and flight doctor, plus full life-support medical equipment. Operating from strategically located regional airbases, the maximum flying time to hospital from anywhere in the region is less than fifteen minutes.

The organisation also has a critical care car, based in Birmingham and the Black Country. The critical care paramedic on board attends medical emergencies such as cardiac arrests, heart attacks, sepsis and strokes.

Patients like Natalie rely on Midlands Air Ambulance Charity in their greatest hour of need, and are taken to the most appropriate hospital for their injuries, which might not necessarily be the nearest hospital. This greatly increases their chances of survival and enables patients to make the best possible recovery.

What is not widely known is that Midlands Air Ambulance Charity does not receive any Government or National Lottery funding. Each year, the charity starts every year with zero funds and must generate over £9 million from local businesses, groups and the public.

A simple commitment will make a big difference. Donate now: www.midlandsairambulance.com/donatenow